THE BEST OF LIVING CHEAP NEWS

PRACTICAL ADVICE ON SAVING MONEY AND LIVING WELL

LARRY ROTH

CB
CONTEMPORARY BOOKS
A TRIBUNE COMPANY

Library of Congress Cataloging-in-Publication Data

Roth, Larry.
    The best of living cheap news : practical advice on saving money
and living well / Larry Roth.
       p.   cm.
    ISBN 0-8092-3188-3
    1. Consumer education.   2. Home economics—Accounting.
I. Living cheap news.   II. Title.
TX335.R7497   1996
640'.73—dc20   96-16029
                                            CIP

Cover design by Scott Rattray
Interior design by Terry Stone

Copyright © 1996 by Larry Roth
All rights reserved
Published by Contemporary Books
An imprint of NTC/Contemporary Publishing Company
Two Prudential Plaza, Chicago, Illinois 60601-6790
Manufactured in the United States of America
International Standard Book Number: 0-8092-3188-3

10   9   8   7   6   5   4   3   2   1

This book is dedicated to
Amy Dacyczyn.
I may not always agree with her,
but I will always admire her.

CONTENTS

INTRODUCTION

One of the questions I am asked most frequently is, How did *Living Cheap News* come about?

In a way, the birth of LCN began back in the 1950s when, as a child, I spent a great deal of time at the home of my grandmother. She had emigrated from Sweden in 1912, married after World War I, and struggled with my grandfather to farm in Colorado. Driven from farming by the dust bowl of the 1930s, they wound up in Oklahoma City, continued practicing the frugality that had served them so well, and made it into the American middle class (my grandfather even owned two Packards before he died in 1955). They sold their farm in the 1950s, when the dust bowl was only a memory, retaining mineral rights whenever possible. Our family still owns some of these mineral rights. I was impressed by my grandmother's history as well as the frugality that enabled her to manage in difficult conditions.

In the early 1960s, I had a paper route, which taught me a lot about how to keep costs low in order to maximize profits. Eventually I expanded to three paper routes. As a high school student, I was saving $125 a month. And that was in the 1960s. My savings would go a long way toward paying for my college education. Through a fluke, I wound up in a high school economics class. I found I was a natural at the dismal science, and I decided to study it further.

In college economics, my professor explained the theory of MPC, or marginal propensity to consume. He said that, as a person's income rises, so does that person's consumption, or MPC. It occurred to me that if I could keep my MPC down and instead increase my savings, I would be ahead of the game. To the extent possible, I followed this plan. When I got a pay raise, I tried to increase the amount that was going to savings by the after-tax amount of my raise. This approach served me quite well, and, in spite of my high savings level, I enjoyed a very comfortable and affordable standard of living. Until 1981. In that first year of "Morning in America," our twelve-year national daydream, the country's concern for the environment receded, and my job as a branch chief with the Office of Surface Mining in Kansas City came to an end.

I wound up moving to Burbank, California, where I rented a two-bedroom unit in an illegal duplex for $535, which was $40 more than I was able to earn in rent on my eight-room Tudor house in Kansas City. (Selling it was impossible in 1982. There just weren't any buyers in those days of 18 percent interest.) I resolved then and there to get myself into a position where I would not be dependent on an employer and where I would never have to leave an area I liked again. In early 1995 I left my job in corporate America, moved back to Kansas City, and made my avocation, writing, my full-time career.

Had I not lived a frugal life, I would have been unable to leave a high-paying job to make a career of writing without a predictable flow of income. On the face of it, my choice may seem unwise, but I was, after forty-five years of following the advice of others, finally following my heart. And I made my move with a safety net. I made sure that I would have enough interest income to feed me if my writing didn't.

In 1989 a thirty-three-year-old friend of mine who had been going to school at night for years completed her BA degree. She was offered a paralegal job paying $20,000 a year. At that time, a starter home in the San Francisco Bay area, where my friend and I lived, could easily run $300,000. The starting pay for a college graduate was totally out of kilter for the area. Happy I had gotten my start twenty years earlier, I began calculating the price increases I had absorbed. My salary had increased five times, but my housing costs had increased more than eleven times, and a new car cost six times what I paid for one in 1971. It occurred to me that Americans could not continue to survive their expenses outrunning their means for much longer. This observation was the inspiration for my first book, *Living Cheap: THE Survival Guide for the Nineties*, which was born in March 1990.

Late in 1990, I subscribed to a frugality newsletter. It was very good but did not really lend itself to the urban life I knew. It seemed to get bogged down in reusing frozen juice container lids and recycling dryer lint. I kept saying to myself, *Someone* should do a newsletter like this for city people—families in which both spouses work and suffer a daily commute, families like those I knew. As I was reading about the other newsletter one morning in a *Wall Street Journal* article that included advice on how to make two rubber bands out of one, I groaned and said to myself, "I could do better than that." I don't usually hear voices, but just then I could almost swear that a voice in my head said, "Well, why *don't* you?" That morning, on my daily walk, I decided to proceed and came up with the name *Living Cheap News*, tying the newsletter to my book, which had just been reviewed favorably in the *Mensa Bulletin*.

Issue Number 1 was printed just after New Year's Day 1992. Just a few days later, Nick Ravo of the *New York Times* called about my book, and I told him about my newsletter. He wound up writing about both. (I was very naive about the press back then. He asked me to send a copy of my book and newsletter to him via Federal Express. There was a loooooooong silence on the phone as I was calculating the cost of responding to this request. Finally he said, "Oh, we'll pay the FedEx charges, of course." One day, I'll have to ask Nick for his picture so I can light a candle in front of it every January.)

THE EVOLUTION OF *LCN*

Another question I'm often asked is, Has *Living Cheap News* evolved the way I hoped it would? Considering that my plans were just to leave copies in local libraries and see what developed, it's been successful beyond any expectations I had at the time I started it. The newer issues are much better than the older ones. I feel much more relaxed nowadays when I write. At one time, I tried to please everyone. In the early months I paid attention to letters that today would immediately find themselves in the circular file. Some readers took it upon themselves to nitpick, and quite a few questioned the ethics of nearly everything I suggested.

It was a difficult period, but fortunately I got through it with the help of other newsletter editors. Most newsletter editors in the New Frugality movement, I quickly learned, do not look upon each other as competition; with a couple of exceptions, we consider each other colleagues. I was happy to learn that every newsletter editor has to contend with frustrated writers who disguise themselves as kindly, concerned souls and who have no clue about the work involved in putting out a newsletter (which looks so easy unless you're actually doing it!). One editor finally printed a long letter from one of these folks and responded, "If you don't like my newsletter, why don't you put out your own [expletive deleted] newsletter?" That pretty much summed up my feelings on the matter, too. I've had to learn to put out the newsletter I want to write and take my lumps if some readers don't like it.

Quite frequently I'm told *LCN* is not like other thrift newsletters. I take that as a compliment. I'm not trying to imitate anyone else, and I know my style of writing is unique.

REACTIONS TO *LCN*

Many people wonder why *LCN* is more likely to contain political commentary than the other thrift newsletters. The answer to that is what goes on politically affects all of us economically. To produce *LCN*, I read *The Wall Street Journal*, a local newspaper, several magazines (including *Money* and *SmartMoney*), several "alternative" newspapers and magazines, and books of all political stripes.

From all these publications, I try to develop the most logical approach to any number of pertinent issues. Sometimes my views result in articles that may appear conservative, as in the articles on Social Security. Some readers may think I'm promoting liberalism, as did a couple of folks when I came out in favor of a national health care system. I prefer to think of my political approach as pro-consumer. Congress is just one more thing we buy with our tax dollars. I like to try to see that we get our money's worth.

Broderick Perkins, a reporter for the *San Jose Mercury News*, remarked once that the best suggestions in LCN come from my readers. While he based that remark on one issue, I agree that I have extremely intelligent readers. And, if their ideas are better than mine, who cares as long as all my readers learn new tricks to save money? How else would most of us have learned to save and freeze margarine and butter wrappers to use to grease baking pans? That's something I would never have thought of. Yet it takes no time to do, and it is using something that would otherwise be thrown out. It's free—in the sense of time, effort, and money.

Another reporter, during an interview for National Public Radio, asked, "If people just use common sense, do they need to subscribe to your newsletter?" This was a rather difficult question. What, after all, is common sense? And how does one define a need? I believe I use common sense, yet I have learned from my readers there are ways to save money that I would never have thought of. And while one would certainly be able to live a fairly normal life without *Living Cheap News* or, for that matter, National Public Radio, both make life more interesting, and both offer ideas not readily available elsewhere.

I hope you enjoy *The Best of Living Cheap News*. My goal is to provide my readers with ways to make their hard-earned dollars go further. Along the way, I'd also like to provide some entertainment and some things to think about. There's no reason frugality should be tedious or dull. I would love to hear from you, and I would love to have you as a subscriber. Write me at LCN's address, 7232 Belleview Avenue, Kansas City, MO 64114.

Thanks for reading, and keep cheap.

1
WHAT IS PRACTICAL PARSIMONY?

In the early days of the New Frugality movement, everyone seemed to be coming up with ways to save money. One of my readers suggested spreading used coffee grounds on a cookie sheet, drying them in an oven, and reusing them. I never tried this because it was not worth it to me to do all this to save a few cents. (Anyway, given that I would be heating up my oven to dry the grounds, I wondered whether I'd spend more on gas than I'd save on coffee grounds.) I began to ask myself, "Is this what people expect of me?" Such time-consuming ways to save a few cents simply are not practical for most people.

To better explain my own philosophy on frugality, which I call "practical parsimony," I wrote the following article.

Have you ever been on a diet? Most of us can answer yes to that one. Well, I liken becoming frugal to going on a diet. If you go on an extreme diet, you're going to feel deprived, and you won't stick with it. A commonsense approach works better. The same is true of some of the more extreme suggestions put forth in the name of frugality nowadays. I have read serious discussions about reusing dryer lint. Some people suggest making wind chimes using metal lids from frozen juice containers. I live in a townhouse. All I need is a bunch of my neighbors putting up wind chimes. To me this is using garbage to make garbage.

Practical parsimony is a way of thinking. It requires us to realize that we must, because of federal, state, and local taxes, earn as much as $1.88 in order to have a dollar to spend. That $10 lunch you just had may have cost you $18.80 in earnings. Practical parsimony does not mean doing without. It does, however, mean realizing the true cost of things. And, realizing the true cost of things, it means buying only what you really need. Or want. And buying used whenever possible.

How many of us have bought things we thought we wanted, only to get them home and never use them? I have several unused appliances, a coffee grinder among them (I'm never going to spend five bucks a pound for coffee beans). Practical parsimony is making sure you really want the things you buy. It means being frugal whenever possible in order to be able to do the things you really enjoy. I believe you can have fun and grow as a person while remaining frugal. I have traveled to Australia and New Zealand as well as Eastern Europe. I rather imagine some people may consider such travel extravagant. But travel is a chance to learn how other people live.

My frugality in most areas of my life lets me do what I enjoy. I believe people should be frugal with their lives as well as with their money. Being frugal means avoiding unnecessary expenditure. If you find something rewarding, do it. Don't waste your life. Just avoid unnecessary expenses of money, time, and effort when you can so you'll be able to do more of what you love!

2

FRUGALITY AS A MEANS TO AN END

Sometimes it seems as though frugality has a bad reputation. Many people envision those of us who are frugal as spending our mornings rewashing plastic bags, aluminum foil, and coffee filters and our afternoons counting our money.

They see us as joyless souls meagerly measuring out our morning oatmeal, our midday rice, and our evening beans. They see us as housebound in our ragged clothes, which we found in a thrift shop Dumpster, spending the best years of our lives figuring out how to hold our ramshackle homes together with duct tape.

There may be some people like that in our crowd, but I doubt they make up the majority. However, those people and those kinds of activities are all too often what the media look for when they want to portray—or, more accurately, caricature—someone who is frugal.

I may be going a bit overboard here, but I was recently interviewed as part of a class project on frugality for one of the schools in the California State University system. I was happy to take part in the project, but I was shocked by the view of us frugal folks the students had.

They came to the interview, which was done by telephone, with articles about those of us who have been designated by the media as frugal. I'm afraid, at least in my case, they left disappointed. My life is pretty much like anyone else's. It just costs me less. The most amusing moment of the interview came when I was asked if I ever eat out. The answer is yes—at least once a week. The silence was deafening. It seems one of the students had read that eating out was taboo. She had read that one frugal person even left the home of relatives in a huff when it was suggested that they all go out for pizza. Maybe the incident happened, but more than likely it was an exaggeration.

The fact of the matter is most of us who are frugal do a lot of the same things as people who are not so frugal. We just give what we do and how we do it a little more thought. And sometimes we will give up those things that are not important to us so that we can have the things that we value without going into debt. We know we can't "have it all," so we try to have what's important.

A question frugal folks are commonly asked is, But what do you do with all your money? This is often asked with the insinuation that, if you aren't spending all your money, there is something "wrong" with you. I was asked this very question on a talk show a couple of years ago, but I wasn't given the time to answer fully.

I'd like to answer the question now. What I did with my money was buy bonds, which paid interest. Eventually I earned enough interest to live on, and I left my job to live where I wanted and do those things I really enjoy. My frugality, in other words, bought my freedom. My liberation was my goal. Frugality was my means of reaching that goal, which brings me to my point.

Frugality is not an end in itself. Most people are not cheap solely for the sake of being cheap. Some of us enjoy "beating the system," so to speak. We've found ways to live as well as other people at a lower cost. Frugality is a way to "beat the system."

I, for example, "beat the system" that said I had to remain with a dysfunctional employer until I reached the officially sanctioned retirement age of sixty-five.

Some of us are environmentally concerned. We believe that, by buying fewer things, especially overpackaged things, and by buying pre-owned things when possible, we will be able to "beat the system" and keep our landfills from overflowing.

Some of us live on a limited income. We are frugal because we want to be able to live well on a low income. We are "beating the system" that says you must always earn more.

Some people (and I am not one of them) as an act of conscience have learned to live on an income so low they can avoid paying income taxes. They believe that, by doing this, they can "beat the system" of supporting a government that does things of which they do not approve.

And many of us, in this age of corporate downsizing and Social Security instability, are building a secure retirement for ourselves. We realize no one else has the stake in our retirement that we do. We are "beating the system" that would have us eating cat food in our twilight years.

3
SABOTAGING OURSELVES

"I've had it with my job," my friend Steve says as he slumps into the chair across from mine. "But I'm dependent on it." Later he confides he feels in danger of having a heart attack.

I can understand his frustration. His company has had repeated cutbacks over the last three years, and Steve has had to pick up the slack. It's not unusual for him to work ten-hour days, and a two-day weekend is usually out of the question. Three years ago Steve was put on medication for high blood pressure. Last year he began taking insulin. Steve is forty-five.

His job is killing him.

But he does everything he can to make sure he needs that job. His hobby, boating, is expensive. It's been months since he's seen his boat. It's a three-hour drive to where it's docked. But he still has to pay insurance, marina fees, and so on. Last year he spent $10,000 on the engines.

When I first met Steve, he had one American car. One weekend he stopped by a Volvo dealership and left with a new Volvo. One day we went to lunch. Steve saw a sports car with a For Sale sign. Two days later he called me to give him a ride so he could pick it up (he turned the Volvo over to his wife, who turned it over—but that's another story). Neither of these automobile purchases was planned. And neither car was purchased for cash.

In 1986 he bought a house for $150,000. In the red-hot California real estate market of the late 1980s, the value of his house shot up to $300,000. He refinanced his house, increasing his mortgage to $250,000.

He's had it with a job that's literally killing him, but he'll stick with it because he thinks he needs all these things.

He's sabotaging himself. He's been distracted from his long-term goal—independence—by short-term "fixes."

And, I can't be so smug either. Earlier this year, I was in Kansas City and happened on a very nice house that I could have bought by putting $3,000 down and taking over an FHA loan. I really liked the house and came very close to buying it as an "investment." I've been able to rationalize some pretty dumb things over the years by calling them investments. My emotions nearly got the better of me again. The house would have resulted in at least a $300 monthly negative cash flow as far as the eye could see. In the end I decided it was a very nice house but not nice enough to trade my independence for.

These days it's not smart to be overly dependent on an employer. Layoffs are epidemic, and, as Steve has discovered, sometimes those who are not laid off are not necessarily the lucky ones. They have to do their work as well as the work of those who left.

Try to keep in mind that buying things—that going into debt—keeps you in your dependent situation. This behavior results in voluntary bondage.

Abe Lincoln made slavery illegal. But many of us insist on enslaving ourselves.

Keep your goal in mind. Don't be deterred by a temporary material "fix."

Don't sabotage yourself.

Less than three years after this article was written, Steve underwent triple-bypass surgery. He was forty-eight at the time.

4

THE JOY OF DOING WITHOUT

A few years ago, my friend Steve sold his boat. Steve netted a good deal of cash from this sale. He was able to stop paying marina fees, insurance on the boat, and the various maintenance and repair costs that these floating money pits always seem to require. (Steve estimates his savings at $1,000 per month.) Steve also saves the three-hour (each way) commutes to the marina he used to take on those rare occasions when he was able to use his boat. Steve has discovered what I call the joy of doing without—in his case, doing without a boat.

Another friend has horses. He bought a three-acre spread here in Northern California. He commutes thirty-seven miles each way every day on a road known for its twists, turns, accidents, and delays. He built a barn and bought the truck, trailers, and other equipment he needs to accommodate his interest in horses. This man is committed to having horses—his house is full of the trophies his horses have won over the years—and he can afford his hobby. But when he tells me about each new expensive adventure with his horses, I experience the joy of doing without horses.

That's not to say I haven't had my own follies. I recently discovered the joy of doing without a cleaning service. *LCN* keeps me very busy, and early last year I fell so far behind in keeping my house clean that I hired a service to do it for me every two weeks. That was a big mistake. After getting the house ready for the service, caging the dogs, putting out the supplies the service required before they cleaned, and rearranging things they moved, repairing things they damaged, and generally getting very angry and stressed every other Wednesday, I began to realize I was spending a lot of time and energy on something that was supposed to be saving time and energy.

The service pulled a lot of dumb stunts. Once they accidentally turned my computer on. As if that weren't enough, they just left it on. They managed to wear a hole in the vacuum cleaner bag. The dust was going in the vacuum cleaner and out the hole. Once they claimed they couldn't clean because there had been a power outage (what actually happened was a circuit breaker that had never shut off before or since was turned off). Somehow, though, they managed to find their check in the dark. Amazingly, according to the owner of the service, none of these things were the service's fault. It was my fault the computer was left on because I should have had a separate extension switch so the one on the computer wouldn't function. It was my fault the vacuum cleaner hole had gotten so large because I didn't tell the service about it. And, incredible as it may seem, they claimed they didn't even know what a circuit breaker was! If only they'd been as good at cleaning as they were at making up excuses and trying to shift the blame for their mistakes to me!

The final straw was the *second* time the dishwasher overflow cap got knocked loose. The first time it happened, the service was there. They called me, and I came running home. I showed them what was wrong and tightened the cap. That time, they cleaned up the mess. Weeks later, I loaded the dishwasher, turned it on, and went to bed. Fortunately, I heard the cap when it flew off its mount. The service's people had loosened it again. As I mopped up the kitchen that night, I decided it had become more of a chore to have the service than it would be to do the cleaning myself. And that is a foolish position for anyone to put his customers in these days in California, given our deep and prolonged recession. Evidently, this service thought it was indispensable. It wasn't.

I got rid of the service, I'm managing the cleaning quite well, I've eliminated the repairs I'd almost gotten used to, I'm saving money, and a source of stress is now out of my life. Once again I've discovered the joy of doing without.

In his book *Cashing In on the American Dream: How to Retire at 35,* Paul Terhorst reminds us to spend on ourselves—not on our infrastructure. A way to avoid building an expensive infrastructure is to examine where each purchase will lead. Will owning something, like a boat or horses (or a new car or a new house), require you to spend more money just to continue to own it? If so, you might want to think twice before you make that purchase. It might just be time for you to discover the joy of doing without!

5
THE LIMITS OF CHEAP

Early in 1992 a reporter from one of the nation's better-known sleazoids called me about helping her with an article on saving money. At least that's the way she put it. When I began giving her my standard repertoire—pay off debts, buy used, etc., she interrupted.

"No, no. I'm looking for something *interesting*," she said. "In Chicago people are stealing parts of freeways and selling these parts as scrap metal. In Montana people are stealing road-killed deer. And 1989 was a banner year for bank robberies. I'm looking for things like that."

After I explained that such tactics—especially bank robbery—were hardly things I could recommend to my readers, she hung up, probably wondering what such a boring person could offer his readers.

In the past four years I've learned that different people have different standards of what is really cheap and what is merely amateur cheap. As *LCN* enters its fifth year, I want to explore the limits of cheap. One of my readers who uses a one-cubic-foot refrigerator and a hotplate, and lives without a car in a very small apartment tells me I am not really cheap. I have a seventeen-cubic-foot refrigerator, a stove, a microwave, a car, and a four-bedroom townhouse (which, at 1,450 square feet, doesn't seem all that large to me—especially now that two bedrooms are devoted to *LCN*).

Another reader in West Virginia is homeless by choice because he doesn't believe in paying for a place to live (and I hope one day he will tell me how he manages this). And I've read about a man who jacks his old Volkswagen off the ground at night to save wear and tear on his tires and another who times his bowel movements so they happen only while he is at work (saving him toilet paper)—and no, the article did not tell what he does on the weekends.

These people have made the choice to be on the fringes of frugality. Their choice does not affect anyone else, and I applaud their efforts.

Every once in a while I hear from people I cannot applaud. In fact, I often feel like washing my hands after reading their letters. These are people who are cheap at the expense of others. Some don't tip in restaurants because of some "principle," hurting not the restaurant owners but waiters and waitresses who are incapable of doing anything about the fact that both their employer and the IRS presume their wages are supplemented by tips. If these folks do not believe in tipping, they should not eat out. Others make toll calls when they know people are not at home, leave a message on their victims' answering machine, and take advantage of the returned call. (An obvious flaw here is that the victims should be able to figure this one out pretty quickly and either not return the call or put the "clever" cheapster down as a hopeless clod.) One woman, upset at having to send a self-addressed, stamped envelope for a sample copy of *LCN*, informed me she was a "true tightwad," and as a "true tightwad" it was her *duty* to get as many things as possible without paying for them.

If anyone believes I support this perverted noblesse oblige, I want to set the record straight. I believe in a "win-win" approach to life. Taking advantage of everybody and everything to the maximum extent possible is "win-lose." In the long run, as these people accumulate "free" things that take up space and complicate their lives, their win-lose approach will ultimately leave them empty. Their win-lose approach to other people, in other words, will wind up being lose-lose.

In this chapter you'll read about some modern masters of parsimony. But first a caveat. In most cases these people go far beyond my comfort level. If these approaches appeal to you, that's fine with me. But I believe many modern urban lives involve a certain amount of drudgery, and I'm not encouraging anyone to engage in anything that would add to that drudgery. In other words, if Dumpster diving, for example, isn't fun for you, don't do it.

The bottom line here is: Be as cheap as you want to be as long as you enjoy yourself and your cheapness doesn't hurt anyone else.

💵 RESOURCES ON THE FRINGES OF FRUGALITY

The Art & Science of Dumpster Diving, by John Hoffman (**$14.95 plus $4 shipping and handling from Loompanics Unlimited, P.O. Box 1197, Port Townsend, WA 98368**)—Loompanics will send you their $5 catalog of books, some of which were written for the seriously deranged, free with your order. Mr. Hoffman tells how he uses soap, shampoo, towels, bath mats, cologne, shaving cream, deodorant, watches, furniture, jewelry, and food he salvages from Dumpsters. And this is just the first page! After telling why it makes sense to salvage others' throw-aways, Mr. Hoffman gets down to the nitty-gritty. He tells how to stake out promising Dumpsters, how to dress, and how to "Dumpster dive" safely (this looks like good exercise as well). Mr. Hoffman advises that the big three Dumpster sites are those near bakeries, grocery stores, and bookstores (these are followed by seven more sites he considers "promising"). Mr. Hoffman says that once you have met your own needs, Dumpster diving can even provide an income. He tells about reselling Dumpster finds, and then he discusses some of the pictures he's found at photo development places (the moral here is, be careful what you have those folks develop). The book is definitely interesting, but some of the finds he discusses would have been better left unrecorded (there are things people throw away I'd rather not know about). The language at times is beyond crude, and I'm not sure how I feel about Mr. Hoffman's killing and eating a duck that was competing with him for some bakery items in one of the Dumpsters. He talks about Dumpster diving as a way out of the nine-to-five grind, but is he trading a dog-eat-dog world for a diver-eat-duck one?

As long as there is traffic, Tom Squier will never go hungry. His *Wild and Free Cookbook* (**$23.95 gets an autographed copy from him at 4925 Ashemont Rd., Aberdeen, NC 28315**) on how to cook road-kill (he says, "If I can't save them, I am going to sauté them") and other wild foods starts off with a bang. He believes meat is meat, "whether you get it with a gun or a Goodyear."

What can one say about a guy who's so cheap he walks to a bank for a free cup of coffee, gives leftover flowers from funeral homes to his fiancée, and separates two-ply toilet paper? When Roy Haynes first read about me, he immediately sent me a letter saying he was the cheapest man in America. And I didn't even know there had been a contest! Now he's written a four-page tip sheet for the really cheap ("attend Bon Voyage parties aboard cruise ships regardless of whether you know any of the passengers . . . the food is free"). **For the tip sheet, send $4** (I'd recommend sending a check) **to Roy Haynes at 150 Dorset St., South Burlington, VT 05407.**

Death is something that has touched or will touch our lives. The modern American approach has been to insulate ourselves from it. We seem to believe that, if we ignore death, maybe it will go away. Aiding and abetting us in this fantasy, the funeral industry now prepares the dead for burial and makes their bodies look lifelike—at a high cost. Lisa Carlson's book *Caring for Your Own Dead* **($12.95 plus $3 shipping from Upper Access, P.O. Box 457, Hinesburg, VT 05461, or call toll-free 800-356-9315)** presents the case—both emotional and financial—for preparing and burying our own dead. Ms. Carlson's first husband died suddenly, and she could not afford a "conventional" funeral. So, despite her grief, she did it herself. After her experience, she researched the subject and produced this book, which includes essays by others with experience in do-it-yourself funerals, a historical perspective, state-by-state regulations, and names, addresses, phone numbers, and prices of low-cost crematoria across the country.

6
REAL ESTATE

A home is the largest single investment most of us will make. Here are some ideas on how to save money on this investment.

🤑 MORTGAGES?

Earlier this year a reporter asked me for some recommendations for an article she was writing on income taxes. I advised that people not do dumb things to save taxes. An example of a dumb thing I gave was to deliberately not pay down (or pay off) a mortgage when one's income allowed one to do so. My comments appeared in a supplement to Sunday newspapers across the country.

I was very surprised at the reaction that advice caused. One would have thought I had questioned the existence of Santa Claus—or, even worse, the Easter Bunny!

We have all been fed certain axioms over our lifetimes, and one of those axioms is, Never pay off your mortgage. I have known people who did not need extra money but who refinanced their home just prior to retirement. That may make sense for some people, but let's look at the other side of the coin.

Many people keep a high mortgage for the tax advantages. One man I know who pulls down a six-figure salary in a high-level position with a local defense contractor said, "If it's a question of giving my money to the bank or to the government, I'll give it to the bank." Well, on the one hand, he's seen firsthand how the Department of Defense wastes our tax dollars, but, on the other hand, his six-figure salary is indirectly paid from those tax dollars. I hope his bank will be able to help him out if his government contract is canceled.

Ignoring for the moment whether you support what our government does with your money, let's take a look to see just how much of a tax advantage a mortgage is. If you are married and filing jointly, your (1996) standard deduction is $6,700. If you're single, it's $4,000. These are the amounts you get to deduct without itemizing—or, putting it another way, whether or not you actually spend this money, you can deduct it. Only if all of your other deductions equal or exceed your standard deduction is all of your mortgage interest deductible. If your mortgage interest and your other deductions don't equal your standard deduction (and mine didn't on my first home), consider paying your mortgage off if possible. You're getting no tax advantages from the interest.

But let's assume all your mortgage interest is deductible. You pay the bank, let's say, $10,000 a year in interest. If you're in the 31 percent tax bracket, you'll save $3,100 in federal income taxes (if you pay income taxes in your state, chances are you'll save there, too). What a deal! There may be a Santa Claus, Virginia, but he doesn't live at the IRS! If anyone wants to pay me $10,000 in return for my paying them $3,100, well, you've got my address. Seriously, doesn't it make sense to pay the $3,100 in taxes and keep the $10,000 you'd pay in interest?

As long as we're on the subject of taxes, let's look at another angle. Here in San Jose, I know of a property that recently sold for $170,000 and for which the fair market rent is $1,400 per month. Let's say you owned that property free and clear. Deducting the expenses you pay as an owner that you would not pay as a tenant—property taxes ($150 per month) and estimated maintenance ($100 per month)—your net rent (if you were renting instead of owning) would be $1,150 per month, or $13,800 per year. If you owned this $170,000 home free and clear, that's $13,800 per year that you are *not* paying in rent. That is equivalent to getting an 8.1 percent yield on your savings. And this 8.1 percent is tax-free!

In my opinion, having a mortgage if you don't have to does not make financial sense. In my book *Living Cheap: THE Survival Guide for the Nineties* (most libraries have it), I described the psychological reasons for paying off mortgages. Among these is not having to be quite so dependent on a paycheck to keep from being homeless and having the resultant freedom to be less inhibited in your job (which, I have found, often makes a person a better employee) or to leave a job you may not like.

I'm certainly not going to advise everyone to rush out and pay off his or her mortgage regardless of other financial obligations, but I do want everyone who has a mortgage to stop and decide for him- or herself whether it makes sense to needlessly continue carrying it. Banks pump a lot of advertising dollars into our economy. Whether for that reason or because of media naïveté, we frequently see articles on whether it is better to have an adjustable- or a fixed-rate mortgage, or a fifteen-year or a thirty-year mortgage, but we rarely see articles that examine the rather basic question of whether or not to have a mortgage at all. This is one more reason we all need to learn to think for ourselves.

SHORT SALES

I saw the Austin, Texas, real estate boom and bust firsthand. I hope it is the closest I'll ever come to witnessing a full-fledged panic like that on Wall Street in 1929. It started almost imperceptibly. I had moved from Los Angeles to Austin, where I witnessed housing prices rise so high that they were comparable to those I had left in Los Angeles. However, Austin had plenty of room to spread out, and Los Angeles was limited in that respect. Houses had stopped selling for some time before anyone seemed to notice. The oil glut had begun, but conventional wisdom had it that Austin would be all right because it was the state capital and home of the University of Texas, two entities that did not depend on oil. Prices didn't start falling right away. The market was like a jet with engines that had stopped. Everything was quiet, but everything seemed all right— except that no one was buying. And no one was lowering prices. Then, all of a sudden, as would happen with a plane with stopped engines, gravity overcame inertia. The market headed down.

Now that I'm back in San Jose, I have researched the market here. The same thing seems to be happening to the San Jose real estate market. Many people are now trying to sell homes they bought just before the 1989 Loma Prieta earthquake, and many of these carry mortgages that exceed the value of the home. Fortunately for Californians, this state has an antideficiency law, meaning that if you walk away from your mortgage, your credit will be ruined for seven years, and you will have lost all that you have put into your house, but your bank can't come after you to make up any loss it incurs. Texans don't have that luxury.

If you find yourself in a situation where you are trying to sell a house that is worth less than the loan, try talking to your lender about a "short sale." This is a sale in which the lender agrees to accept less than the amount owed on the loan. Lenders don't want to own property, and that means you'll be able to approach your lender with this option from a position of strength. After all, your only other option is to turn the property back to the lender. What have you got to lose? If your lender won't work with you, the Dumb Idea of the Month award goes to him or her, because your alternative is now pretty much limited to walking away from your mortgage, and your lender won't be able to tally his or her losses until after your house has been foreclosed and resold. And that could be a long process!

SELLING YOUR HOME IN A SLOW MARKET

Your home needs to be the best it can be. Priced right. Looking good. You must be ready to do what's needed to sell. Dress your house for success. Overstuffed rooms and closets look smaller than they are. Clear them out. Spruce up the outside—paint and clean up your yard, garage or carport, fences, roof, patio, etc. Repair windows, doors, exterior and interior walls, floors, etc. Carpets must be clean. Check the lights, wiring, plumbing, heating, and cooling. Bathrooms and kitchens are most important to women. These rooms should be light.

These tips were provided by Pat Tice, a Realtor in the Kansas City area. I'd like to emphasize her point that property must be priced right. I've looked at a few houses this year, and it seems sellers generally believe every house in town except theirs has lost value. One Realtor tried to justify a high price by *telling me the sellers paid $280,000 for a house that is now worth $230,000. When that house was built, it cost $17,000. And $17,000 has no more relevance to the current value of that house than $280,000. The only thing that matters is how much the house is worth now.*

SELLING YOUR HOME WITHOUT A REALTOR

I sold my townhouse in San Jose without a Realtor in 1994. On the one hand, I gained a genuine appreciation of just how tough a job it is to be a real estate agent. On the other hand, I did save the commission. Here are some tips to follow if you want to try selling your house yourself. (These are based on what worked for me in a very difficult market; California has been in a recession for five years, beginning with the 1989 earthquake and continuing through defense layoffs and corporate downsizing, and home prices are down at least 20 percent from their 1989 peaks here in San Jose.)

Talk to Realtors to find out what prices are in your area. Realtors can generally tell you what is for sale in your area and what the asking prices are. In many areas, they can also tell you what sold and what the selling prices were. This will give you the information you need to price your house. Some of you may think this is unethical; if that's the case, you don't have to do it. However, if you don't succeed in selling your house yourself, you will probably list it with a Realtor, and this is as good a chance to meet Realtors as any. In my case, I had been cheated to the tune of $1,000 by an unethical real estate agent when I bought my place, so I figured I was just making him earn part of that $1,000.

Have a professional sign made. Forget classified advertising. It is expensive, and it doesn't work. Instead, invest in a professional sign. Mine cost $72 (and I had easily thrown away twice that amount on ads before I decided to try the sign). The people most likely to buy your house are those who already know and like your neighborhood. They've already decided where to buy. Now it's a matter of which particular house. Your sign lets people know your house is available.

Use your sign to narrow your prospects. Remember, your goal is not to get hordes of people to look at your house. Your goal is to find that one person who is going to buy your house. On your sign list (1) the number of bedrooms and bathrooms your house has, (2) the price of your house, and (3) your phone number. Giving the size and price of your house will keep most of those who are not interested or qualified from bothering you.

Remember your goal. Remember that you are looking for one buyer. Don't be discouraged if you don't get hundreds of calls.

Decide in advance how you are going to handle real estate agents. I priced my house to include a 3 percent "co-op" fee. (The "co-op" fee will be half the going Realtor commission in your area. In most areas, the going rate is 6 percent. However, there are areas where this varies—in Kansas City, for example, it is 7 percent.) Some Realtors were willing to work with me. Others were not.

Be prepared to hear from a lot of real estate agents. Talk to them. You may find one you will want to work with should you not be able to sell your house yourself.

Be patient. And be prepared for the unexpected. The person who bought my place did so four months after she first looked at it.

When you get an offer, try to find out what the buyer really wants. In my opinion, this is the one area where selling your house yourself is better than doing it through a Realtor. In my case, the buyer wanted the unit for a specific price, which gave her all the real estate commission savings. I agreed to her price, but I negotiated a below-market rent back for the few months it would take me to move. Additionally, I saved all the fix-up costs (painting, for example) that I had anticipated spending. This was truly a win-win outcome, but it was an outcome that would probably have been impossible to negotiate through a third party (or, if two agents had been involved, a third and fourth party).

Use "faux" agents for advice. Mortgage brokers and escrow companies want your business! A mortgage broker works for points (each point is 1 percent of your buyer's loan). And your escrow company will be paid very well for handling your closing. Both of these entities can advise you on what it takes to get your paperwork done correctly and legally. (They are not agents, of course, so when you sell your house yourself, don't expect them to be responsible for any errors you may make.) The mortgage broker for the person who bought my house provided her with the real estate contract and helped her write her offer. And he provided me with the disclosure forms I needed to "keep legal."

Examine your closing documents carefully. Once you sign these documents, you have no recourse (unless you can prove fraud, and that is nearly always impossible). These documents supersede the real estate sales contract, and usually the instructions to the escrow agent are given verbally by the selling agent (or the "faux" agent). The agent (how can I say this tactfully?) may not always have your interests in mind when he gives these instructions. This is how I was cheated (it's a long story), but you can learn from my experience. The next time I sold a house, I merely advised the "faux" agent I would not sign at closing if the statement did not agree with the contract.

Question closing costs that seem too high. In the past I had filed my own documents for recording, and I knew how little effort is involved in doing this. (The forms are preprinted, and all that is required is that the blanks be filled in correctly.) Imagine my shock when I saw a "document preparation" charge of $50 on my closing statement. I was all fired up and ready to chew up and spit out an escrow officer. I didn't have to. When I mentioned those costs, the escrow officer immediately said, "Oh, we'll waive those." Imagine! All that anger and no place to go with it. I wanted to say, "No! No! I want to argue about this for a while!" But I didn't. Since my closing, I have read in a couple of articles that such charges are called "garbage fees" in the real estate business and that, if the fees are questioned, they'll generally be waived.

IN SEARCH OF CHEAPER HOUSING

This article appeared after I moved from San Jose to Kansas City.

A friend from California recently spent a week here in Kansas City. This was her second trip to the Midwest. The first had been years ago, and that was to a small town in Ohio to meet her husband's family. That trip was unpleasant, and the marriage eventually ended in divorce. From that time until now she associated the entire Midwest with that unpleasant experience in that small town and that failed marriage. And she would never consider living in the Midwest.

She came convinced Kansas City was small-minded, small-town, and homogeneous. She left—after visiting many of our attractions and museums, sampling various ethnic restaurants, driving through the various neighborhoods the city has to offer, and looking at homes—in love with the place. She found a lovely home listed for less than $50,000. She's back in California now, but she's put Kansas City on her list of places where she may want to live when she retires.

Her trip was interesting for me, too. I "discovered" Westheights, an area in Kansas City, Kansas, where truly stately homes built at the end of the First World War (some designed by Lewis Curtiss, a Frank Lloyd Wright protégé) cost less than $30 per square foot. And homes there are likely to remain cheap because Realtors tell prospective buyers, "Everyone wants to move out of Kansas City, Kansas—not in." Westheights may just be the place for someone who wants a lot of house for his or her money.

Bill Robinson recently "discovered" another part of the Midwest— North Dakota. I've never been there, but his letter follows this article.

After living here a few months, I've not given much thought to California real estate prices, but every once in a while I get a query from someone asking, "Are there homes in your area suitable for a family for less than $150,000?" In a word, yes. Many.

A few years ago, *Money* magazine had an article on how to live on 20 percent less. One of their suggestions was, if you live in an area with a high cost of housing, you should consider moving. They interviewed a family who had moved from Orange County, California, to upstate New York.

I'm not suggesting that everyone move. And I'm certainly not suggesting everyone in California move to Kansas City. But I am suggesting that, if you are considering moving, you should not automatically eliminate the Midwest. There are many cities here that offer, to coastal minds, a lot for the money. Admittedly, we have hot summers, cold winters, and no oceans, but we also have friendly people, lower prices, and a more laid-back pace of life. My next-door neighbor, an attorney, works on a schedule that gives him every other Friday off. And his employer never asks that he forgo this day off. The concept of sixty hours' work for forty hours' pay is still relatively unknown here, where employers as well as employees still believe work is only one part of a well-rounded life. And more coastal residents seem to be "discovering" the middle part of the country. Moving away from the country's high-cost coastal cities may eventually become the norm.

Even if a move is not in your plans, you may be able to find lower-cost housing where you now live. As I mentioned, Westheights in Kansas

City, Kansas, offers a lot of house for the money. There may be similar areas where you live. These may be in school districts that do not have stellar reputations. If you have no children, such an area may be ideal for you. Even if you have children, before you pay twice what you have to for a house, check out the price of private schools in your area. It may be much less expensive to pay for private schools for a few years than to pay the mortgage on a needlessly expensive house for thirty years!

If you and a friend are both looking for a home, consider buying a duplex together instead. You'll need a contract outlining how you'll handle maintenance and the eventual sale of the building, of course. However, since land prices are a major contributing factor to high housing costs, you'll be able to buy living space for much less than if each of you bought a house. In effect, this is a do-it-yourself condominium.

There are alternatives. Look for them. And happy house hunting.

BILL ROBINSON'S EXCELLENT NORTH DAKOTA ADVENTURE

Bill Robinson of Bandon, Oregon, wrote the following about a trip he took to North Dakota:

I drove 4,200 miles, and I am proud to say I have accomplished something few Americans these days even try: My route from the Oregon coast to northwestern North Dakota was made on local roads—i.e., minor two-lane federal highways, state highways, and even county highways. I always avoided metropolitan areas. This is not only more relaxing but is more interesting, and one sees the true nature (and real people) of the area rather than the artificial interstate establishments which seem to be the same almost from coast to coast.

One unexpected bonus of the route I followed was a great savings in money. In September, along the Oregon coast, one never expects to find a decent, clean, and safe room for the night for less than $80 (and $100 to $140 is common). However, the moment I crossed to the Washington state side and left Highway 101, this expense picture changed. In almost every case I picked one of the nicest motels or hotels available (in every case in a small town—i.e., one from 2,000 to 12,000 population). My average lodging cost per night was not quite $30! One of my most pleasant and luxurious rooms was also the least expensive—$18.50 in North Dakota. My most expensive was a small town in Montana, in a luxury casino hotel (the only establishment available), where I paid $40.

Though my travel in North Dakota was limited to the northwest part of that state, the landscape was a surprise to me and, I think, would be to anyone because of the conception of the state as featureless and flat. When I entered Williston (near where the Yellowstone River enters the Missouri), I was amazed at the lovely clean towns, full of trees, usually in a small river valley. Often I would explore the local streets, and seeing the neat lawns, with children playing in the streets, and well-tended trees everywhere, was like stepping back in time. A lot of these towns reminded me of small Ohio towns as they were in the 1950s when we lived there. Everywhere, in the country between the towns, there were beautiful river valleys with trees, hills, and many lakes.

North Dakota (at least the northwest part of that state) has made a practice of locating all highways one to three miles from all the villages. This has avoided the ugly strip development that is so common along other highway towns throughout the West. Such a town, when I stayed for the night, seemed quiet and isolated from even the bustle of the small, local, state highways I used. Seeing children playing freely everywhere was refreshing, since I know, from visiting my grandchildren, that few California children are safe even in their front yard without an adult constantly watching.

Minot, North Dakota, was the farthest east I traveled, and, to my surprise, it is a beautiful city—almost on a par with many European cities I have seen and visited. Should things continue to deteriorate in Oregon (thanks to the huge California invasion), we shall pick either Minot or Crosby, North Dakota, to eventually move to. Lovely three-bedroom houses sell for $30,000 to $45,000. The winters, of course, would be cold, but, as my family and I learned from three years in Montana, the cold winters are probably exaggerated. Another winter advantage would be the availability of natural gas (as we had in Montana). Our only choice in Oregon is wood (hard work) or electricity (fairly expensive).

Bill touched on some good points. Of course it gets cold in North Dakota in the winter, but he is not letting that stop him from considering that state as an alternative to where he lives now. And, as he pointed out, heating a home is less expensive in North Dakota than in Oregon. I've lived in many parts of the United States, and I found the climate to be much less important than the people. In fact, in many places, a less-than-desirable climate was an advantage. It united people. It gave them a sense of "we're all in this together." It gave people something to talk about, and they didn't have time to concentrate so much on other people's business.

REAL ESTATE RESOURCES

Bob Easter is the President of Easter and Easter, Inc., an Austin, Texas, real estate firm. He has used his experiences in the topsy-turvy Austin market to write a guide for home sellers, *14 Home-Selling Secrets: The Mistakes Everyone Makes* **($9.95 plus $3.50 shipping)**. This 94-page book succinctly covers how to avoid making your house one of those that "age" once it is on the market. While generally very good and well written, the book did have one suggestion I found dumb—that you "remove" all pets from a house for sale. Just where does he want you to "remove" them to? For many people, this is simply not possible. Aside from this one nit, I'd recommend this book to people who are considering selling their homes.

Another good book for potential home buyers is Easter's 172-page *Home Buying Power* **($12.95 plus $3.50 shipping from Easter and Easter, 4212 Lostridge Dr., Suite 1100, Austin, TX 78731, or toll-free 800-848-5593)**. Easter offers some helpful information in this book including how to write a low offer and how to negotiate to win. He also includes a very interesting chapter on future housing trends wherein he predicts that good indoor air quality, home office space, and security systems will be among those things buyers of the future will look for. He also discusses co-housing, which is currently popular in Scandinavia. Note: If you order either or both of these books *and* mention *Living Cheap News*, you will not be charged for shipping.

If you're on the other side of the real estate table, trying to buy a home, there's a new option out there for you. It's called a "buyer's agent." Until recently, general practice was for all real estate agents to be considered seller's agents. The rationale behind this was that the seller pays their commission; therefore, all agents work for the seller (and anything and everything a buyer said to them, even in confidence, was relayed to the seller). I'm sure you can see how questionable this logic is. The buyer gives the seller the money to pay the commission. Without a buyer, there is no commission! Now there are agents who work strictly for buyers. There are different types of buyer's agents. Some still accept listings from sellers. Others, including Denver-based **Buyer's Resource (for an agent near you, call them at 800-359-4092)**, work only with buyers.

If I were a first-time buyer, I would seriously consider looking for a buyer's agent. Having been through buying a home a few times, though, I prefer dealing directly with an owner or with the selling agent (and asking the selling agent to reduce his or her commission, since half is all he or she would have been paid had I used an agent to help me buy the place).

On the subject of buying a home, Dearborn Financial Publishing sent some helpful books recently. (**Dearborn's address is: 155 N. Wacker Dr., Chicago, IL 60606-1719; their toll-free number is 800-245-2665.** Shipping costs are $5 for the first book. If you order more than one book, they suggest you call first to get the exact shipping charges.) Robert Irwin's *Buy Your First Home* (**$14.95 plus shipping**) is a 196-page paperback pretty much for those who are looking for their first home. The book is up-to-date, even discussing the relatively new concept of the buyer's agent. William L. Ventolo's *Your Home Inspection Guide* (**$15.95 plus shipping**) is a 260-page book that not only discusses the usual things to inspect such as heating and plumbing systems, but also advises that soil composition, topography, house and lot orientation, etc. be looked at. Earlier this year in a Kansas City suburb, two new homes collapsed as a result of spring rains weakening the soil under them. This book offers a lot of good detailed advice. Mary Callegari's *Your Home Mortgage Answer Book: 100 Questions and the Answers You Need* (**$14.95 plus shipping**) is a 178-page paperback that does answer 100 questions about mortgages, including refinancing and mortgage insurance. The book also includes charts that help buyers determine what their payments would be for various amounts and interest rates, and there is a 45-page glossary for prospective mortgagors.

Edith Lank is a syndicated real estate columnist, and now the third edition of her book *The Home Seller's Kit* (**$15.95 plus shipping**) is available from Dearborn. The book is comprehensive, even to the point of discussing, without condescension, selling your home without an agent.

Thomas C. Steinmetz and Phillip Whitt have written *The Mortgage Kit* (**$17.95 plus shipping**), which in 268 pages gives a comprehensive guide to everything you ever wanted to know about mortgages. Ingrid Ritchie and Stephen J. Martin offer *The Healthy Home Kit* (**$19.95 plus shipping**), which deals with environmental hazards in your home. In 384 pages they cover such things as asbestos, radon, lead, formaldehyde, and, well, you get the picture. A. M. Watkins has written a jewel of a book, *Manufactured Houses* (**$14.95 plus shipping**), in which he discusses how far manufactured houses have come in recent years. He also offers a directory of manufactured-home builders, in case you want to pursue your own manufactured home.

Squeeze Your Home for Cash: 101 Great Money Making Ideas for Homeowners, by Ruth Rejnis (**$14.95 plus shipping**), discusses how to make money from your home, from long-term projects such as remodeling to such short-term cash-flow enhancers as renting a room (and she notes that many people travel and are in town only sporadically, so you might be able to rent a room to someone who may use it only once a week). Among her other suggestions are allowing your home to be used for movies or commercials, allowing your home to be part of a neighborhood tour (if it's an older, interesting home), and running a bed and breakfast. Her money-saving tips include planting a garden, having a garage sale, and teaching classes at home. She concludes by discussing reverse mortgages, how to save on insurance, and how to challenge your property tax bill. All in all, this 228-page book is refreshingly innovative.

The Home Inspection Troubleshooter, by Robert Irwin (**$14.95 plus shipping**), discusses what to inspect before you buy a home. Beginning with a one-hour inspection list, he covers pretty much everything from the roof to the foundation. The 190-page book is well written and concise. It could well help you avoid buying the dream house from hell.

If you're like I am, you often find yourself doing home remodeling in the wrong order. For example, I added a patio cover to my townhouse when I lived in San Jose. Then I had to replace the patio after the 1989 earthquake (believe me, it's much easier to do the patio first!). Now there's help for us in the form of Robert Irwin's *The Home Remodeling Organizer* (**$15.95 plus shipping**). The 227-page paperback discusses various remodeling projects from a practical viewpoint. He even discusses finding a fixer-upper house and redoing it. I was a tad disappointed with his short discussion of landscaping, my next project, but I suppose that's a minor nit.

If you're a buyer, once your contract is negotiated, chances are you're going to need a mortgage. Julie Garton-Good has written *All About Mortgages: Insider Tips to Finance the Home* **($19.95 plus shipping)**. This 288-page book even addresses the benefits and disadvantages of renting versus buying and paying cash (though you might imagine which way the book is slanted on both issues!). Written in a question-and-answer style, the book is easy to follow and thorough.

As long as we're on the topic of real estate, no list would be complete without Mitchell Levy's well-considered challenge to conventional wisdom, *Home Ownership: The American Myth* **($14.95 from Myth Breakers, 19672 Stevens Creek Blvd., Suite 200, Cupertino, CA 95014)**, in which he questions one of the axioms of our time: Is buying really better than renting? There is no one answer, but Mitchell gives you the formula for making an informed decision.

An excellent resource for those who might want to reconsider the wisdom of keeping a high mortgage is Marc Eisenson's *The Banker's Secret* **($17.95 from Good Advice Press, Box 78, Elizaville, NY 12523)**. Marc not only explains what a bad deal a mortgage is, but shows how easy it is to start paying one down.

Both Good Advice Press and Myth Breakers offer software to make their respective analyses easier. Contact them for more details.

If you're thinking of relocating to a place you know little about, Location Guides may be able to help you. They offer *Location Reports*, which provide statistics on population, crime, employment, and so on for more than 800 cities. Their *Location Guides* offer information on state and local points of contact, schools, fun things to do, etc. in your proposed new area. *Location Guides* **are $9.95**, and *Location Reports* **are $27.95**. Each order (one or both books) costs an additional $3 shipping. **Location Guides' address is P.O. Box 58506, Salt Lake City, UT 84158**.

I recently read *For Sale by Owner*, a new book from **Nolo Press (950 Parker St., Berkeley, CA 94710)**. I figured it might come in handy if I ever decide to sell my house (and the book's $24.95 price is a lot cheaper than a Realtor's commission). Although the book is informative, it's definitely for the novice, and it's pretty much for California sellers only—although some of the information might be helpful to sellers in other states.

Picket Fence Productions has come up with a videotape called *How to Sell Your Own Home* (**$28.90 postpaid from them at 1 Kennedy Dr., Suite U7, South Burlington, VT 05403, or toll-free 800-761-6060**). As you might guess from the location, the tape is geared toward sellers in the eastern United States. Sellers in other parts of the country may still find this tape useful, provided that you remember to substitute "escrow agent" in place of "attorney." My local library rents videotapes for $1 for two days, and they have a great selection of how-to videotapes. If your library offers something similar, I highly recommend that you ask your library to purchase Picket Fence's videotape. Picket Fence also sells For Sale signs, though I stand by my recommendation that you have a professional make a sign for your specific house.

If a home purchase is on your To Do list, Joseph Eamon Cummins's 260-page *Not One Dollar More* (**$21.45 postpaid from Kells Media Group, P.O. Box 60, Oceanville, NJ 08231, or toll-free 800-875-1995**) is a must-read. The book is well written and intelligent and offers a lot of tongue-in-cheek humor as well as a lot of really good advice. Mr. Cummins discusses the art of being a negotiator without appearing to be negotiating. For example, when prospective buyers are faced with an agent's telling them that someone else is interested in a particular house, Mr. Cummins advises that the prospective buyer politely ask the agent to get back in touch if the other prospective sale falls through. In other words, the buyer should call the agent's bluff.

7
RENTING
VERSUS
BUYING

The *Wall Street Journal* recently had an article about baby boomers who are selling their homes and moving to apartments and rented townhouses. People are not doing this in droves, but in many parts of the country people have learned that buying a house can no longer be considered an investment. And they are basing their decision to buy or rent on how they feel about owning their own space.

To many of us, myself included, owning a home is more than a financial decision. It gives us a sense of control—a sense that in our own place no one can tell us what to do and no one can raise our rent. This is a false sense of security, of course. Our property taxes can certainly go up, as can our utility costs. And every locale has zoning and use restrictions. But we can still feel that the place is ours. It is certainly ours when it comes to maintaining it, and that maintenance can be expensive. I doubt that there is a homeowner alive who at one time or another has not thought about how nice it was to have a landlord. But until recently we've at least been able to tell ourselves that our home was a good investment.

California real estate has declined in value about 20 percent since 1989, and renting now looks pretty good to those of us who bought there during the 1980s. My timing worked out all right; I made a small profit on my townhouse, but its value, on paper, resembled a bell curve. I bought on the left side of the curve and sold on the right. Its peak (on paper) was about $70,000 higher than it actually brought. I'm fortunate I didn't buy at the peak.

Mitchell Levy, who lived not far from where I lived in California, has published a book titled ***Home Ownership: The American Myth (Myth Breakers, 1993),*** in which he provides the means for you to determine whether renting is better than buying in your area. Mitchell, who owns his home, should be given a great deal of credit for broaching the subject and pointing out that buying is not always the best choice.

If you are not living where you plan to retire, you may well consider renting. If you know where you want to retire, you might consider buying a home there and renting it out until you are ready to retire. This will give you some tax write-offs, including depreciation, insurance, and travel to inspect your retirement home, that you would not have if you occupied your home. If you could rent your retirement home for as much as you pay in rent where you live, you would come out ahead.

Renting has another advantage. You won't spend money on major remodeling. My townhouse had one of those avocado kitchens that were popular for about fifteen minutes in 1974. It was dark and dank, and I had it redone to the tune of $10,000. I did get my money back when I sold the place, but I suspect I would have done just as well to have left well enough alone. And, had I been renting, I would have left well enough alone.

Before I bought my townhouse, I had been renting another one that I actually liked better for $900 a month, or $10,800 a year. When I bought, I assumed a VA loan for $11,000, and the payments were about $1,400 a month. I lost the interest on $11,000 and paid $500 more a month. But wait. That was not all! I also paid the homeowners' dues of $121 a month. My "bargain" cost me this much per month:

Payments	$1,400
Homeowners' dues	121
Lost interest @ 8%	73
Total	$1,594

If I take into account tax deductions for interest and property taxes, the bottom line was probably around $1,100 a month, or $200 more than if I had continued renting.

I eventually paid off my mortgage, but I had $145,000 on which I was not earning interest. At 8 percent, even though my house was paid for, it was costing me:

Interest missed	$ 967
Homeowners' dues	121
Total	$1,088

I was paying nearly $200 a month more than if I were renting. After the kitchen redo, the total came to $1,155 (adding in the lost interest on the $10,000 it cost to remodel the kitchen).

Figuring my average after-tax cost to buy instead of rent was $200 a month, I lost $16,800 during the seven years I lived in my townhouse. When I sold it I cleared about $15,000 on paper. Of that, more than $5,000 went to Uncle Sam and the Great State of California. In retrospect, renting would have been a much better choice.

Marc Eisenson, author of *The Banker's Secret*, which tells what a bad deal a mortgage is and how to get rid of yours early, lives with his partner, Nancy Castleman, in a charming rented home in the Hudson River Valley. From their home, they now produce *The Banker's Secret Bulletin*. Marc and Nancy have decided that, for them, renting makes sense.

The bottom line here is that renting may be your most sensible financial option. There will always be areas in which housing prices will, for a time, increase. However, the baby boom generation, which escalated prices simply because too many were looking for a diminishing supply of homes, is pretty much housed by now, and the demand that drove prices is no longer there. In fact, when the baby boom generation no longer needs all the houses that have been built, prices may well decline.

KEEPING A LID ON RENT COSTS

I have been both a landlord and a tenant. If you decide to be a long-term renter, here are some things you can do to keep your costs down:

Find a place you really like. Even if you have to pay a little more for it, living in pleasant surroundings will help your mood and your overall sense of well-being. You will also be less likely to look for something else, which will save you time, energy, and money. Moving is expensive and tiring. Renting space you like in the first place is a way to avoid moving.

Rent from an individual, if possible. If you rent in a huge complex run by a computer and a manager, you're going to face periodic rent increases no matter what you do.

Have an application form already completed. You will give the appearance of having your act together, and you won't have to go looking for your account numbers and other details.

Get to know your landlord. Realize your landlord is human and let him or her know you are, too.

Don't make your landlord sweat the small stuff. If something simple needs to be done, do it yourself. But let your landlord know you've done it yourself.

Help out. If garbage cans need to be set out, do that yourself. Save your landlord work.

Always pay your rent on time. Landlords appreciate punctuality. They have bills to pay, too.

Keep your place neat. Landlords like to rent to people who will take care of their property.

What, you may be asking, are the advantages of all this? Simple. You may well be able to live in your home for years without a rent increase if you follow these steps.

I have never raised the rent on a good tenant—I know how hard they are to come by. If you are paying $500 a month and your landlord is thinking about raising your rent by 10 percent, or $50, believe me, he or she will think long and hard before risking that you will find somewhere else to live. If you move, and if your unit is vacant one month, it will take ten months at the new rate to make up for the loss. And the odds against the new tenant's being as good as you are, from the landlord's perspective, are about 90 percent (and I say this from experience).

So if you rent and turn out to be a good tenant, you might not have to deal with frequent rent increases.

🏅 RESOURCE

If you're trying to decide whether to buy or rent a home, issue number 5 of *The Banker's Secret Bulletin* (**$5.95 from Good Advice Press, Box 78, Elizaville, NY 12523**) is a must-read. Those of us who came of age in the 1970s and 1980s basically learned to cope with a housing market that was an anomaly. And eventually, we accepted this anomaly as the norm. Unprecedented inflation and baby boomers looking for places to live drove housing prices out of sight for many. The market of the 1990s may be a return to that of the very early 1970s, when the decision to rent or buy boiled down to whether one wanted to be encumbered with a house (yes, it really was that simple once upon a time—I actually knew people who sold their house and moved to an apartment because they didn't want to be bothered with the upkeep).

I realize this is the second time I have mentioned *The Banker's Secret Bulletin*, but Marc Eisenson's research on the rent-or-buy question is so impressive that issue number 5 is well worth a special mention.

8
AUTOMOBILES

The first question we should ask ourselves regarding automobiles is, Do I need one? I have recently seen ads for very low-mileage cars. One, a 1977 Pontiac, had 72,000 miles; another, a 1979 Buick, had 35,000 miles (the asking price for each of these, by the way, was $2,500). The Pontiac's owner drove an average of 4,000 miles a year; the Buick's owner drove less than 2,200 miles a year. Given the depreciation, insurance, and maintenance cost of those cars, I wonder if using taxis might not have been cheaper. Most of the people in the world do not own cars, and many people who can well afford cars choose not to own one. Paul Terhorst, author of *Cashing In on the American Dream: How to Retire at 35*, has not owned a car since 1972.

Going a step further, if we already have a car and are thinking about replacing the one we own, we should ask ourselves, "Do I need a different car?"

If you need a car or have a car, this chapter is for you.

BUYING A USED CAR

Richard Peterson of Clinton Township, Michigan, wrote and asked for an article on buying a used car. He emphasized he was not looking for an old clunker. He was interested in a car a couple of years old. Here goes.

As I discussed in my book *Living Cheap: THE Survival Guide for the Nineties*, I have purchased two new cars in my life—a 1971 Volkswagen and a 1980 Buick Regal. Both cars were good, but with both cars I had problems getting the dealers to honor their warranties. When the service manager of the Buick dealership where I bought the Regal told me he would not fix some minor defects because I hadn't paid for a perfect car, I decided that buying a new car was pointless. I bought my current car, a 1986 Oldsmobile Delta 88, in 1988. It had 24,000 miles on it, and it was $6,500 less than a new model. It wasn't perfect, but this time I hadn't paid for perfection.

The potential advantages of buying a used car are many. They cost less to begin with. Because they cost less, there is less sales tax to pay. Because their value is less, license fees and insurance costs are normally lower. There are, of course, some financial risks involved in buying a used car. The car may not have been maintained. It may have been a lemon. There are ways to minimize these risks.

The first thing I do when I am in the market for a used car is decide what kind of car I want. I am somewhat fortunate in that I travel a good deal, and I rent a variety of cars. My decisions to buy the Regal and the famous Oldsmobile were based on my being impressed with similar cars I had rented. I have been impressed lately with Ford's Taurus and the Buick Century. When I'm in the market for a different car (and I don't plan to be in that market for a long time), I'll certainly consider these cars. The April 1996 issue of *SmartMoney* advises that nearly 600,000 1994 Ford cars and trucks, or about 20 percent of Ford's total 1994 retail sales, will be coming off two-year leases in 1996, which should drive used-car prices down until this glut of cars can be absorbed. Additionally, Ford has drastically restyled its popular Taurus and Sable models for 1996, which should drive down prices for previous year models of these cars even further. *SmartMoney* also advises that some leases include free maintenance, offering opportunities for savings on barely used and well-maintained automobiles.

If you don't know what kind of car you will be looking for, a good place to start is your library. You will find such books as *The Complete Car Cost Guide*, which tells you, among other things, which cars depreciate fastest. (Remember, when you're buying a used car, you are making depreciation work for you.)

Car rental companies are a good place to look for a used car. Usually they don't offer their problem cars to the public, their cars are well maintained (normally they will even show you the records), and they almost always come with some sort of warranty. And the car rental business is very competitive. They're not looking to alienate any customers. My sister bought a 1985 Oldsmobile this way. When she tearfully parted with it last year, she had put 200,000 trouble-free miles on it. By the way, if you rent a car you really like, ask if it will be put up for sale soon. I did this once and found out the car was scheduled for sale that month. (Note: Some car rental companies no longer sell directly to the public. They sell to dealers who resell these cars as "program" vehicles. You should be able to locate these dealers by telephoning car rental companies in your area or by watching for the word "program" in car dealers' ads.)

Another good place to look for cars is the used-car lot of a new-car dealer that sells a different brand or type of car. I bought the Oldsmobile from an Acura dealer. Its first owner wanted something more stylish, and the Olds didn't fit in with the kinds of cars an Acura dealer would typically offer. So it was priced to move.

The classified ad section of your newspaper is another good place to look for used cars. This is how I located the famous Olds in the first place.

Put out the word that you're in the market for a car. You never know whose brother, aunt, or cousin may have one to sell. If you're dealing with an individual, though, be extra careful. Not everyone is out to sell you a lemon, but individuals are not counting on repeat business, so their incentive to be honest with you is less than that of someone who is in the business and, presumably, has a reputation to protect. Additionally, state laws requiring disclosure of known defects are more easily enforced when a dealer is involved.

Check the value of the car you're interested in. Most banks and credit unions, as well as your library, have the *Kelly Blue Book*, which lists wholesale and retail prices for used cars. Use this as a guide. If you're dealing with someone who has unrealistic expectations and who won't negotiate, walk away. (But leave your telephone number—he or she might decide to be more reasonable later.)

Before you buy, find out how much car insurance is going to cost you. And find out if there are any "flukes" that make your choice of car more expensive than other models. In my case, for example, I found out (too late) that the two-door model I bought costs more to insure than a four-door model. It is not logical, but it's a fact.

After you've found your car and checked the price you'll pay to insure it, have a mechanic check it out. Any reputable dealer or individual will let you do this. You may have to put down a deposit to take the car off the lot, but by now you should be considered a serious customer. Only a dolt of a salesperson will throw a monkey wrench into the deal at this point. If you run into one of these dolts, speak to his or her manager.

FUEL SAVINGS TO MAKE YOUR CAR LAST

Nutz & Boltz™ is one of the best automotive newsletters I've seen. They accept no advertising, so their allegiance is to their readers. And they pull no punches. If there's something dumb or underhanded going on in the auto industry, you're likely to read about it in *Nutz & Boltz* first. The 16-page monthly newsletter is $25, and the fact that they keep you up-to-date on "Secret Warranties" could well make this newsletter a good automotive investment. Their address is **P.O. Box 123, Butler, MD 21023-0123 (phone 800-888-0091)**.

The following fuel-saving tips to help your vehicle last are an excerpt from *Nutz & Boltz* newsletter (reprinted with permission from Volume VII, Number 3):

- **Keep your tires inflated at the correct pressure.** Underinflation causes tire wear and wastes fuel.

- **Do not carry unneeded weight in your vehicle.** Excess weight puts a heavier load on the engine.

- **Avoid lengthy warmup idling.** Once the engine is running smoothly, begin driving—but gently. Remember, however, that on cold winter days it may take a little longer to warm up your car.

- **Accelerate slowly and smoothly.** Avoid jackrabbit starts. Get into high gear as quickly as possible.

- **Avoid long engine idling.** If you have to wait and you're not in traffic, it's better to turn off the engine and start again later.

- **Avoid engine lug or over revving.** Use a gear range suitable for the road you are traveling.

- **Use your air conditioner only when absolutely necessary.** The air conditioner puts an extra load on the engine, increasing fuel consumption.

- **Avoid continuous speeding up and slowing down.** Stop-and-go driving wastes fuel.

- **Avoid unnecessary stopping and braking.** Maintain a steady pace. Try to time the traffic signals so you have to stop as little as possible or take through streets to avoid traffic lights.

- **Keep a proper distance from other vehicles to avoid sudden braking.** This will also reduce wear on your brakes.

- **Avoid heavy traffic or traffic jams** whenever possible.

- **Do not rest your foot on the clutch or brake pedal.** This causes needless wear, overheating, and poor fuel economy. *[Editor's note: Resting your foot on the brake also causes your brake lights to go off and on without any logical reason; this may cause people driving behind you to give you the universal hand gesture that does not mean "Have a nice day."]*

- **Maintain a moderate speed on highways.** The faster you drive, the greater the fuel consumption. By reducing your speed, you will cut down on fuel consumption.

- **Keep the front wheels in proper alignment.** Avoid hitting curbs, and slow down on rough roads. Improper alignment not only causes faster tire wear but also puts extra load on the engine, which in turn wastes fuel.

- **Keep the bottom of your vehicle free from mud, etc.** This not only lessens weight but also helps prevent corrosion.

- **Keep your vehicle tuned up and in top shape.** A dirty air cleaner, improper valve clearance, dirty plugs, dirty oil and grease, brakes not adjusted, etc. all lower engine performance and contribute to poor fuel economy. For longer life of all parts and lower operating costs, keep all maintenance work on schedule, and if you often drive under severe conditions, see that your vehicle receives more frequent maintenance.

💰 BUYING A NEW CAR

Although even *The Wall Street Journal* has reported a mass price-driven switch from new cars to used, we'll take a look at new-car shopping. If you're in the market for a new car, there are a couple of shopping services out there that claim they can save you money as well as time. Generally, you need to be able to tell these services exactly what you want, and they'll get bids from various automobile dealers. The first is Car-Bargains (800-475-7283). They charge $135 for their service. The second is AutoAdvisor (800-326-1976). Their charge ranges from $335 to $359, depending on how soon you need your car (they did throw in a coupon good for $35 off the price of their services in their mailing).

You may well be able to do something similar on your own. A friend of mine decided a couple of years ago that he wanted to buy a new truck. He decided exactly what he wanted on it, including a special paint job, and he sent his specifications to all of the Ford dealers in the San Francisco Bay area. He was very pleased with the results, and what he spent in postage was more than offset by the cost of the fuel he didn't use truck shopping.

💰 CAR REPAIRS

Mark Eskeldson, the host of "Shop Talk: America's Radio Car Clinic," sent me a copy of the second edition of **What Auto Mechanics Don't Want You to Know** (**$11.95**; to find a bookstore that sells the book, call

Technews Publishing, 800-788-3123). According to the 234-page book, the world of car repair is not only unethical, it's become a business that, in some cases, is institutionally corrupt, with franchisees and store owners being pressured to increase parts turnover, which means the cheerful salesperson you give your car keys to may try to sell you repairs you don't need. The book covers some of the better-known undercover investigations, including the infamous Sears fiasco, but it points out that an estimated 75 percent of all repair scams are carried out without suspicion. On the bright side, the book lists Nissan and Toyota "secret warranties" as examples of situations where the car is out of warranty but the manufacturer made such a major error that the manufacturer will pay to have the problem fixed anyway.

DUMB IDEA OF THE MONTH

The coveted award this month goes to Sears for their Die Hard battery. This battery costs around $80 and has a prorated guarantee for six years. Not only does it allegedly never need maintenance, there is no way for the average person to open it to add water. Does it last six years? Not in my experience. Does Sears live up to the guarantee? You bet, and that's the scam. Sears is not selling a six-year battery for $80; Sears is selling a battery for $1.11 per month. And the only way to get your $1.11 per month battery is to go on buying and buying. If you don't have a Die Hard, don't buy one. If you do have a Die Hard, the next time it dies, think hard about getting out of the Die Hard replacement cycle. Check the prices elsewhere, especially at places like Price-Costco, Sam's, and Wal-Mart before you sign on for another Die Hard. Wal-Mart sells six-year batteries for about $48. And it will replace a battery that lasts less than three years at no cost.

READER'S CAR TIPS

John Gast of Chandler, Arizona, shared some thoughts on managing automobile expenses. After demonstrating that automotive expenses for a person driving 15,000 miles per year could top $5,000, Mr. Gast recommended that owners:

Keep a yearly record of all expenses. Maintain the vehicle by changing the oil and filter every 3,000–4,000 miles, changing the automatic transmission oil and filter every 30,000–40,000 miles, changing the air filter when dirty, changing the antifreeze every couple of years, maintaining the tire air pressure, checking the belts and hoses for deterioration, keeping battery connections and cables clean and in good repair, checking gas mileage frequently and getting a tune-up when gas mileage drops, and repairing small problems before they become major problems. Park in covered parking as much as possible. It makes no sense to leave a $15,000 asset out in the weather because the garage has $1,000 worth of stuff in it.

(This is good advice from another perspective as well. A garaged car is harder to steal, and some insurance companies give discounts if a car is garaged at night.)

When buying a car, buy unused miles. For example, a 1988 Honda with 44,000 miles for $5,000 should last another 106,000 miles, so the cost per 1,000 miles would be $47.16. Buying a car takes patience, but if a deal is missed, there will always be another one down the road. When buying a used car, have it inspected. This is a small cost and it could avert a financial disaster. Control the "I want a new car" desire by washing and waxing the old car, changing the appearance of the old car—get new wheels, tint the windows, add pinstriping, etc., and by checking the expense record of your current car and balancing it against the cost of owning a new car.

💰 AUTOMOTIVE TOLL-FREE NUMBERS

The following are the customer service numbers for various automobile companies. All the numbers except the one listed for Alfa Romeo are toll-free.

Acura	800-382-2238
Alfa Romeo	407-856-5000
Audi	800-822-2834

BMW	800-831-1117
Buick	800-521-7300
Cadillac	800-458-8006
Chevrolet	800-222-1020
Chrysler Corporation	800-992-1997
Ford Motor Company	800-392-3673
Geo	800-222-1020
GMC Truck	800-462-8782
Honda	800-633-5151
Infiniti	800-662-6200
Isuzu	800-255-6727
Jaguar	800-452-4827
Land Rover	800-346-3493
Lexus	800-255-3987
Mazda	800-222-5500
Mercedes	800-222-0100
Mitsubishi	800-222-0037
Oldsmobile	800-442-6537
Pontiac	800-762-2737
Porsche	800-545-8039
Saab	800-955-9007
Saturn	800-553-6000
Subaru	800-782-2783
Suzuki	800-447-4700
Toyota	800-331-4331
Volkswagen	800-822-8987
Volvo	800-458-1552
	or 800-526-4785

And, finally, the NHTSA Auto Safety Hotline (to find out if your car is involved in a recall) is 800-424-9393.

9
ENTERTAINMENT

"But what do you do for fun?"

That's the question I get asked the most by media interviewers. And it's a question that is really difficult to answer because my work is fun. I love to read, I love to write, I love to figure out ways to "beat the system," and I love to show others how to do the same. And *Living Cheap News* gives me the opportunity to do it all.

Every day, unless the weather is really miserable, I take my dogs for a two-mile walk. I enjoy this chance to watch the seasons change, to see what changes my neighbors are making to their homes (my neighborhood comprises houses mostly built in the 1920s). This alone can be quite amusing as I think about all the families who have lived in these houses. The house I lived in during the late 1970s (in this same neighborhood) had a fence at the front of the house which had to be opened before I could put my car in the garage. I moved the fence back to the garage (my neighbor at the time told me that's where the fence had been when she moved in). The fence is now back to where it was when I bought the house. I think of all the changes that have been done (and undone) in the past seventy years. I imagine the wonder of the homes' occupants as the first radios were brought into the living rooms. I think about how the inhabitants adapted or were defeated during the Great Depression, how anxious families waited for news of loved ones during World War II, and how recent history has been received within these walls. It occurs to me that these houses, which have undoubtedly out-lived their first owners, are merely temporary containers for their human inhabitants, just as our bodies are temporary containers for our souls.

These houses keep me humble. Too often we believe that all his-tory has occurred simply to bring us to our time. We believe, so to speak, that our time is the ultimate destination of the train of time, when in reality our time is merely a whistle-stop on a route that has eons to go. And this should be comforting to us. We don't have to do everything. What we don't do will be done by the next generation. Or the next. All we really have to do is to be. And so my entertainment is being. Being myself, being a writer, being a resident, finally, of where I want to live, and being independent.

Which is not to say I don't "do." I enjoy travel. I enjoy eating out. I enjoy jazz. I enjoy theater. In short, I enjoy pretty much the same things others enjoy. But I enjoy them on the cheap. I find I don't have to spend a lot of money to be entertained.

Most cities have areas that can be enjoyed simply by walking through them. One such area that comes to mind is Alexandria, Virginia's Old Town. Cobblestone streets and eighteenth-century buildings, many of which are now shops, provide a scenic walk for those of us who delight in urban scenes. If you prefer the more rural scene, you can drive to the country or, if your city has one, you can walk (or jog, if you're into such masochism) the increasingly popular nature trails that are sprouting up on rights-of-way once populated by riders of now-defunct streetcars, interurbans, and passenger trains.

Ethnic areas have developed in surprising places. Many recent immi-grants are discovering the Midwest; as a result, we who live in the cities on the prairies now have the same access to good Asian, Indian, East-ern European, Ethiopian, and other ethnic restaurants we used to have to travel to the coasts for. Kansas City and its suburbs now have a choice of an incredible variety and quantity of lunch buffets (most of which are priced at $4.95). Finding these can be a challenge, but if your area has one or more of those weekly "alternative" newspapers (these are almost always free), pick them up. These newspapers used to be known pri-marily for their sleazy sex ads, but many of them have cleaned up their act, and almost all of them review new, inexpensive restaurants long before the mainstream newspapers (which seem to specialize in repeat visits to long-time, well-known, and expensive eateries) get around to them.

By the way, I've seen a couple of Chinese buffets in New Zealand, but the buffet concept as we know it is pretty much an American invention. If you go to Germany, for example, expect to pay for everything. Last summer, some friends and I went to a Mexican restaurant in Augsburg. Even the chips and salsa were an extra 8 marks (about $6). The whole meal, for five people, was 136 marks (about $105), but that included drinks—which brings me to the subject of alcohol.

Drinks can add a lot to the price of a meal. If you want a before-dinner drink, I'd suggest you have one at home if you are not the designated driver. With the price of palatable wine at $7 to $8 for five liters, it really doesn't make a lot of sense to buy the same stuff for $2 to $3 a glass, does it? Even soft drinks, tea, and coffee can add a lot to the price of a meal, though I will admit I have a weakness for an after-dinner coffee. If you want to shave the price of a drink off your meal and still appear to be having something other than water, ask for water with a slice of lemon in it.

Two-for-one deals (see the resources described at the end of this chapter) are a great deal for two people. Do remember to tip for both meals, but be advised you should not be charged sales tax for the meal you got free. If I am charged this sales tax, and if the waiter or waitress will not take the tax off without a big hassle, I simply deduct it from his or her tip. This way, the waiter or waitress has a vested interest in correcting the mischarge.

If you're not into buffets or don't have a two-for-one coupon, you can still save on restaurant meals. Remember, lunch is almost always cheaper than dinner, so eat out at noon if possible. Some eateries have "early-bird" specials. Call ahead to see if such is the case where you plan to have dinner.

Some of the best food deals can be found at "happy hours." Many of these offer meat, vegetables, chicken wings, cheese, and so on. Usually you have to buy a drink (and a soft drink is perfectly acceptable), but the food is free.

For other entertainment, bookstores are certainly a possibility. And many bookstores now have coffee bars as well. I especially enjoy used-book stores, and as the price of books goes up, a new breed of used-book store is coming into being. You won't find dusty copies of *A Texan Looks at Lyndon* in these shops. These have only slightly used copies of recent books (a lot of these are review copies). And they usually have a coffee bar and reading rooms as well. And, if you find the shop nearly empty, you can get to know the owner. In addition, if you have some books to sell or trade, you might be able to take home some goodies without having to shell out any cash.

When it comes to books, your library is hard to beat. I recently read *Balkan Ghosts* by Robert Kaplan. Kaplan refers often to John Reed's little-known 1916 book *The War in Eastern Europe*. John Reed went on to write the well-known *Ten Days That Shook the World* about the Russian Revolution. He eventually chose to live in the Soviet Union, where he died in 1920. His life was the subject of the lengthy Warren Beatty movie *Reds*. Robert Kaplan said he had to pay several hundred dollars for his copy of *The War in Eastern Europe*. Just out of curiosity I decided to see if I could get this book from my local library. Sure enough, they had it (at another branch), and I was able to check it out. It's the first (and only) edition, it's been in the library since 1918, it was rebound in 1944, and it's available to anyone who has a library card!

I also wanted to read another book mentioned in *Balkan Ghosts*. This book, *Athene Palace* by Goldie Horowitz writing under the pen name "Countess Waldeck," is a unique view of the Nazi occupation of Romania by a naturalized American citizen who was Jewish and who had emigrated from Germany just as Hitler came to power. The book was written just before the attack on Pearl Harbor and published in February 1942. I was able to get this book also from the public library. That is not as amazing as is the fact that the last time the book had been checked out was in April 1948. Who else would keep an unread book for forty-seven years?

And your library is not just for books anymore. Most libraries now offer compact discs, books on tape, and videotapes. Many have for years offered art that you can check out and hang on your wall for a while. Some have discussion groups. All of them have great reference sections. And, if the library does not have the book you're looking for, the odds are you can get it through the Interlibrary Loan Program. Some libraries charge 50¢ or $1 to get a book for you from another library, but that's still a pretty cheap way to read.

Check out your local adult education program. You'll be surprised at what some of these are offering. Kansas City's Communiversity, for example, has offered courses on meeting single members of the opposite sex, advice for cross-dressers (no, you didn't read that wrong), living within your income, retiring rich, barter groups, and alien abduction, and a variety of psychic courses, as well as tours of historic and ethnic areas of the city. (Would you believe right here in the heart of the Midwest we have a Serbian Orthodox church that offers services in Serbian conducted by a priest from Serbia?) Whatever your interests, odds are there's a course for you. Taking these courses is not only a way of learning more about a particular subject, it's a way of meeting people who have similar interests. And the courses are cheap. Communiversity courses cost from $5 to $9, and the tours are only slightly more expensive.

Believe it or not, even though I am not crazy about our twentieth-century temples, shopping malls, I do get a kick out of shopping. I enjoy estate sales. I like wandering through old homes, and occasionally I do find a bargain. I don't really go to these things to buy but, rather, for entertainment. I enjoy the reaction of some people to what's available, and you see all kinds of people at these sales, from antique dealers to people who think they'll die if they don't get into one of the rooms before you do. Garage sales are also fun sometimes, but true estate sales must sell everything to settle the estate. People who have garage sales can just put their unsold stuff back in the garage.

If you do go to estate sales or garage sales, don't assume the asking price is the final price. Unless the item is something you really and desperately want, or unless it is already a bargain, ask if the price is the least the sellers will take. The worst they can say is that the price is firm. Be prepared to walk away, leave a bid, or leave your phone number.

But please don't forget your manners. I was somewhat shocked by the approach taken by the customers at the first (and probably only) garage sale my parents had a few years back. None of us was prepared to deal with rudeness. As a result I developed the following ten commandments for garage sale shoppers:

1. Remember, you're at someone's home.

2. It is not polite to throw things on the floor/ground if you think the price is too high.

3. If you must bring your children, control them. (One of our customers left in a huff when I asked her little darlings not to fight around the glassware.)

4. You can achieve a lot by speaking civilly to the sellers. Chances are their goal is as much to get rid of stuff (and this becomes more true after a couple of days of putting the stuff out and bringing it back in) as it is to make money.

5. If you honestly believe something is overpriced, by all means, make a lower offer.

6. If something is priced right, don't negotiate. If the seller wanted to give it away, he or she would already have done so.

7. If you find a fantastic bargain, don't gloat to the seller.

8. Don't criticize the items for sale. If you don't like them, don't buy them.

9. Don't ask to use the rest room; you are not at a service station.

10. If you don't need an item, it's not a bargain—even if it's cheap.

Another form of entertainment you might want to think about is developing a hobby. Gardening is an example of a hobby that could save you money. Consider your garden edible landscaping. Wine making or beer brewing are certainly hobbies that could save money (if you already drink wine or beer). Before you choose a hobby, make sure it is something you want to do, and approach it slowly. I have friends who have tried several hobbies. With each one they bought everything it would take to pursue that particular hobby. As you might imagine, their pursuit of hobbies has led to an attic full of unused stuff.

I mentioned that I enjoy theater. To me there is something about a live performance that is just so much more invigorating than watching a movie. But I like to enjoy theater as inexpensively as possible. So I go on preview nights, and I take advantage of two-for-one deals such as those offered in the Entertainment coupon books. The regular price for a play at my favorite local theater is $15. Preview nights cost $11. I know even the regular price would be a bargain in New York, where $50 to $60 is now common (and even TKTS's price would still be more than twice the local price), but I look on it as "pay $33 for three and see one almost free" (the regular price for two is $30).

I also mentioned I like jazz, and in that I am fortunate because Kansas City is a big jazz town where many of the greats (Charlie Parker, Count Basie, etc.) got their start. We have many jazz events throughout the year, and we have a couple of radio stations that get a certain number of free tickets (to give as prizes to their audiences) to these events, probably in return for advertising the sessions. If I'm home in the daytime, listening to a jazz station, I have a pretty good chance of getting through when they give these tickets away. So I can get a free seat at a live performance. Of course a lot of radio stations offer similar deals to rock concerts, New Age music sessions, etc. It's a good way to get pricey entertainment free.

Museums offer entertainment to those so inclined, and many museums have days they don't charge admission. Call the museum you are interested in and ask about "free" days. By the way, if you're overseas, hungry, and in a museum, museum snack shops are often good and inexpensive places to eat.

If you have a college or university in your area, you may be able to go to lectures, concerts, or plays cheap or free. Often, area newspapers will list what's going on at local campuses. Check to see what the schools offer, and, if possible, get on their mailing lists.

Each of us has his or her own idea of "entertainment." We can be entertained at a high cost, or we can generally find the same entertainment in a less expensive manner. It's up to us to look for alternatives.

ENTERTAINMENT RESOURCES

The folks at **Entertainment (2125 Butterfield Rd., Troy, MI 48084, or call 810-637-8400; this is not a toll-free number)** sent me a coupon book for the San Jose area. I've been a customer of theirs off and on since 1971, when I bought my first book in Columbus, Ohio. Since then, I've used their coupons in Kansas City, Los Angeles, and San Jose. The coupon books have come a long way in recent years. They're much bigger, and many restaurants now offer 50 percent off for single diners rather than sticking to "buy one and get one free," which implies only couples dine out. The selection of savings is also much better, including 50 percent off at some bakery thrift stores. The savings on meals and entertainment are considerable. (I can thank Entertainment for an even greater savings. Years ago, I invited a young woman to dinner, and she accepted—provided I did not use one of my Entertainment coupons. She said she wanted to be more to me than just the free meal on a coupon. Well, that was the end of that. It was obvious we weren't compatible, and I didn't have to spend a fortune to find out!)

If you're in one of the cities for which there is an Entertainment book (there are 119 editions, including ones for London and Europe), and if you dine out, go to the movies, or buy tickets to sporting events, you might consider buying one. Many charities sell them. The Entertainment books are in the $30 range as of the 1996 edition, and many groups offer discounts to that price. I was able to buy mine for $28.

Now Entertainment has a little brother that may actually be a better deal. These are the Gold C coupon books sold by many schools to raise money for various activities. They are $10, and they have many of the same coupons as the Entertainment books (mine has three bakery thrift store coupons, each worth $5, so I'm already $5 ahead on my book). I don't know about you, but I'd much rather buy one of these than the typical overpriced candy, cookies, or magazine subscriptions schools have traditionally had their students push. And if I'll buy one, nearly anyone else should be an easy sale! If you have any influence with your local schools, you might want to take a look at Gold C. The address of their "Youth Division" is the same as Entertainment's address. The Youth Division phone number is 810-237-9727. If you can't easily find a book, write them or check your local white pages under "Entertainment Publications."

One of the best books I know of that deals extensively with inexpensive entertainment is Shel Horowitz's *The Penny-Pinching Hedonist*. The book is **$20 plus $.85 Massachusetts sales tax, if applicable, from AWM, P.O. Box 1164, Northampton, MA 01061**. To order with a credit card, call 800-683-WORD.

10
FOOD

When it comes to food, we in America are fortunate indeed. Food is available. Food is plentiful. And food is wasted. This would shock many people in this world, believe me. I saw the food lines in Eastern Europe. I was with friends there when one man carrying about two dozen eggs attracted the attention of all his neighbors, who wanted to buy part of his bounty. In that area of the world, the price of food was not of primary importance. Food was simply hard to find at any price. And food—the search for it, the waiting in many lines for it, and the paying for it—took a large percentage of both the money and the time of the people of that world. Our world is different.

For most of us, food takes a small percentage of our income. And the only time involved is the time it takes us to go to the store, select and pay for our groceries, and return home. And what a selection we have! We are indeed fortunate. We can select high-price convenience foods, or we can select cheap basics. And, if we know where to look, sometimes we can even find free food.

I was in the checkout line behind a person who was using food stamps one day. The person didn't really buy anything frivolous, but everything was a brand name, and nothing was on sale. I thought to myself, "If I could just spend some time with that person, I could help that person make those food stamps go twice as far." But, of course, I didn't butt in. Then.

But now I'm going to pretend you are that person.

I occasionally buy frozen convenience foods if I have a coupon and they are on sale. But I know, even then, the prices are high. If you want to cut your costs, cut down on convenience foods.

Skip by the store's deli, the salad bar (unless you are looking for cheese; sometimes the salad bar price of cheese is lower than the dairy case price), and the bakery (unless they have a day-old section). Find out if your store has areas for bread, cheese, and meat that are nearing their "sell by" dates. If they do, you'll be able to save 50 percent or more by shopping these areas. Don't be shy about combining coupons (or, better, double coupons) with these marked-down products. In fact, don't be shy at all about combining coupons not only with sales prices, but with store coupons (generally, you can't combine two manufacturer's coupons on one product, but you can use both a store coupon and a manufacturer's coupon) and, when it is really a sale, with "buy one, get one free" deals. (Watch out for these, though. Quite frequently, you buy one at twice the regular price and get one free.)

Check out places like Sam's, Price-Costco, etc. If you have an Aldi's in your area, you're one step ahead. One day a week (usually Wednesday or Thursday), your newspaper will have the food stores' ads as inserts. Look through them for items you can use. Stock up when the prices are really good. Don't shop at all if you can help it when the prices are not good. If your store is out of a sale item, get a rain check. (If they didn't advertise the price as "good while supplies last," they owe you a rain check.) Try store brands, generics, etc.

For snacks or quick meals, think cheap and easy. One of my quick working lunches is a can of green beans and a cup of water brought to a boil to which I add a package of ramen noodles and flavoring. A quick breakfast is oatmeal, which takes about three minutes to fix, and peanut butter. It's great in the winter, and it tastes a little like peanut butter cookies.

And be sure to check out the SHARE program (discussed at the end of the chapter) if it is available in your area.

WHAT YOU SHOULD KNOW ABOUT FIXED AND VARIABLE COSTS

Manufacturers have two basic kinds of costs to worry about. Their **fixed costs** are those they must pay whether they sell one widget or a million widgets. Their property taxes, the cost of their facilities, and so on fall into this category. Their **variable costs** are the costs that actually go into their products. Let's take tomato sauce, for example. Variable costs would include the cost of the can, the cost of the tomato sauce, the cost to process the can, and so on.

When setting prices, a manufacturer is obviously going to include variable costs as well as profit. But how does a business handle those fixed costs? Someone has to estimate how many products the company will sell, then add an amount to the price to cover fixed costs. If the company's sales are less than the estimate, fixed costs will eat into profits.

Our benefits as consumers come when a manufacturer sells more than what was estimated. The manufacturer can then sell the product for only the variable costs plus profit. Consumers get a bargain, and the manufacturer still makes money.

Many manufacturers' accounting years end in December. This is the reason the early part of the year is a good time to stock up. Tomato sauce, for example, has been selling in San Jose for 14¢ per 8-ounce can this January (it's usually 34¢), and frozen orange juice, usually well over $1 for a 12-ounce can, has been as low as 69¢. Look for bargains this time of the year, and stock up if you find a deal on something you would normally buy anyway. (Remember—it's not a bargain if you don't need it.)

CHEAP COFFEE

Here is an idea that will save money without any extra effort on your part. I have a Mr. Coffee–type coffeemaker. After the grinds cool down, I refrigerate them and just add new coffee to the existing grounds. I use three and a half scoops for the first pot, and, for each subsequent pot, I add two and a half scoops until the filter is full. I then throw it all out and start over. I can't tell the difference between the first pot and the last. This may work for you. It's worth a try. I've been using this method since the great coffee shortage of 1976.

Mrs. Ruth Glicker of Florida wrote the following after I revealed (and the nation's presses reported) that I reuse my coffee grounds:

. . . Don't throw your coffee grounds out when your filter is full. Put the grounds in the freezer. They absorb odors, and you won't have to buy baking soda! I also put my scouring pads in the freezer. I can get them to last a year that way. *(Makes sense—they won't rust there.)*

BOX WINE

If you buy box wine (and I've seen Franzia's five-liter boxes as low as $5.99 lately), you should know that a good deal of wine remains in the pouch after the spigot stops dispensing. To get all the wine, wait until the spigot stops dispensing, remove the pouch from the box, cut a corner off the pouch, and pour out the remaining wine.

TUNA SALAD EXTENDER

One of the most overlooked bargains I know of is canned mackerel. I recently bought some for 59¢ per 15-ounce can. I mix one can of drained mackerel with one can of drained tuna, mayonnaise, onions, peppers, etc. to make a good-size fish salad. The taste is a little different from that of regular tuna salad, but the cost per ounce of fish is reduced to 5.6¢ versus 9.8¢, or nearly 43 percent, assuming you can find a 6-ounce can of tuna on sale for 59¢. In addition, it seems that mackerel is good for you as well as cheap. Both *Bottom Line* and *Delicious!* report mackerel is high in omega-3 oil, a healthful fatty acid.

Caution: Try one can before you buy in quantity. I like it, but you may not.

🪙 WHEN YOUR FAMILY WANTS DOUGHNUTS

You're at home, it's a weekend morning, and your family wants something sweet. Before you grab your car keys and rush off to Dunkin' Donuts, try what my mother used to fix for us—cinnamon toast. To toast, add butter or margarine, a little sugar, and cinnamon. Microwave it for about 15 seconds, and, *voilà*! Cinnamon toast. You control the ingredients, so besides being cheaper and faster, your snacks are also better for your family.

💵 CHEAP SPICES AND PICANTE SAUCE

Those stale spices you find in the expensive little cans in the grocery stores are enough to send anyone to the doughnut shop. I buy my spices at **Planters Seed Company, 513 Walnut, Kansas City, MO 64106.** Their phone number is **816-842-3651**, but I recommend you send them a postcard asking for their price list. Planters has been in business for many decades, and, as with most midwestern businesses that have been around a while, they are strictly no-nonsense and no-pretense. Their wood floors are bare and show the scuff marks from many years of visits from local farmers. Their cabinets are painted green. Planters is decidedly not a place where the elite meet, but their prices reflect that fact. When I'm in KC, it's a must stop for me.

They also sell a picante sauce mix. Although my ancestors came from countries proud of such bland ethnic dishes as lutefisk and mamaliga, I love picante sauce. But I don't love the price of the commercial varieties (I recently saw Pace on sale for $1.99 for 16 ounces), so I use the dry mix to make my own. The mix at Planters Seed Company, when combined with tomato sauce and water and heated, tastes quite good. If you like yours chunky, use canned diced tomatoes instead of tomato sauce. You'll have great picante sauce—cheap.

💰 SOFT DRINKS

The Wall Street Journal recently reported that generic and store-brand soft drinks were gaining market share. A "taste test" was discussed. It seems that most of the tasters could not tell the difference between Coke ($1.19 for a two-liter bottle), Pepsi ($1.29), and several store brands (ranging in price from 69¢ to 78¢).

It's great that more people are giving store brands a chance, but I question the value of buying soft drinks at all. They are, after all, water, sweetener, artificial flavoring, etc. What's there that's worth even 69¢ for two liters? Try to make do with tea, coffee, or even water (yes, it's still available—even in California).

STRETCHING YOUR MEAT BUDGET

Remember the great meat revolt of 1974? The price of meat had taken a sudden jump. (Having learned from the first oil embargo how a shortage could translate into higher prices, suppliers engineered a meat shortage, which was followed by a sugar shortage later that year and a coffee shortage in 1976.) I lived in Ohio at the time, and with midwestern common sense, the people there just stopped buying meat. That was one shortage that backfired. People discovered that not only could they make do with less meat, they liked their new diets better. So, although prices came back down, consumption remained lower.

Meat is still expensive, but there are ways to stretch your meat dollar. One way is to buy from your store's reduced-price counter if they have one. I do this all the time. On the rare occasions the meat turned out bad, I took it back and got a refund. Just because the meat is reduced does not mean you have to pay for inedible food. Another way to save on meat is not to use any a couple of days a week. Have pasta, eggplant parmigiana, rice and beans, or other vegetarian dishes instead. Canned fish is a staple for me because of both convenience and price.

A TRIP TO THE GROCERY STORE

I took my notebook along with me to my local Safeway store recently. It's getting to where nothing I do surprises the people who work there anymore. A local talk show asked me to give them the specifics on how much one can save by buying store brands instead of name brands. The show wound up not using the information, but I found it interesting. Safeway's paper towels were 14 percent cheaper than name brands, and you could save 15 percent on peanut butter, 19 percent on a cereal like Grape-Nuts, 20 percent on raisin bran, and 33 percent on a Rice Krispies look-alike. (Better yet, you can save big on cereal by buying from bulk bins.) Frozen orange juice (which was on sale at the time) was less than half the price of name brands. By the way, frozen orange juice is almost always cheaper than buying the ready-to-serve juice; use your own water and save.

Speaking of juice, this tip was passed along to me by a newspaper reporter. Use four cans of water instead of three when making juice from concentrates. This not only saves money, it is actually better for those of us who must watch our diets (actually I've gotten to the point that juice made with the recommended three cans of water tastes too sweet).

In the December 1983 issue of JoAnn Kunz's *Hearts and Homes*, which is no longer published, there was an article entitled "Cut It in Half." It told the story of a bathroom cleanser company that doubled the number of holes in the top of its container to get people to use more cleanser (it worked). The article made the point that the package recommendations often encourage waste and passed on tips to do more with a lesser amount of product or energy.

💵 MORE STRETCHING TECHNIQUES

Just about the same time I read Ms. Kunz's article, Bill Robinson of Fiat Lux Publications wrote with the following great ideas:

If you buy and use instant pudding mix, here's a tip the company does not want you to know. The most popular brand calls for adding two cups of cold milk. Three cups can be added, and the pudding will congeal just as well and just as rapidly, and you have an extra cup of pudding. Not only is the flavor as good, but it is not so oversweetened. Four cups of milk work also, but it takes longer to set. The truly adventurous might want to add some healthy ingredients such as shaved coconut.

The same stretching technique works with those packets of instant gravy. Most of these call for one cup of water, which produces a small amount of salty, rather bitter gravy. Instead, add two cups of water—double the suggested amount. To this add a small amount of Kitchen Bouquet and a small tablespoon of cornstarch to assist thickening. To improve flavor, add a small teaspoon of beef or chicken bouillon (as appropriate) to the gravy. Using the same technique, and by increasing the above additions, a single packet of gravy mix can be extended to three or four cups. In fact, as you become more adventurous in your additions, you may find you can do without the base packet of gravy mix completely.

Ramen noodles—you know the kind—the little cheap packets where you add that little envelope of flavor after they are cooked—call for adding the noodles to two cups of boiling water for three minutes, then stirring in the flavor. This is too bitter, too salty, and too strong. Always use 3¼ cups of boiling water. Since they're too hot to eat anyway after three minutes, let them sit for ten or twelve minutes. During this time the noodles swell. This gives you more volume and a better taste. *[Editor's note: After I mentioned that I found this much water didn't work well for me, Bill wrote that he poured off a lot of the water because he didn't like the salty taste of the ramen seasoning.]*

Ramen noodles are a good place for diced, leftover chicken scraps, beef scraps, veggies, etc. All these enhance the flavor of the ramen. Add enough of the leftover stuff (and maybe a few of your own noodles) and stretch the recipe to four cups.

We use cheese on a lot of Mexican food, sauces, and Italian food. There's a problem with cheese stored in the refrigerator too long, though. It sometimes acquires a very unhealthy-looking mold in various hues of green. No more. We haven't seen mold on cheese for many months. The secret is simple. Store your cheese block in aluminum foil. But first, on the aluminum foil, place a square or two of paper towel. Sprinkle a few drops of vinegar on the towel. We use good-quality white wine vinegar and have *never* yet detected any vinegar flavor. Now securely wrap the cheese with the towel and the foil. The acidic content and fumes of the harmless vinegar will never allow mold spores to germinate. When I use the cheese the next time, I add a few more drops of vinegar—only two or three.

I was particularly glad to get Bill's tips on ramen. I had just bought a bunch of the little packets on sale for 10¢ apiece.

Here's a way to save half your money on dish soap and other liquid cleaners. These are mostly water anyway, so I just add more water.

I find a fifty-fifty mix works just as well as 100 percent soap. Also, when it comes to cleaners, check out the generic brands at stores such as Kmart. Their Very Pine liquid is about half the cost of Pine-Sol, and how different could it be?

💰 SWEET NEWS

If you use artificial sweeteners, you should be aware NutraSweet's patent on aspartame has run out, and other, much cheaper brands of aspartame are coming to market. One is Sweet Mate, which I understand has been on sale for 10 percent of the price of NutraSweet (if you buy it in the bulk package, not in the individual serving sizes). Be aware, though, that aspartame breaks down when it's heated, so it's best not to cook with it.

When it comes to cooking, Europeans have been turning to Sweet One, which is not a brand of aspartame, for years, and now Americans can, too. Sweet One offers a free booklet of recipes—just call 800-544-8610 and ask for it. Even the call is free.

🦃 MAKE THE MOST OF THAT TURKEY!

No, I'm not talking about that Southern California "thrift" newsletter many of you have written me about. There's nothing I can do about that, so let's concentrate on the traditional Thanksgiving bird. Turkey is an excellent buy in November. Last year I saw many stores advertising it as low as 27¢ per pound! I managed to cram three birds in my small freezer and finished the last one in March of this year. You can bet my freezer will be bare in anticipation of this year's bargains! And, when one of these bargain babies leaves my house, about all that's left is, as my father says, the "hoof, beak, and horns."

Cooking a turkey is easy. Believe me, if it weren't, I wouldn't do it. I wash the bird thoroughly inside and out and season it with whatever looks good (usually pepper, celery seed, and perhaps a little cayenne pepper). I don't use salt, but a lot of people season their turkey with that, too. Once that's done, I cook it for an hour at 450°F and then turn the heat down to 350°F and cook it three more hours. (The cheapest turkeys—the ones I buy—usually weigh sixteen to twenty pounds.) I use a roasting pan, and while basting is recommended, just between us, I don't baste. Once the turkey is done, I put aside enough for my Thanksgiving meal. Then the fun begins.

What is excess to the holiday meal gets cut up and frozen for sandwiches for future lunches. And, to make sure there's no waste, I cut up as much as I can while the turkey's still in the roasting pan. Then I lift the carcass out of the roasting pan. What is obviously scrap (no bones, of course) becomes my dogs' Thanksgiving meal. That is their reward for quietly smelling the cooking bird all morning.

I use the drippings in the roasting pan (and remember, all those shavings that fell in the drippings while I was slicing the turkey for sandwiches are still there) to make gravy. I pour the drippings into another pan, add a can of chicken broth, and heat. Once it is near boiling, I add flour (about a cup and a half) and stir until all the lumps are gone. I season it to my taste and use it for a series of midwestern-style biscuit-and-gravy breakfasts. I will admit this is a high-fat breakfast, but I only do it when I cook a turkey. And is it good!

Remember the carcass? While I've been making gravy, it's been boiling on another burner. After it has boiled for about forty-five minutes (or longer), I remove the bones (warning: some small bones may remain even if you thought you'd found them all), pour the liquid into three or four containers, and freeze. I use this broth later to make turkey rice (just substitute it for an equal part of water when you make rice) or turkey noodles (ditto), to which I add frozen vegetables (peas go great with turkey rice) or whatever looks good.

As you can see, the only things I actually throw away are the bones. If anyone knows how to make use of them, I'd sure like to hear from you!

You may have noticed I did not mention stuffing the turkey with dressing. I don't. If I make dressing, I do it as a side dish. I know people have cooked stuffing inside the turkey for years and lived, but one dose of food poisoning is enough to convince most people it's better to be safe than sorry. And I've had more than one dose of food poisoning.

CEREAL

It's come to the attention of some of our congressional representatives that, at $5 per box, cereal prices are ridiculous. I have no idea what our congressional representatives want to do about it, but the Quaker Oats Company is offering an alternative. They now offer "Quaker by the Bagful," which they say is about half the price of boxed cereal. The varieties they offer in bags are all high in sugar (it was the second listed ingredient in the bag of Fruity OHs they sent me).

Boxed cereal is not my choice of breakfasts. I tend to agree with Laura Martin-Buhler, who, in the April 1995 issue of ***The Gentle Survivalist* (for a sample, send $3 and a self-addressed, stamped envelope (SASE) to Box 4004, St. George, UT 84770),** described packaged cereals as boxes of air. If you have to have this stuff, you might want to try Quaker's new product, but there are alternatives.

Most major stores carry their own brand of cereal, which is nearly always cheaper than any brand name, no matter how that brand name is packaged, and many stores have bulk bins that offer such basic cereals as raisin bran and flaked wheat or corn by the pound.

Another way to save on cereal is to buy from the bulk bins in many stores. You can find wheat bran for around 49¢ per pound; I recently bought oat bran on sale for 75¢ per pound. I mix the bran in with other bulk bin finds—wheat germ, etc. You can get a lot of stuff from the bulk bins for the price of one box of cereal. Check it out. By the way, storing your bulk finds is an excellent use for those coffee cans you've been wondering what to do with!

The best buy in cereal is hot cereal. I've seen 42-ounce boxes of oatmeal for as little as 99¢. And that's forty-two ounces of *dry* oatmeal. Remember, when it's cooked, it absorbs water, so, compared with the boxed cereal, that's dirt cheap. It takes about three minutes to fix, but it's also more healthful (zero preservatives and the only sugar is what you add) than the boxed stuff. You can also be inventive with cooked cereal. Try my favorite, peanut butter, or add fresh or dried fruit. If time is an issue, you can cook a few days' supply and refrigerate it.

And oatmeal is not your only choice. If you can find a health food store that sells in bulk, millet and buckwheat are also good for breakfast, as is any other grain (or mixture of grains) that might catch your fancy. Like oatmeal, other grains absorb water and are a much cheaper alternative to boxed cereals.

Millet is a grain I learned to like a lot on my recent trip to Russia. Yes, millet is the main ingredient of birdseed. It is also 11 percent protein and contains a greater variety of amino acids than any of the grains commonly consumed in the United States. This is important if you are trying to reduce the amount of meat in your diet. I found it locally for 39¢ per pound (for "organic" millet—I suppose it would be even cheaper if it were not organic).

For a hearty breakfast, add one part millet to four parts water. Bring to a boil, then simmer for twelve minutes. (It tends to boil over during these twelve minutes; to avoid a mess on your stove, lift the lid now and then.) Turn off the heat, and let it sit for twenty minutes. You can even cook up a week's worth and reheat it in the microwave. I like it with just a little butter or margarine. That's the way my hosts served it in Russia.

And, of course, your choices for breakfast are not limited to cereal. Eggs, cheese, and fruit are certainly options, and I've read that some folks consider pizza the way to start their day.

I even saw "spaghetti on toast" listed as a breakfast entree in Australia. And people were ordering it.

FOOD RESOURCES

Marcie Rothman's *The $5 Chef* (**$7 postpaid from Five-Spot Press, P.O. Box 160663, Sacramento, CA 95816**) is 129 pages of cooking cheap. When I first heard about the book, I thought, "Five dollars a meal is not all that great." Well, it turns out the five dollars is for a meal for four people. When I heard that, I sent for the book. It's written clearly enough so even I can follow the directions. (You may have noticed my food recommendations don't require a lot of cooking—there's a good reason for that.) About the only thing I question is Ms. Rothman's recommendation that you shop in one place. If you live in an area where stores are close together, I still recommend you take advantage of all the bargains you can (keeping in mind there is a trade-off in extra transportation costs, of course).

Margaret Engel sent me a copy of *Food Finds*, the book she and Allison Engel wrote. Published by HarperCollins, it costs $16. If you can't find a copy, the book is available from **Book Call, phone 800-255-2665**. This is a large book. Actually, this is a very large book—346 pages, 8½″ × 11″. It gives alternatives to pricey places like Hickory

Farms and Swiss Colony. There are literally too many bargains in this book to go into here, but one that gets my vote is Deer Mountain Berry Farm, P.O. Box 257, Granite Falls, WA 98252. They sell four 1-pound jars of jam (strawberry, raspberry, gooseberry, blackberry, boysenberry, loganberry, or blueberry) for $9.20 plus shipping.

Lois Carlson Willand sent me a copy of *The Use-It-Up Cookbook*. Subtitled *A Guide for Minimizing Food Waste*, it looks to me like a guide for eliminating it. She has arranged the book in sections, "Breads, Grains, and Pasta," for example. If you have leftover bread, just look in this section, and you have nine pages of recipes. The book is spiral-bound, **costs $12.95 (postpaid), and is available from Practical Cookbooks, 145 Malcolm Ave. SE, Minneapolis, MN 55414.**

I wheedled a copy of Georgia Ryan's *250 Wonderful Ways to Serve Ground Beef* ($12 including postage and handling—prepaid order only) from GCR Cookbooks, 6424 E. Baker Pl., Denver, CO 80222). Ms. Ryan says many of her friends told her they were getting tired of chicken and fish and that, frankly, fish was getting too expensive. Ms. Ryan talked to the manager of her store's meat department, and he confirmed that people were buying more ground beef in spite of the bad press beef has been getting lately. He gave the current economy as one possible explanation. Ms. Ryan had experimented with ground beef recipes for nearly forty years, and she compiled them into this 150-page spiral-bound book.

This for That: A Treasury of Savvy Substitutions for the Creative Cook, by Meryl Nelson ($7.95 plus $2.50 shipping and 8.25 percent California sales tax, if applicable, from R & E Publishers, 468 Auzerais Ave., Suite A, San Jose, CA 95126, or phone 408-977-0691), solves a problem I'm sure all people who cook run into. You're in the middle of a recipe, and you don't have an ingredient. Instead of running to the store (using expensive fuel and wearing out your car), consult Ms. Nelson's book. Out of food coloring? Use a dry soft-drink mix (like Kool Aid). Want to make gravy, but you're out of flour? Try cornstarch and bread crumbs or instant potato flakes. This book is 100 pages of "this for that," and I'm sure every cook will find it invaluable.

I recently came across Donna McKenna's *The $30 a Week Grocery Budget*. Ms. McKenna has been feeding her family of *six* for $30 a week *or less*. (The only exception, she says, was when the family encountered hard times and had to accept food stamps—she was allotted more than $80 a week at that time, and, even then, she donated $35 in excess food per week to charity.) In her 59-page book, she tells how to shop and how to keep your freezer running efficiently (keep it full of something), and she gives many recipes for simple, cheap food. Hats off to this amazing woman for sharing her secrets with us! Volume II includes some of her philosophy as well as several pages of recipes, even some vegetarian ones. **Volumes I and II are $9 postpaid from 106 Bedford St., Statesboro, GA 30458.**

Patti Anderson sent me a copy of her monthly newsletter, *Frozen Assets* **($12 a year from 6005 North 116 Plaza, Omaha, NE 68164-1429—if you'll send her a long SASE, she'll send you a sample).** She advocates cooking once a month and freezing meals to be used throughout the rest of the month. Using her method and the seven pages of recipes in each issue, you can shop once a month, buy in bulk, and spend more time with your family each evening instead of rushing home to cook. This sounds ideal for the increasingly common two-income American family.

375 Meatless Recipes **($7.95 plus $1.65 shipping and handling from TEACH Services, Rt. 1 Box 182, Brushton, NY 12916, or toll-free 800-367-1844)** offers more than one meat-free recipe a day for a year.

Barbara Nosek sent a copy of her 21-page booklet, *Sloppy Joe and the Whole Gang* **($4 postpaid from The Source, P.O. Box 81645, Spring Valley, NV 89180—additional copies to the same address are $3; Nevada residents add 6 percent sales tax).** This booklet has twenty-five recipes for making sloppy joes with ground beef, ground turkey, ground lamb, ground pork, ground veal, Italian sausage, ground camel (I am not making this up), peanut butter, and tuna.

Rhonda Barfield is also back with a much updated and expanded version of her cheap-shopping book, *Eat Well for $50 a Week* **($12 including postage and handling and Missouri tax, if applicable, from Lilac Publishing, P.O. Box 665, Dept. L, St. Charles, MO 63302-0665).** Her $50 a week, by the way, feeds her family of six, and she shares many of her cost-cutting recipes in this book.

Linda Slater, who retired from editing *The Thrifty Times*, offers a $5 booklet, *Save Every Day on Your Groceries* **(checks should be** made payable to her and sent to 6135 Utica St., Arvada, CO 80003).

Acorns and Eat 'em, by Suellen Ocean (**$12 postpaid from Ocean House, 28970 Sherwood Rd., Willits, CA 95490—CA residents add $.73 sales tax**), is the kind of book I really enjoy telling my readers about. Ms. Ocean tells how to take acorns, which are available in vast quantities—free—wherever oak trees grow, and make them edible. She provides several recipes—including one for bread made without sweetener—that make use of acorn meal.

The holiday season is a difficult time of the year for vegetarians. To help vegetarians during the holidays and the rest of the year, **The Vegetarian Resource Group** is offering the 224-page book *Simply Vegan* for $14. **Their address is P.O. Box 1463, Baltimore, MD 21203.**

I've mentioned the high cost of cereal. Now Stephen Jewett has written *Make Your Own Breakfast Cereal (or Save Money on the Cereal You Buy)*, which is **$12.95 plus $2 shipping and handling from Armstead Publishing, 190 E. Eighth St., #3063, Holland, MI 49422-3063**. The book contains a great deal of information on where to get cereal ingredients cheap as well as recipes for a variety of cereals, even one of my favorites, millet.

Several people have asked about how to find food cooperatives in their area. I have good news. Kris Olsen of **Co-Op Directory Services** will help you locate your nearest wholesaler for co-op food-buying clubs and retail co-op stores if you will send a self-addressed, stamped envelope to her at **919 21st Ave. S., Minneapolis, MN 55404**.

The American Friends Service Committee's SHARE Program enables you to buy $25 to $35 worth of food for $13 to $15 plus two hours of community service. Your service can be anything from working with the Boy Scouts to helping bag food for the SHARE Program. The areas in which I know SHARE operates (and the phone numbers associated with those areas) follow:

Northern California	800-499-2506
Southern California	619-525-2200
Colorado	800-933-7427
District of Columbia	301-864-3115 or 3506
Florida	800-726-7427
Georgia	404-873-2322

Illinois	217-529-2500
	or 309-637-0282 or 0288
	or 815-961-7328
Iowa	515-673-4000
Kansas	913-234-6208*
Maryland	410-636-9615
Massachusetts	617-828-5151
Michigan	517-482-8900
Minnesota	612-644-9339
New Jersey	201-344-2400
New York	212-518-1513
North Carolina	800-758-6923
Ohio	216-253-8806
Pennsylvania	215-223-2220
Virginia	800-253-7842
	or 703-381-1185
Wisconsin	414-783-2500

*Kansas City–area residents must dial the area code and the number. Trust me on this one.

If you are interested in SHARE, call the area nearest you. Many of these cover a large territory. The number listed for Kansas, for example, is in Topeka, but the geographic area for that office includes all of Kansas and parts of Oklahoma and Missouri (including Kansas City).

Some centers are stricter about the two-hour community service than others. Some require a signed time card from an "approved" organization. The Kansas center is on an honor system, which has both positive and negative aspects. On the one hand, many people probably don't get involved in their community. On the other hand, it lets those individuals so inclined decide for themselves what they can do to help their community, whether or not their service of choice is under the auspices of an "approved" organization.

11

TO COUPON OR NOT TO COUPON

The material in this chapter was originally published in three parts.

💰 PART 1: THE UNANSWERED QUESTION

To coupon or not to coupon? That is the question left largely unanswered in my mind by *The Super Coupon Shopping System*, by Susan Samtur. This $5.95 paperback published by Hyperion should be available in libraries, bookstores, and garage sales in your area. You may have seen Ms. Samtur on television. Usually she is filmed approaching the check-out register with a basketful of groceries for which she pays, after coupons are deducted, $1.98 or some such amount. Well, I was certainly interested in Ms. Samtur's system.

Unfortunately, while there is a lot of good information in this book, there is also a lot of self-promotion. Ms. Samtur is the editor of ***The Refundle Bundle* ($19.87 for two years—twelve issues—from P.O. Box 141, Centuck Station, Yonkers, NY 10710)**, a fact we're reminded of early and often. Additionally, I was turned off by Ms. Samtur's approach to manufacturers' "freebies." She brags that freebies such as children's toys and frisbees with product logos are "scattered through-out the house," and, as if that weren't enough, she goes on to describe some of the freebies that fill her attic. How nice for her. While she advises the list of freebies "could go on and on," fortunately it doesn't. My experience with manufacturers' freebies has been that they are generally of such poor quality and little use that I am embarrassed to give them to Goodwill (and many of these items are now being made by Chinese prison labor). I have actually asked companies just to send what I ordered and forget the free gifts.

The most disappointing, if not misleading, aspect of Ms. Samtur's book is her insistence that store brands and generic products are somehow inferior to name brands, when they are in fact often identical items packaged under different labels. Although this book does have a lot to offer (I learned a lot about rebates, including the fact that a person may get a "rebate receipt" in lieu of cash register tapes when more than one rebate will be claimed), a lot of Ms. Samtur's assertions should be taken with a grain of generic or store-brand salt.

PART 2: THE STORE-BRAND ALTERNATIVE

In the last issue I took exception to the unsubstantiated and self-serving implication by Susan Samtur, author of *The Super Coupon Shopping System*, that name-brand products are better than generic or store brands. The fact is store brands are often the same products produced by name-brand manufacturers. They just have a different label.

As a case in point, let's look at the dandruff shampoo sold by Long's drugstores here in California. The first time I bought a bottle of this shampoo, I couldn't get over how similar it was to Head & Shoulders. The bottle is identical, the color of the product is identical, and even the smell is the same. Recently, Head & Shoulders was on sale, and I had a coupon. The combination of the sale and the coupon brought the Head & Shoulders price below that of the store brand, so I bought the Head & Shoulders. I put the two bottles side by side to try to figure out the difference. I'm pretty sure there isn't any.

The final clue is the listing of ingredients. The label on Head & Shoulders (Normal or Dry Hair) lists the following:

Pyrithione zinc in a shampoo base of water, ammonium laureth sulfate, ammonium lauryl sulfate, glycol disterate, cocamide mea, dimethicone, fragrance, ammonium xylenesulfonate, tricetylmonium chloride, cetyl alcohol, stearyl alcohol, DMDM hydantoin, sodium chloride, and FD&C Blue No. 1.

Long's label reads:

Pyrithione zinc in a shampoo base of water, ammonium laureth sulfate, ammonium lauryl sulfate, glycol disterate, cocamide mea, dimethicone, fragrance, ammonium xylenesulfonate, tricetylmonium chloride, cetyl alcohol, stearyl alcohol, DMDM hydantoin, sodium chloride, FD&C Blue No. 1.

The only difference is the deletion of the *and* before the last product! And, remember, ingredients must be listed in descending order based on the proportion of the product they comprise.

Oh, and Head & Shoulders' label advises their formula is "protected by US Patents 4 345 080, 4 379 753, 4 704 272, and 4 741 855." Do you suppose Procter & Gamble, the maker of Head & Shoulders and the holder of those patents, would allow such blatant infringement by a regional drugstore chain? I think not. My suspicions are that P&G's overproduction of Head & Shoulders is sold at a discount and given a different label. And I suspect the same is true of almost any store brand. Manufacturers are no different than we are. If they have something they cannot use, they'll sell it cheap rather than throw it out.

In my years of buying store brands, I've had only one bad experience, and I got my money back. Consider store brands one more alternative.

PART 3: MAKING COUPONS WORK FOR YOU

In the past two issues, we've looked at using coupons on name-brand products versus using store-brand or generic products. By now you may think I am anti-coupon. I'm not. Using coupons can certainly save money, and of course I use them when it makes sense to do so.

One thing that seems to surprise many people is that sometimes you can use more than one coupon on an item. For example, in the Bay Area,

Safeway frequently issues coupon books. The coupons in these books, labeled "Safeway Coupon," are *store* coupons. The coupons you see in the newspaper are generally labeled "Manufacturer Coupon." A recent Safeway coupon book had a coupon that let me buy Kellogg's Corn Flakes for 69¢. I had a manufacturer coupon for 75¢ off Kellogg's Corn Flakes. By combining the two, I was able to make 6¢ by buying a box. Of course, these deals are rare, but they do happen.

You may run into a clerk who will question whether you can actually use two coupons on one product. Since the manufacturer reimburses the store for their coupon, it should not matter to the clerk, so if this happens, ask the clerk to explain to you why you cannot use both coupons. Then ask to speak to the manager.

Here's the last word from me on coupons (at least for now): Use them when they are for a product you would buy anyway. Don't use coupons to save a few cents off a product you would not buy if you did not have a coupon. (Believe me, this is advice I have difficulty following. I fight my tendency to use superfluous coupons by not clipping coupons that I might find too "tempting" once I'm in the store.) Before you use coupons, check the prices of store-brand and generic products. Don't let anyone tell you store brands are inferior. As we have seen, they are often brand-name products sold with a different label. If you buy a store-brand product that you don't like, take it back. You don't have to keep something you don't like, and you don't have to return it immediately, either. Just put it somewhere with your receipt, and take it with you when you make your next shopping trip. You don't even need to be out any extra fuel.

ADDITIONAL RESOURCES

Two really good ways to keep up with what's going on in the world of coupons and refunding are **Trash-to-Treasures ($22 per year from P.O. Box 1117, Waldorf, MD 20604)** and *Centsible* **($23.95 per year from P.O. Box 234, Lowell, MA 01853)**. Both of these newsletters are published monthly and have gobs of information on coupons, mail-in rebates, and free items available, often simply by calling a toll-free number.

12
CLOTHING

Clothing depreciates pretty quickly, so it follows that good places to look for cheap clothing are thrift stores, clothing resale stores, garage sales, estate sales, and consignment stores.

Thrift stores vary from city to city and from location to location. Some are clean and well lighted; others are dark and filthy. If you find some you feel comfortable with, don't bother yourself with the ones you don't like. Know your prices, though. Don't automatically assume all thrift store prices are bargains. Quite frequently these stores hire people who have no concept of what a reasonable price is, and the prices wind up unreasonable. (On the other hand, the prices can wind up incredibly low.)

Recent articles in all three Bay Area newspapers have discussed various aspects of shopping for clothing in thrift stores. One article was devoted to children's clothing. It pointed out that children outgrow clothing before they wear it out. One woman was quoted as having purchased an Oshkosh B'Gosh jacket for $5. The price for a new jacket was $38.

Teresa Black of Oklahoma City, a very talented friend of mine who writes and performs music for various groups as well as in contests, writes that she buys her costumes in thrift shops. She advises that bridesmaids' dresses are usually pleated and have lots of extra material in the skirts. She says with the help of Hancock Fabrics and a leotard top, she can look like an 1890s dance hall girl in no time. (Even if that isn't exactly the look you're after, it sounds to me like bridesmaids' dresses may be a good source for skirts.)

Garage sales are probably the cheapest place to buy clothing, but they're also the most time-consuming. Your family's sizes have to be the same as those of the family having the sale. And you have to be able to live with their tastes in clothes. Further, your selection will be pretty limited. On the other hand, if you run into some clothes that will work for you at a garage sale, you'll save around 90 percent of the retail price.

Estate sales offer similar challenges, and because the items being sold are frequently those that had belonged to an older person, they may also present some style challenges. But if you can find something you can use at an estate sale, the prices should be attractive. In more than twenty years of going to estate sales, I found only one that had some clothing I could use—three good-quality winter coats, for which I paid $5 each.

Consignment stores have been around a long time, but it seems they were an enclave of the very wealthy, who don't stay wealthy by throwing their money around. Consignment stores are a good place to sell, as well as buy, good-quality used clothing.

A fairly recent addition to the used-clothing alternative is the for-profit resale store. Most of these specialize in men's, women's, or children's clothing. A few years ago, CBS invited me to become part of a "cheapskate challenge." The challenge was to get the most back-to-school clothes for $100. With the help of a for-profit children's resale store, The Rubber Ducky in San Jose, California, I was able to buy seven outfits, some books and toys, and a stuffed animal for $88. We borrowed the producer's niece for this segment, and the crew was so surprised by how low the resale shop's prices were (about 80 percent below retail) that everyone stayed behind to do some additional shopping after the segment was filmed.

To locate used-clothing stores in your area, I suggest you first try the Yellow Pages under "Clothing—Used." Ask the customers in the stores you visit if they know of any other good thrift stores. Also, ask your thrifty friends if they know of any good thrift shops or consignment stores. Don't be afraid to make an offer below the asking price when you're in these stores. (But please do make fair offers. I really don't subscribe to the win-lose approach to dealing with people; remember, these stores must make a profit, or they won't be there for you for very long.)

Before we leave the topic of used clothing, let me address the "Ew, gross!" reaction so many people seem to have to wearing something that's been worn by someone else. First, remember all those clothes you've tried on and rejected in the department store fitting room? Well, the odds are someone else has tried on the clothes you buy at department stores, too. So, even your "new" clothes have probably been on someone else. Second, when we think of our daily activities—sitting in other people's cars, using office furniture that others have used, handling public rest room doorknobs, etc.—how likely is it that wearing clothes previously owned by someone else is any less sanitary (especially if we wash or dry-clean these clothes before we wear them)?

One of the funniest comments I ever read about this "Ew, gross!" reaction was in Amy Dacyczyn's *The Tightwad Gazette*. She commented that on one talk show people seemed overly preoccupied with how disgusting it would be to wear used clothing. The next day the same talk show featured the subject of spouse swapping. It is an interesting commentary on our society that wearing someone else's used clothing is considered more disgusting than going to bed with someone else's spouse.

💰 NEW CLOTHING

I find it difficult to find clothes that fit, even in the "Big and Tall" section, so you can imagine that trying to find used clothing is, for me, almost a lost cause. So I buy new clothing, but I buy it cheap.

I shop a local Penney's outlet store. This store has a section for returned goods and a section for catalog overstock items. Just recently the store had a sale, and I bought two pairs of jeans and a name-brand flannel shirt that is almost heavy enough to be a jacket for $36, tax included. The retail price on one pair of the jeans would have been pretty close to the price I paid for all three items. If you have a genuine outlet store in your area, check it out. But beware of stores that call themselves outlet stores. Quite frequently the prices at such places are pretty close to retail.

You can save even if you don't shop outlet stores. Buy clothes out of season. You'll be a bit behind in fashion, of course, but I don't know of anyone in our times who would notice.

THE CLOTHES IN YOUR CLOSET

Once you've bought your clothes, take care of them. The longer they last, the less you'll have to spend on clothes. As your clothes wear out, make them the clothes you wear around the house for painting, doing house-work, etc. If your elbow goes though a sleeve or your knee goes through your jeans, consider making your shirt into a short-sleeve shirt and your jeans into cutoffs.

As your clothes disintegrate, consider using their remains as clean-ing or dusting rags. Try to find uses for your clothes before you throw them out. I give my worn-out tennis shoes (one at a time) to my dogs for a chew toy.

And if you've made a mistake and bought something that you won't wear, don't torture yourself by keeping it in your closet. If it's too late to take it back, take it to a consignment store or give it to charity. If you're in doubt about whether you want to get rid of an item, put it in a box and see if you forget about it. If, after a year, you haven't used it or even thought about it, it's safe to assume you can live without it!

13
TRAVEL

The world is divided into two types of people. People who divide the world into two types of people, and people who don't. No, no, I mean people who love to travel and those who don't.

I love to travel. But I also like to travel as inexpensively as possible. I've made three trips to the South Pacific and three trips to Europe. None of them cost a fortune. The following articles are some thoughts on travel, starting with the great American tradition—a trip by automobile.

MY 2,000-MILE CAR TRIP

Well, it wasn't a vacation exactly, but I did travel nearly two thousand miles by car with my two dogs last year. It had been seven years since I had done anything similar, and things have changed somewhat since 1988.

I usually don't enjoy long car trips, but, after five cross-country trips by air in two months, it was nice to have some legroom. And it was nice to have access to a variety of meals after having been at the mercy of airline food. (I swear one "breakfast" on TWA was a muffin and a fruit drink—not even juice. I know people who have begun to pack their own meals.)

I had the famous Olds, now nine years and 73,000 miles old, checked out before I started. I had to have a heater hose and the water pump replaced. These were unexpected expenses, but a breakdown on the trip would have been much more expensive. I suggest that having your automobile checked for possible needed repairs is a good prerequisite for any long trip by car. This sounds like common sense, but you'd be surprised at how many people pile into the family car not knowing its condition.

The Olds did very well. It "pinged" like crazy going over one mountain pass between I-5 and Bakersfield, but a switch to a higher grade of unleaded solved that problem. I also learned to turn the cruise control off going through mountain passes. Trying to maintain a constant speed going uphill and around curves is too hard on the engine and too costly in fuel consumption. Besides, with all the trucks on the road, it's also too dangerous.

We all get those mailers (mine come every Tuesday here in Kansas City, and they came every Tuesday in California as well) that have coupons for KFC, Subway, Pizza Hut, etc. I rarely use them when I'm home because, even at the sale prices, the stuff is still pretty expensive. But I saved a bunch of them and took them with me on the trip. Now, obviously, if your coupons say they're good only in your area, you needn't try using them elsewhere, but a lot of those coupons just say, "Good at Participating Locations." The Subway coupons are an example. After making certain the coupon was good, I used one I had received in the mail in San Jose at a Subway in Tucumcari, New Mexico.

Fast food on the Interstates is improving. I remember the days when my family traveled on the Oklahoma Turnpikes. It was Howard Johnson's (at outrageous prices) or nothing. We generally chose nothing. Now there is Burger King, McDonald's, Arby's, Hardee's, and the aforementioned Subway. Many of these have "99¢ specials," even at their Interstate locations. I took advantage of Burger King's 99¢ Whoppers (pretty good, but drippy), McDonald's 99¢ Big Mac (pretty awful), and Hardee's 99¢ Swiss Mushroom Melt (not bad, but I wouldn't make a special trip for one). And, as I said before, I used a coupon at Subway for their seafood sandwich. To me, Subway was the best find because they seem to offer the greatest variety (and, therefore, the greatest opportunity to buy healthful food), and if you ask for "the works" on their sandwiches, you essentially get a small salad for no extra charge. While Subway's prices are not outrageous, they're not exactly cheap either, so I'd suggest you use those coupons. Don't leave home without them!

Traveling with pets is not the big deal it used to be. I'm happy to report that Motel 6 accepts pets. Usually the limit is one, but they don't do a bed check. I stayed at Motel 6s in Needles and Tucumcari. The costs were $24.19 and $26.69, respectively. Both were functional for what I needed—a place to get a few hours' sleep. And both had free coffee. (I'd steer clear of that, though.)

Speaking of free coffee, many states' visitors' centers (usually the first rest stop in the state) not only offer free coffee, they have free booklets about what to do and see in their state. One of the best on my trip was Oklahoma's visitors' center near Sayre. One of their freebies is a 29-page booklet with a whole slew of recipes using peanuts (it's put out by the Oklahoma Peanut Commission). The Kansas visitors' center has booklets with money-saving coupons for activities in Kansas, Oklahoma, and Missouri. It costs nothing but a few minutes to stop at these centers, yet the people are almost always friendly and knowledgeable about their state, and you never know what you'll find.

TIPS FOR CAR TRAVEL

A reader sent me some "Cheap Advisor" columns by Ed Haugland, who writes for *The Single's Trumpet* in the Denver area. I contacted Mr. Haugland, who advised he is compiling some of his columns into a booklet. When he finishes, I'll let you know how to get a copy. One of his columns deals with travel by automobile with a family. Among his tips:

Limit restaurant meals. Mr. Haugland admits the need for an occasional hot meal served in pleasant surroundings, but he advises that you eat out only once a day and take advantage of breakfast specials, which often can be had for under $2. (As an aside here, some restaurants will allow you to order off the lower-priced breakfast menu any time of the day. All you have to do is ask for the breakfast menu.) Mr. Haugland advises that you fill out the rest of the day with fresh fruits and vegetables, cold cereal, milk, trail mix, peanut butter, crackers, etc. He also advises that you take an electric skillet or hot plate with you to use in your motel.

Don't take a vacation from frugal shopping habits. Take your coupons along—you might find some double- or triple-coupon deals. Scan local newspapers for specials, and look up freight salvage, warehouse-type grocery stores, and day-old bakeries in the phone book.

When traveling country roads, look for produce stands, farmer's markets, and "U pick" places. (Another aside: In rural Ohio, as well as other places, you may even find some untended produce stands where you take what you want and just leave the money. Be honest, or these places may disappear.)

Control the kids. Children's requests for expensive snacks (and souvenirs) can nickel-and-dime you to death. Give them nutritious food and an allowance. Once they've spent all their money, that's it. This teaches children money management as well as taking away from their parents the burden of saying no hundreds of times a day. As another aside, I spent a week a year at a church camp when I was young. Parents were charged a set amount of money for snacks. Each snack was deducted from the allowance, and, if there was money left over at the end of our week's stay, we children got to keep the money. I was always surprised at the number of kids who had gone through their allowance early in the week. You probably won't be surprised to learn I always got money back. Even as a child, I wanted money more than soda pop.

Plan ahead for freebies. Write to state tourist commissions for information on industrial tours. Breweries and wineries are notorious for handing out free samples. Some companies that process food also are generous with samples. Even if these places don't hand out samples, many will have factory stores that offer discounted prices. Take advantage of grand openings and sample offers at grocery stores.

Check out books on native edible plants. Make every rest stop a foraging opportunity.

Mingle with the natives. Listen to local radio announcements and read the community affairs section of the local newspaper to uncover information about church bazaars, bake sales, potlucks, picnics, and flea markets.

Check the brochure kiosk in your hotel. Some of these will have discount coupons. (This is very good advice; I recently went to a play and missed a pamphlet in the lobby that would have given me a $5 discount.)

Plan your route to include stops with family and friends. But don't be a freeloader. Help with yard work, baby-sitting, errands, etc.

Reduce costs by reducing your food intake. Most people don't burn a lot of calories when they're traveling. You'll save money and avoid gaining weight.

HOW I KEPT CHEAP ON MY RUSSIA-HUNGARY TRIP

All right. Many of you have asked how I was able to go to Russia and Hungary and still stay cheap. Here's how I did it.

The air fare to and from Europe was free via American Airlines' AAdvantage program. The only air fare I paid was between St. Petersburg and Budapest, and I'll get to that later. Airline frequent-flyer programs are a great deal. As far as I know, it costs nothing to join any of them, and you don't even have to leave the ground to accumulate miles! American is affiliated with MCI (the telephone company), and you get five AAdvantage miles for each dollar you spend with MCI. Citibank has a Visa card that gives you one mile for each dollar charged. (It costs $50 a year, and you don't get mileage for interest, so there's still no reason not to pay your card off each month!) You can also accrue AAdvantage miles on TWA (and some other airlines).

Other airlines have similar affiliations, but since San Jose is an American hub, I concentrate my flying with them. If you're, say, in the Denver area, you might want to check out United. Delta may work better for you if you live near Salt Lake City or Atlanta (and Delta's miles don't expire).

The best way to get free trips is to concentrate on one affiliate group. But don't pay higher prices just to accumulate miles. I still fly Southwest Airlines when I'm traveling one of their routes because they almost always have the cheapest fares.

A good way to get an appreciation for air fares in this country is to fly within Europe. When I began to check air fares between St. Petersburg and Budapest, I found I could fly either Aeroflot or Malev, the Hungarian airline, for $535. And that was either one way or round trip. And, no, I am not making this up. When I commented to Malev that I found that absurd, they gave me the name of a travel agent who, they said, could get me a better deal. I wound up paying $295. The moral here is, if something seems stupid, say so; maybe there's a way around the stupidity.

For the Russian part of my trip, I went through **American Home and Host (2445 Park Ave., Minneapolis, MN 55404, phone toll-free 800-SOVIET-U)**, who arranged for me to stay in private homes in Moscow and St. Petersburg. This arrangement has many advantages, not the least of which is it is a lot cheaper than staying in hotels. It's a good way to get to know the Russian people. The hosts speak English (which is now a required subject beginning in the third grade). The program guarantees a private room, and American Home and Host offers anything from just a room to a package that includes meals, sight-seeing, and night life (theater, opera, symphonies, ballet, etc.). The all-inclusive program is what I opted for, and it cost about half what I would have paid just for a hotel room. American Home and Host will give *LCN* readers an additional 10 percent discount.

One disadvantage is you may not get along with your host. (American Home and Host gives you numbers to call if there are serious problems.) I was lucky. My Moscow host was the charming widow of a TASS reporter. She had lived in New York, London, and Canberra, Australia, and spoke excellent English (she translates articles for a magazine). But I did have to insist on seeing Ismaylovsky Park, and having street vendors constantly approach me was embarrassing for her. (My solution for her embarrassment was to spend several hours on Arbat Street by myself one day when she had to work.) When I left Moscow, she gave me a scarf and ski hat to keep me warm in St. Petersburg. And she packed a lunch for my train ride north. My St. Petersburg family was charming. Igor and I talked politics late into each night, and, while I did not learn to drink vodka like a Russian (a shot glass in one gulp), I did learn to drink it.

The Budapest part of the trip was something of a letdown. Staying in a hotel was not as much fun as getting to know the natives. And the hotel was a disappointment. The Steigenberger Reservation Service (800-223-5652) offers similar (and, I hope, better) spa vacations in several countries.

Now to the bottom line. My four weeks in Europe cost just under $2,300, not including souvenirs and gifts. That's about $82 a day for the works.

⬡ RESOURCES FOR TRAVELERS

How did I know about the Sunday flea market at Ismaylovsky Park when my host didn't? I'd read *USSR: A Travel Survival Kit*, published by **Lonely Planet Publications (Embarcadero West, 155 Filbert St.,**

Suite 251, Oakland, CA 94607). Lonely Planet publishes a variety of travel guides, and their "On a Shoestring" series is great for cheap travelers. I copied pages from my 824-page guide and took them with me. My St. Petersburg host was amazed at the detail the guide provided. And their *Eastern Europe on a Shoestring* gave me a good guide for self-directed cheap sight-seeing in Budapest. Many bookstores carry Lonely Planet's guides. If you can't find them, send a postcard and ask for their catalog (or check your library).

Travel Smart (**40 Beechdale Rd., Dobbs Ferry, NY 10522-9989**) is $44 a year, but sometimes they offer a special price, so write to them before sending any money. This is how I learned about the Gellert Hotel special in Budapest. But *Travel Smart* only reports the specials; they're not responsible for them. Some public libraries will order newsletters like this, so check yours; if they don't have it, you have nothing to lose by requesting that they order it.

Of interest to the health-conscious is *Traveling Healthy and Comfortably* (**$29 per year for six issues from 108-48 70th Rd., Forest Hills, NY 11375**). This newsletter contains a lot of information about staying healthy while traveling. For example, it reminds you to wash your hands after handling paper money in developing countries, as paper money can contain diarrhea-causing organisms. (That's a good enough reason for me!) For a sample copy, send a self-addressed business-size (#10) envelope with postage affixed.

The Diabetic Traveler (**$22.95 a year, four issues, from P.O. Box 8223, Stamford, CT 06905**) provides important tips on traveling with diabetes. The newsletter advises, "Safe and enjoyable travel by a person with diabetes demands that a 'plan ahead and be prepared' approach be utilized." And it provides the details of that approach. For a sample copy, send a self-addressed business-size (#10) envelope with postage affixed.

For those interested in really cheap travel, M. L. Endicott has a book for you. His *Vagabond Globetrotting: State of the Art* (**$8.95 postpaid from Enchiridion International, Cullowhee, NC 28723-2589**) even tells how to find cheap shelter, work, and study abroad.

Beth Hubbell's *Luxury Travel for the Unrich and Unfamous* (**$7.95 plus $1.50 shipping from Jeremiah Publications, 1158 Woodside Dr., #109, Haslett, MI 48840**) gives tips on making travel fun for the whole family. From survival items to how to pack, this book addresses it (including the best advice of all on packing: when in doubt, leave it out). It certainly took me back to my childhood, remembering how difficult it was to pack our 1953 Pontiac for a three-day trip. Where was this book then?

The following companies are airline ticket consolidators, who buy up unsold seats and resell them cheap. They deal mostly with international flights, but occasionally they have something domestic. At any rate, it costs nothing to call them: Council Charter (800-800-8222), Travac Tours and Charters (800-872-8800), TFI Tours International (800-745-8000), Unitravel (800-325-2222), and Euram Tours (800-848-6789). There are also travel clubs that offer discounts to travelers looking for cheap charters, tour packages, and cruises *and* who can depart on short notice. The trick here is they usually charge a membership fee, so try to find out if they have something you can use, then join if the membership fee is less than your savings. The clubs I know of are Encore (800-638-0930), Worldwide Discount Travel (800-446-9938), Travelers Advantage (800-255-1488), and Vacations to Go (800-446-6258).

The folks who used to publish *The University Residence Guide* have come out with a much-expanded **Budget Lodging Guide ($16.95 postpaid from B & J Publications, P.O. Box 5486, Fullerton, CA 92635, or 800-525-6633)**. At more than 600 pages, it lists more than 8,000 cheap places to stay, including colleges and universities, YMCAs, bed-and-breakfast inns, home-exchange programs, youth hostels, inexpensive motels and hotels, etc. worldwide (including Russia but excluding much of the rest of Eastern Europe). This may be one of the travel guide bargains of the year. You'll also find sources for additional discounts as well as free information on your destination. One night's savings could make up for the cost of this book.

Lynie Ardeen sent a copy of her brand-new book, *Travel Free: The Ultimate Guide to Bargain Travel* **($14.95 postpaid from TWN Publications, 242 E. Main, Suite 38, Ashland, OR 97520)**. This 109-page book is packed with information on how to travel cheap. Unlike many travel books, Ms. Ardeen's often takes a walk on the wild side, even telling how to deal with coupon brokers who buy frequent-flyer awards and sell airline tickets obtained with those awards (I don't know if I would recommend doing this; I've heard of people being stranded overseas because the airline wouldn't honor their return ticket.) She also discusses buying two super-cheap discount tickets and not using the return flights if this is cheaper than buying one ticket and using "hidden city" discounts (airlines don't like these practices, either). The book doesn't stop at airline fares, either. She discusses discount lodging, alternative lodging, and even driving for free. (Volvo has a program that will let you buy a new Volvo in Sweden, use it in Europe, and ship it home when you're done. You'll not only save money on the car, assuming you were going to buy one anyway, you won't have to rent a car while you're there.) All in all, there's a lot of good information in this book.

This past year I've had the opportunity to review several of the mass-market travel guides, among them the Frommer's series, *Let's Go* by a subsidiary of Harvard Student Agencies, and "The Real Guide" series. They're all generally helpful, but the best guides I've read—and used—remain those published by Lonely Planet. Their "On a Shoestring" series is especially helpful to those of us who are looking to save money around the world. The hotels they review include the fancy as well as the plain. (If you're willing to share a bath, as are most Europeans, you can save a bundle and meet someone other than Americans while you're abroad.) The last time I went to Europe, I copied the appropriate pages from my Lonely Planet guidebooks. Even the natives with whom I stayed were surprised at the depth of the guidebooks (and, in Moscow, my host learned about an interesting—and free—attraction within walking distance of her apartment). These books will probably be in your library or bookstores. If you cannot find them, Lonely Planet's address is Embarcadero West, 155 Filbert St., Oakland, CA 94607.

Apollo Publishing Company sent a copy of Mauris L. Emeka's *AMTRAKing: A Guide to Enjoyable Train Travel*. Mr. Emeka, a former Amtrak employee, advises, for example, that passengers bring their own blankets, if they're traveling overnight, and he reminds passengers who have paid for a sleeper berth that their meals are included in their fare. The 132-page book is available from **Apollo (P.O. Box 1937, Port Orchard, WA 98366) for $8.95 plus $3 shipping**. It should also be available at your local bookstore or in lobby shops at train stations.

If you're thinking of spending time in San Diego in the near future, Sally Gary, who wrote **San Diego's Best Freebies & Bargains** and who teaches a class titled "Living Well in San Diego on $25,000 a Year," has a deal for you. And the price couldn't be better. If you'll send a SASE to **Free List, 2726 Shelter Island Dr., Suite 94, San Diego, CA 92106**, she'll send you a list of 25 free things to do in San Diego. What a deal!

If you're thinking about traveling with your dogs, there's actually a newsletter for you. *DogGone* **($24 per year—six issues—from P.O. Box 651155, Vero Beach, FL 32965-1155**; for a brochure and an order form, send a SASE). The Air Transport Association also offers a free brochure on travel and pets (send a business-size SASE to them at 1301 Pennsylvania Ave., NW, #1100, Washington, DC 20004). If you're traveling to or within California with your dog, you may be interested in Maria Goodavage's *The California Dog Lover's Companion: The Inside Scoop on Where to Take Your Dog in the Golden State* **($16.95 from bookstores or $20.45 including shipping plus California sales tax if applicable from Foghorn Press, 555 DeHaro St., #220, San Francisco, CA 94107, or toll-free 800-364-4676).**

Finally, *Wheels and Waves* by **Genie and George Aroyan ($13.95 postpaid from Wheels Aweigh, 17105 San Carlos Blvd., A6107, Ft. Meyers Beach, FL 33931)** is a comprehensive guide to cruises for the handicapped traveler. Ms. Aroyan, a world traveler, is paraplegic.

VACATION AT HOME?

A reader in Key West, Florida, caused me to do some thinking about taking vacations away from home. She said when you travel, you're paying for two places to live—the home that's sitting vacant and wherever you're staying when you travel. I certainly can't argue with that logic. And I've had some good vacations without leaving town.

Admit it. You've never done the "touristy" things right in your own area, have you? I grew up in Oklahoma City, and I'm there at least once a year. But I've never seen the Cowboy Hall of Fame. I lived in New York, but I never visited the Statue of Liberty. I've driven by San Jose's Rosicrucian Museum, but I've never seen the inside. And I confess I've never been inside the Winchester Mystery House. There are so many things to see right in our own backyards. Many cities have made museums out of the homes of their once-prominent citizens.

Finding these attractions is often as easy as checking the front pages of your phone book. (San Jose's tourist attractions are listed under "Places to Go" at the front of the Yellow Pages.) Most cities have a visitors' bureau. A phone call or visit there could provide days of touristy activities in your home town. You'll find that many of these local attractions are cheap, and some are free.

I first discovered vacationing at home when I lived in Kansas City. I had three weeks of vacation time to use or lose, so I started visiting the various museums and galleries I never had time to visit when I was working. And, in three weeks, I still hadn't taken advantage of all the local offerings!

If you exhaust all the things you want to do in your immediate area, there are likely to be other areas close to you that offer additional attractions. Those of you who live near the Pennsylvania Dutch country have an opportunity to see a different way of life as well as some of the most beautiful scenery this country has to offer. Virginians have Williamsburg, the James River country (also gorgeous countryside), and, if you've never seen Jamestown, well, shame on you! Ohio has its famous Indian Mounds, Michigan has Mackinac Island, Missouri and Arkansas have the Ozarks, Kansas the Flint Hills. Colorado has the Rockies, Arizona the desert (with Flagstaff for contrast). California has the Sierras, the Pacific Ocean, and a host of interesting towns from Eureka (with its famous Carlson mansion) to San Diego. I could go on, but my point is simply that you don't have to travel long distances to do something out of the ordinary.

I would be the last person on earth to discourage overseas travel, but I've been on my share of tours that were so scheduled a drill sergeant would feel at home. One that comes to mind was a "bargain" tour of Britain I endured a few years ago. The tour bus was packed, every night was spent in a different hotel in a new town, and some of these hotels had small rooms and uncomfortable beds. Getting home, getting permanently unpacked, and sleeping in my own bed was the best part of that vacation. While I'm happy I was able to visit Britain, I have no desire to go back, and I know the memories of that tour are one reason I'm Anglophobic when it comes to travel.

Taking advantage of the home you have, visiting at your own pace in your own car the things that are right in your own backyard, is a much more pleasant experience than many tours that make work out of play.

FOREIGN TRAVEL NEAR HOME

If you don't want to cross an ocean but do want to visit a foreign country where the language is usually English, the people generally friendly, the scenery varied, and where Americans do not need a visa or a passport, Canada is right next door. And the exchange rate is favorable (about $.86 U.S. will buy $1 Canadian). This may not last forever; I visited Montreal in 1974, and the exchange rate was not favorable then, so now may be a good time to see Canada.

Call 800-565-0267 for information about Prince Edward Island (home of L. M. Montgomery's Anne of Green Gables), 800-563-6353 for Newfoundland and Labrador information, 800-661-0788 for information on the Northwest Territories, 800-341-6096 for Nova Scotia information, 800-561-0123 for information on New Brunswick, and 800-363-7777 for Quebec. Each of these toll-free numbers will get you a tourist guide (Nova Scotia's is 300 pages), and most provinces include a road map in their packet.

ORGANIZATIONS THAT HELP YOU TRAVEL CHEAP

Just before my last trip to Kansas City, I discovered a reservation service there that promises the lowest prices on hotel rooms. I checked, and, sure enough, they got me a room for $5 less than the hotel had quoted. I then found out that Kansas City is not the only city with this service. The following are the toll-free numbers for discount hotel deals in these areas:

Kansas City	800-877-4386
Washington, D.C.	800-847-4832
San Francisco	800-677-1500
Los Angeles	800-356-1123
Las Vegas	800-733-6644
Boston	800-332-3026
Chicago	800-468-3500

The following offer reservations in several cities:

Miami, New Orleans, New York, Orlando, and San Francisco	800-950-0232
Atlantic City, Chicago, Las Vegas, New York, Philadelphia, and Washington, D.C.	800-950-0232
Charleston and Hilton Head, South Carolina; Savannah, Brunswick, Atlanta, and Augusta, Georgia; Charlotte, North Carolina; and Jacksonville and Daytona Beach, Florida	800-486-6483
Boston, New York, Washington, D.C., Chicago, Los Angeles, San Francisco, New Orleans, Maui, London, and Paris	800-964-6385
Boston, New York, Philadelphia, Washington, D.C., San Francisco, Los Angeles, Cincinnati, Chicago, Dallas, and Denver	800-221-3531
New York, Washington, D.C., San Francisco, Los Angeles, and London	800-782-2674
Cheap(er) rooms in Western Europe, Asia, North America, and the Caribbean	800-846-7000
Discounted rooms in Asia	800-477-7172 or 800-245-0050
Cheap rates in the United Kingdom	800-235-0909

The following are travel clubs that offer last-minute discounts, primarily on cruises and package tours: Discount Travel International, which costs $45 per family per year, can be reached at 215-668-7184. Vacations to Go is $19.95 and can be reached at 800-338-4962. Worldwide Discount Travel costs $50, and their phone number is 800-446-9938. Moment's Notice, which costs $45, can be reached at 212-468-0503.

If you'd like to cruise without being surrounded by, well, a bunch of tourists, you might want to check out **TravLtips Cruise & Freighter**

Association ($12.50 per year for six issues from P.O. Box 218, Flushing, NY 11358), which tells how to cruise on a freighter. Most freighters carry no more than twelve passengers, and the cabins are more comfortable than most cruise line cabins. And not incidentally, since the main purpose of the ship is freight, they're cheaper than the Love Boat. According to TravLtips, prices start at about $70 a day.

Another organization to contact is **Campus Travel Service** (for their expanded *US and Worldwide Travel Accommodations Guide*, **send $14 to Box 5486, Fullerton, CA 92635, or call toll-free 800-525-6633**). This group gives prices (many from $15 to $30 per day) and lists of dormitories and residence halls that are available to the public during summer sessions. (And, remember, summer in the Southern Hemisphere is our winter.)

Originally designed for students, Airhitch is now available to anyone (although their brochure says, "[I]t helps to be able to think and travel like [a student]"). If you can be flexible about the date, airline, and airports you can use, Airhitch might work for you. You register, give them a date range, wait, and follow orders when you get your assignment; this must be done *in both directions*. This is travel at its cheapest but not necessarily its most convenient. For more information, write **Airhitch at 1341 Ocean Ave., Suite 62, Santa Monica, CA 90401**.

A tax-deductible vacation? It's possible through Global Volunteers, but you've got to work to earn that tax break. The cost to you is from $300 to $2,350 for one- to three-week slots in Russia, Poland, Tanzania, Indonesia, Tonga, Jamaica, Guatemala, Mexico, and Costa Rica as well as the Mississippi Delta and along the Rio Grande in Texas. For more information and a catalog, call toll-free 800-487-1074.

Speaking of Costa Rica, there are a couple of books out touting the virtues of the place as a retirement haven as well as a vacation spot. I've never been there, but the books make the place sound fascinating. *Choose Costa Rica*, by John Howells, is **$12.95 from Gateway Books, P.O. Box 10244, San Rafael, CA 94912**. *The Official Guide to Living-Visiting-Investing in Costa Rica* is **$12 postpaid from Adam Enterprises, Box 18295, Irvine, CA 92713**. Both books emphasize that there are a number of American expatriates there enjoying a stable government and low prices. Both explain that, because Costa Rica has a large indigenous middle class, political turmoil is not likely to be encountered there.

If you've got your passport in order and can really be flexible, courier travel may be for you. For a variety of reasons many shippers prefer to send items as "checked baggage," which means they need a passenger, or courier, to go along with the baggage. The advantage to the courier is that the flight is cheap (on very rare occasions, it may even be free). The disadvantages include having only a limited stay at the destination and being limited in many instances to carry-on baggage. And travel at the courier fare will be for one person only. Most of the available courier flights are from the West Coast to Asia and from the East Coast to Europe, but there are exceptions. If you'd like to learn more about courier travel, check out (of your library, if possible) Kelly Monaghan's **The Insider's Guide to Air Courier Bargains ($16.95 postpaid from Inwood Training Publications, Box 438, New York, NY 10034, or call toll-free 800-356-9315)** or Mark I. Field's **The Courier Air Travel Handbook ($10.70 from Publishers Distribution Service, 6893 Sullivan Rd., Grawn, MI 49637, or toll-free 800-345-0096)**. You might also want to consider *Travel Unlimited*, a courier newsletter, **which is $25 per year for twelve issues from Box 1058, Allston, MA 02134**.

On my first trip to Australia I didn't have time to see Tasmania, but I did pick up a brochure for Evergreen Tours, which offered a ten-day Tasmanian getaway at a price I couldn't match in the United States. I signed up for the tour even though Evergreen advised the average age of their customers was 55. (I figured half would be around 70 and half would be around 40—my age at the time.) Was I ever surprised to find most of the people on my tour were in their 80s (and it was difficult to keep up with them)! I enjoyed the tour, but if being called "Sonny" as you approach middle age is something that might concern you, the United States Tour Operators Association offers a *free* brochure to help you avoid such surprises. *How to Select a Tour or Vacation Package* is available from **211 E. 51st St., Suite 12B, New York, NY 10022**.

I want to forewarn you on this next one that while it is not illegal, it is on shaky ground ethically. But I believe I would be shirking my responsibility if I didn't at least let you know it is available. *Please* don't write me with all the reasons I shouldn't do this—I don't. Travel agents get a heck of a deal on travel. In fact that's the main reason many travel agents do what they do. Now there are travel agencies that sell travel agent credentials to just about anyone who will pay for the privilege of being an accredited travel agent. One company I am aware of that does this is **Ruben's Network, 74 Grove Dr., Mastic, NY 11950, or phone 516-281-0593**. The charge is $299.99 to join and $29.99 per year to renew.

Shopping is about the last reason I would want to go anywhere, but *The Wall Street Journal* reported recently that **Mid America Dental, Hearing and Vision Center, of Mount Vernon, Missouri**, has become a tourist attraction primarily because it offers low-cost dentures ($195 versus $1,000 in most places). If you're not in the market for dentures but still feel the urge to spend your vacation shopping, there are a couple of new books out on outlet shopping. The first is *Joy of Outlet Shopping* **($5.95 from P.O. Box 17129, Clearwater, FL 34622-0129, or call toll-free 800-344-6397)**. The other, *OutletBound*, is available for **$8.50 postpaid from P.O. Box 1255-LC, Orange, CT 06477, or call toll-free 800-336-8853**. A word to the wise here—just because a store is an outlet, it does not necessarily follow that it is packed with bargains. I have seen outlet prices *higher* than discount store prices. Knowing your prices before you shop outlet stores is the only way to make sure you are getting a bargain.

Anne Pottinger of **Annlin Publications' Home Exchange Unlimited (18547 Soledad Canyon Rd., Suite 223, Santa Clarita, CA 91351; phone 805-251-1238)** may be able to help you travel cheap. It just might be that someone who lives where you want to travel wants to travel where you live. Got that? Well, if that's the case, Anne has a solution. Each of you can use the other's home and save the hotel bill. Write or call her for further details.

Since I first wrote about Home Exchange Unlimited, I've become aware of five other home-exchange services. All of these agencies charge a fee for their services, so check out the price before you sign up. The five are: **Vacation Exchange Club (800-638-3841), Intervac Home Exchange (Box 590504, San Francisco, CA 94159; 800-756-4663 or 415-435-3497), Worldwide Home Exchange Club (806 Brantford Ave., Silver Spring, MD 20904; 301-680-8950), Loan-a-Home (Two Park Lane, #6E, Mt. Vernon, NY 10552; 914-664-7640), and Trading Homes International (800-877-8723)**.

Cheap sleeps include hostels, which are usually like college dormitory rooms (and you have to help clean up in the morning) and go for

$8 to $20 per night per person. For more information, contact **American Youth Hostels, P.O. Box 37613, Washington, DC 20013, 202-783-6161**. In spite of the name, American Youth Hostels cater to travelers of any age, and they sell guides to hostels in Europe, Africa, Asia, and Australia as well as North America (they're $13.95 each).

For a list of North American hostels—both those affiliated with American Youth Hostels and others—send $1 and a stamped, self-addressed business-size envelope (SASE) to **Sugar Hill International House, 722 St. Nicholas Ave., New York, NY 10031**. For a list of members of the American Association of International Hostels, send $1 and an SASE to **Santa Fe International Hostel, 1412 Cerrillos Rd., Santa Fe, NM 87501**.

YMCAs provide cheap lodging to singles and couples in various locales. In spite of the name, lodging is available to both men and women, and I don't believe they discriminate on the basis of religion. For more information, write **The Y's Way, 224 E. 47th St., New York, NY 10017, or call 212-308-2899**.

Bed-and-breakfasts used to be a good way to sleep cheap, but many of them are now more expensive than discount hotels and motels. Nevertheless, there are probably still some bargains out there. If you want to check out bed-and-breakfasts, write **The National Network of Bed and Breakfast Agencies, Box 4616, Springfield, MA 01101**.

DUMB TRAVEL IDEAS

At London's Heathrow Airport, travelers needing a transfer to Gatwick Airport are directed via large, official signs to Speedlink, which at £13.50 (about $21) is priced 50 percent higher than Jetlink (owned by the same company as Speedlink) and nearly 64 percent higher than National Express, which nicks you for a mere £8.25 (about $13). If you don't stumble onto the latter two, you'd think Speedlink was your only option. Why the deception?

Time-shares won the Dumb Idea of 1994 award. A few years ago I took advantage of a free weekend getaway with one catch—I had to endure a sixty-minute sales pitch for a time-share condominium in Colorado. I didn't buy, of course, but the sales pitch was enlightening. The lowest (off-peak) price for a 400-square-foot one-room studio unit was $7,000. And that was for a *one-week* period of ownership. I calculated that, even if all fifty-two weeks sold at the lowest price, this unit's total sales price would be $364,000, or a whopping $910 per square foot! Add to that maintenance fees, management fees, cleaning fees, property tax, and myriad other assessments that were likely to increase over time, and all I could see was a bad investment.

If you get roped into one of these "free" sales pitches, just say no. The salespeople will be good, and they will sound convincing. They will point out that this is all you'll have to pay for a vacation anywhere, forever. True? Maybe. *If* your time-share company has an agreement with another time-share company that has something where you want to go and *if* there is space available, you might be able to take advantage of your "investment." But why bother? Ignoring for the moment the additional fees, if you put $7,000 into an investment that pays 6 percent, and you pay $100 per night for a room, your interest will more than pay for a four-night stay anywhere you want to go. Pay for the other three nights and forget about the headaches of time-share ownership.

If you feel you cannot live without a time-share, buy one from an owner who is reselling it. There's almost no market for these, and you'll save a great deal of the purchase price. However, you'll still be stuck with the carrying costs.

CHANGING MONEY IN EASTERN EUROPE

A very few years ago, you could sometimes get four or five times the artificial official rate of exchange on the black market, and my advice would have been to consider doing so. But the rewards were worth the risks back then. My advice now is that you change only at "official" establishments—banks, hotels, etc. Even the kiosks in Russia are all right. The risks of dealing on the black market now range from losing all your money to getting hurt physically if you catch a sharp trick being pulled by an armed money changer. And the rewards are rarely more than a 15 percent differential, now that nearly every country has a convertible currency (and the world value of the dollar is published every Monday in *The Wall Street Journal*). Don't get greedy for that extra 15 percent. The risks clearly outweigh the rewards in this situation.

🖃 TRAVEL TIPS

Watch those "holds"! In addition to being something of a disappointment, the Gellert Hotel slapped a $1,300 "hold" on my Visa account when I checked in. When I checked out, the bill came to $753. If the hold and the bill don't exactly match, this has a cumulative effect on tying up your credit availability. Holds will come off of their own accord in three weeks or so, but that may not be soon enough for you. In other words, the hotel had canceled out $2,053 of my credit limit. The same thing happened with Avis when I returned to the United States and used a free car rental certificate. They put a $150 hold on my Visa account. The bill came to $23 (I only had to pay tax on the value of the free rental), but this wiped out another $173 worth of credit. You can see I would have been up a creek if my credit limit had been $2,000 (even though my total charges were $776).

If "holds" threaten to exceed your credit limit, demand that the hotel staff (or rental car clerk or whomever) remove them when you check out (return your car, etc.). If you cannot get the hold removed, speak to the manager. As an example of how serious this can get, a friend of mine was awakened by a bellhop in the middle of the night and told he either had to pay cash or leave the hotel because a series of "holds" had used up his credit limit. And the bellhop was quite prepared to help my friend pack if the cash was not forthcoming.

One of the few types of souvenirs I buy are unframed prints of places I have visited and enjoyed. They're easy to pack and unbreakable. But framing them can be pricey, especially if the prints' measurements are metric. Here's a cheaper way to get anything framed. Have your print matted to a standard frame size (11″ × 14″, 12″ × 16″, etc.) and buy a standard frame at one of the art supply stores (Aaron Brothers, Michaels, etc.). You'll normally save at least 50 percent.

Stay out of duty-free stores. I've never found a bargain there. In fact, some of their prices on liquor are higher than those I see advertised in my local newspaper. Cologne is almost always higher than you'll pay at a discount store. And your duty-free purchases are one more thing you have to carry with you. In the Moscow airport's duty-free shop, vodka that could be purchased for less than $1 at kiosks was $11.57. Most airlines offer duty-free shopping on board, and I've never seen any bargains there either. I think duty-free sellers prey on people who don't know their prices and who, therefore, assume they are getting a bargain.

Hotel prices got you down? Another option for the really brave traveler to Eastern European cities is simply to go to the train stations. Often people with rooms to rent are there, holding signs saying, in several languages, "Room for rent." The closer the dwelling is to the central city, the more you'll pay. Taking advantage of rooms that the locals may—or may not—be renting requires traveling without guaranteed reservations, a practice I now avoid after once winding up in Montreal because I had not made reservations in Burlington, Vermont, where I'd planned to stay.

I received a copy of **International Travel News (*ITN*)** just in time for this issue. At more than 100 pages, this monthly newsletter may be the best bargain in travel magazines. While *ITN* does accept advertising, this keeps its cost down. It's $16 a year from **520 Calvados Ave., Sacramento, CA 95815 (or call toll-free, 800-366-9192)**.

Bellwoods Publications (31878 Del Obispo, #330, San Juan Capistrano, CA 92675) is offering a travel resource kit containing sample issues of their **Travel for Less** newsletter and an abridged version of their **Toll-Free Travel Directory** for $1.

🤑 MORE TRAVEL TIPS

A friend of mine let me in on an airline industry secret. He travels frequently from coast to coast and stops to see relatives in Chicago, the hub he flies through. If he were to make his reservations with a scheduled stopover, he'd have to pay more for his trip. So he doesn't schedule the stopover. But he takes it anyway. He gives the attendant his ticket to Chicago, checks his baggage to Chicago, and flies to Chicago. On the day he wants to return to his home, he arrives at the airport early, gives the attendant his remaining ticket, and flies standby. Sometimes he has to wait a few hours, but he has always made it back the day he wants to fly (obviously, he doesn't do this around Thanksgiving or Christmas), and he has never paid extra. He advises the secret is just to present the ticket. You don't call ahead, and you don't make any "official" changes. Doing either would result in being charged for a changed ticket.

After all my years of flying, I finally got to take advantage of "denied boarding" compensation. I was returning to San Jose the Friday before Thanksgiving, and flights were overbooked. American asked for volunteers to wait an hour in return for a $200 voucher good on future flights. I'd never made $200 for simply waiting an hour before, and that seemed like a pretty good deal, so I volunteered, and I wound up getting the voucher for my wait. I later learned there are people who do this kind of thing semiprofessionally, and I suppose the holiday periods would be the best times to get vouchers. The semipros say to buy a ticket for a busy flight day, check in, and ask if they're overbooked. If they are, volunteer to be bumped. Some people say it happens to them all the time, and they've made it profitable (though, as I said, this was my first time).

If you're a member of a fraternal organization, check to see if they offer tours. An example is the **Alliance of Transylvanian Saxons (5393 Pearl Rd., Cleveland, OH 44129)**, which is basically an insurance company that was set up years ago to serve the ethnic Germans who immigrated to the Cleveland area from Transylvania. They've offered a twelve-day escorted tour of Transylvania for $2,100, which includes airfare from Cleveland to Munich, two overnight stays each in Munich and Budapest, and ten days in Transylvania. Now, I'm not advocating Transylvania as your travel destination this year (although it is an experience—rather like touring the Middle Ages at times). Instead, I'm trying to demonstrate that, if you can find a group of people who have a mutual interest, you may also be able to find a good deal on a tour. As another example, a friend of mine is a member of a Jewish charity that organizes tours to Israel. These tours include being introduced to members of the Knesset.

14
CHRISTMAS

In the 1960 movie *The Time Machine*, H. G. Wells's time traveler, played by Rod Taylor, travels to a future in which humans have evolved into two species, one of which breeds the other for food. When the one species needs more food, they blow a whistle. The other species goes into a trance and, in a herd, walks toward its doom.

Every year about Thanksgiving time, I think about that movie as Americans suddenly seem to go into a trance and, in a herd, drive to the nearest mall and financial doom.

Now, I'm not accusing the merchants of America of breeding us for Christmas fleecing, although, in this age of conspiracy theories of all stripes, that one would be no less unbelievable than many others. I will say, though, that a lot of January's financial problems could be avoided by thinking before reaching for those credit cards in November and December. This thinking should begin with an examination of the purpose of Christmas.

BUT WHAT IS CHRISTMAS FOR?

When I was a college freshman, an essay titled "But What's a Dictionary For?" was required reading. The essay dealt with, I believe, *Web-*

ster's Second International Dictionary, which had been released without atlases and a lot of appendixes people had come to expect from an unabridged dictionary. The point of the essay was that the dictionary did its job. It provided information about words. And that's what a dictionary was supposed to do. Custom had come to dictate a dictionary do more. The essay suggested we back off and consider the function of a dictionary, rather than what we had become accustomed to.

Similarly, I think it's time we ask the same question about Christmas. What is Christmas for? Is it a time to go into debt, buying people things they neither want nor need in order to fulfill a perceived obligation? Is it a time to spend waiting in long lines at sterile shopping malls? Is it a time to curse our fellow man because we can't find a parking place?

Christmas is supposed to be an enjoyable time of the year. But how many of us spend November and December wishing it were over and done with for another year, and then spend January depressed because we feel as if we missed it altogether? Could it be we feel that way because the way we celebrate Christmas is not a celebration at all and has little resemblance to the whole purpose of the holiday?

Christmas is a religious holiday. It is the celebration of the birth of Christianity's raison d'être. It is a time for families to get together—especially in our transient society. And it's a holiday for children.

Each Christmas my family gets together in the middle part of the country. For years, each of us engaged in the gift-buying frenzy of trying to guess what the others would like. Each year, some of us would be irritated by not getting as good a gift as we believed we had given. We would worry about how to get the things home, and about where we would store them once we got them there. And each year, the gifts were less and less what we wanted or needed.

After several years of getting things that would be kept for a decent period of time and then donated, thrown out, or used for garage sale fodder, my family finally declared a gift truce. We don't give gifts anymore. If one of us wants something, we buy it for ourselves. We don't have to worry about storage space, schlepping things home on an airplane, or hurting anyone's feelings. The stress caused by worrying about gifts is gone. And we enjoy each other's company. To me, that's what Christmas is for.

And Christmas is for children. But be realistic. Don't go hopelessly in debt to make that one day wonderful for little Johnny and Suzy. Be sensible so they can enjoy the other 364 days of the year.

One of the most miserable Christmases I ever had was when my parents bought me nearly everything a kid could ask for. I had been very ill that year. I had mumps, which became encephalitis—sleeping sickness. Weeks after I left the hospital, my grandfather was killed in an automobile accident, and my grandmother suffered injuries from which she never fully recovered. Six weeks after my grandparents' accident, my uncle died suddenly.

My parents tried to "make up for a miserable year" by giving their children a wonderful Christmas. I was seven years old, and I'd done a lot of growing up that year. I knew they couldn't afford all those things. And knowing that made me miserable.

On the other hand, one of the best Christmases I ever had as a child was the year I got a Candy Land game. It could have been any game. But my parents took the time to play the game with us children.

It isn't how much stuff you give children that counts. It's how much of *you* they get. They may whine that they want more things, but give them your time. The things won't last. The memory of the time you gave them will. In other words, even children can have very nice Christmases without an abundance of gifts.

I suggest you try a Christmas during which you give modest gifts only to your children. Tell the adults you normally buy things for that this is what you plan to do, and ask them to reciprocate. Then go through with it. If they give you gifts anyway, don't feel guilty. They were forewarned. Simply thank them for their gifts and reiterate your position. Sooner or later they will get the message. But don't cave in. Don't let their gifts blackmail you into rejoining the gift war.

I am willing to make one exception to this rule. If you have elderly relatives living on a fixed income, you may buy them gifts, provided you buy them something they can use. This means no knickknacks (how many old people do you see shopping for additional things to dust?), no dishes, and so on. Consider buying them a cooked ham, a cooked turkey, or something they will consume. My grandmother loved to get preserves for Christmas.

Stay out of the malls. Spend time with your family. This is what Christmas is for! Happy holidays.

🪙 READER RESPONSE

Many readers did not like my suggestion that they reconsider the purpose of Christmas. One reader in Pittsburgh even told me my suggestion was illegal. But Deborah Brown of Parsippany, New Jersey, wrote to tell me that her Christmas had, indeed, been simpler and better:

I, along with a growing number of people, am fed up and frustrated after looking closely at my financial picture and watching large sums of money disappear in rent, groceries, and finance charges on credit cards used too much. I have decided to call a halt to it. I took the first steps by stopping credit card use and contacting family and friends about a Christmas truce. Only the children in the family got gifts. This is the first year Christmas did not send me into debt. Everyone I talked to was thrilled to get rid of the financial and shopping burden. I actually had time to do fun things with my kids, and I saved about $1,500 this Christmas.

Ms. Brown brings up an interesting point in her letter. By declaring an end to the "gift wars," you may be giving the greatest gift of all to your friends and family—more time to enjoy their holidays.

A couple of years ago a friend was telling me how frustrating Christmas had become for him. His son and daughter-in-law, and their two children hit my friend's house early in the day, had breakfast and opened presents there (leaving a mess), and hurried off to his wife's parents' house (many miles away), where they did the same thing and ate a Christmas dinner at noontime. Then they returned to my friend's house for Christmas dinner in the evening. My friend lamented that the children were in a foul mood, and all his son could do was collapse in front of the television, leaving my friend and his wife to clean up the mess.

It occurred to me as I was hearing this story that this was no fun for any of the participants. I asked, "Have you ever thought that your son may be doing this because he thinks it is what you want?" My friend's face lit up. He said, "You're probably right! I'm going to talk to him and put a stop to this nonsense." And he did. It turned out this was a situation where everyone was doing what they thought other people expected them to do. And everyone wound up miserable. As it did for my friend, a little honesty could net you much more enjoyable holidays.

💵 A LOOK AT OUR CHRISTMAS TRADITIONS

Years ago an older friend I met in college mentioned she remembered when "Rudolph the Red-Nosed Reindeer" was first released. I had assumed Rudolph had always been around. He'd been there since I could remember, and that was "always" for me. I never thought about it. But now Rudolph is a Christmas tradition, joining many others from various places and times to make up our winter holiday—a holiday that would seem quite pagan to the Puritans. Celebrating Christmas was a crime in their society.

Christ's actual birth date was debated in the early days of Christianity. Various arguments were put forth that it was January 6 (a date still celebrated by Eastern and Russian Orthodox Christians), March 28, April 19 or 20, May 20, or November 17. December 25 was declared the official day by Pope Julius I in A.D. 534. The timing of the holiday was probably inspired by the ancient Romans, who celebrated Saturnalia from the seventeenth through the twenty-third of December. The Romans knew how to party, and Saturnalia was the mother of all their celebrations.

From the Celts comes Christmas pudding, which they made to honor their god, Dagda, who selflessly spent his life stirring a giant cauldron of all the earth's goodies to ensure good harvests.

The Vikings, who celebrated the winter solstice only a little less strenuously than the Romans celebrated Saturnalia (it's colder there than in Rome, and Scandinavian days are very short that time of the year), contributed the yule log, which, in order to ward off bad luck in the coming year, had to be kept burning throughout the holiday. The Christmas ham also comes from these people of the frozen North—they sacrificed a wild boar to their god Frey as part of the festivities. Father Christmas can trace his roots to these folks, too. He began his career as a man dressed up as Winter. Hoping to insure winter would be mild so close to the Arctic Circle (a triumph of hope over experience if there ever was one), the Viking people would invite him to their homes, where he would generally be treated very well.

The Germans were big on worshiping trees. The oak was their favorite, and this tree worship was so deeply embedded in German culture that missionaries finally gave up on trying to get the Germans to change this custom. The missionaries redirected this affinity for trees and made it part of the Christmas celebration. The Germans compromised and made the fir their new favorite—the missionaries convinced them the three points of the triangular shape represented the Trinity. And so we have the Christmas tree.

Glass Christmas tree decorations originated in Bohemia, now part of the Czech Republic, where on one unseasonably hot afternoon a couple of hundred years ago, some glass glowers had a bit too much to drink and began competing to see who could blow the best bubbles. They discarded the results of this contest in a corner, but their wives took the glass bubbles to local markets, where they were sold as Christmas novelties.

The Christmas turkey came to us from Europe by way of Mexico. Hernando Cortés, conqueror of the Aztecs, for whom turkeys were one source of protein, took some back to Spain with him. Over time, the turkey has become the most popular Christmas bird.

Turkey, the country, gave us Nicholas, who became St. Nicholas, who became Santa Claus. Nicholas was a generous bishop who is said to have, among other things, saved an unmarried girl from prostitution by giving her a dowry and resurrected three young boys who had been murdered and butchered. He died on December 6, 345. In many parts of Europe, December 6 is still celebrated as St. Nicholas Day, and the evening before is when presents are exchanged. The story of St. Nicholas was brought to America by the seventeenth-century Dutch, and he became part of Christmas, merging with the Viking-originated Father Christmas. Santa's traditional red and white outfit goes way back. To 1931. Santa as we know him today came from an ad for Coca-Cola.

A mystery that always intrigued me was why Santa had to come down the chimney. I finally found out. This legend comes from Lapland, where the only part of the igloo-type houses that protruded above the snow in winter was the hole in the roof that let the smoke out. This really was the winter entrance and exit of Laplander houses in olden times. Lapland also contributed the eight reindeer. Rudolph would have to wait a few centuries.

Briton Henry Cole, too busy to write his many friends during the holiday season, contributed Christmas cards in 1843. We have him to thank for our writer's cramp this time of the year. And the traditional portrayal of a white Christmas comes from the years 1812–1820, when, for eight years in a row, it snowed in London every Christmas. These years were also the first eight of Charles Dickens's life, and, as the author of *A Christmas Carol*, Dickens established the white Christmas as a British ideal. London has been able to meet that ideal only twice in this century—in 1938 and 1970. Irving Berlin made it an American ideal with his song "White Christmas," which he introduced in the 1942 movie *Holiday Inn*.

Many people believe the practice of giving gifts at Christmas originated with the Three Wise Men. It didn't. If you remember the story, the wise men gave gifts to the Christ child. They didn't give gifts to each other. My grandmother, who grew up in rural Sweden, told of getting an orange and maybe some nuts at Christmas. Adults did not exchange gifts. Our practice of giving gifts is a relatively recent one and primarily a product of advertising. Even in the early part of this century, gifts were simple and mainly for children. As advertising became more pervasive, gifts became more and more expensive.

And so we have arrived where we are today. Our new Christmas tradition is shopping. You know how I feel about this new tradition. I think it detracts from the true meaning of the holiday. It takes a season that should be about peace and joy and makes it a hassle. All I'm going to say to you is this: You have a choice. There is no law that requires you to engage in the gift wars. And one final thing. Happy holidays, no matter what your traditions are or where they came from.

💰 TRADITION!

In the summer of 1995 I visited Romania. Our tour concentrated on the ethnic Germans who colonized Transylvania starting in the twelfth century. The tour comprised people who were descended from these "Transylvanian Saxons." My grandfather was my Saxon ancestor.

Legend has it that these folks were the ones lured away from Hamelin by the Pied Piper, and Robert D. Kaplan's excellent book *Balkan Ghosts* (St. Martin's Press, 1993) has a wonderful chapter discussing the Saxon epoch in Transylvania. This epoch is rapidly coming to an end, and his chapter, appropriately, is titled "Transylvanian Tale: The Pied

Piper's Children Go Back to Hamelin." Of approximately 200,000 Saxons who remained in Romania before the 1989 revolution, an estimated 180,000 have immigrated to Germany. Our bus driver and our tour guide were both Saxons who had immigrated to Germany. And before I joined this tour, I spent a few days with friends who had also immigrated. I'll discuss this visit in a later issue of *LCN*.

Our tour guide's brother is the pastor of one of the "fortified churches" in Transylvania. His church, which we would categorize as Lutheran but which in Europe is simply called Evangelical, is in the town of Sinpetru, although its Saxon inhabitants call it Petersburg. (Many towns in Transylvania have *three* names—Romanians, Saxons, and Hungarians each refer to the same place by a different name.) The churches were fortified when they were built because they were often under siege by, among other peoples, the Turks. One Sunday, as part of our tour, we attended a service at the fortified Evangelical church at Sinpetru.

As we entered the church, the men were directed to one set of pews and the women were directed to another set of pews. The women's pews had no backs, and, since many in our group were in their seventies (and one person celebrated his eighty-ninth birthday on the tour), sitting through a church service without back support was a hardship.

After the service we were treated to homemade schnapps, wine, and a meal that could only be described as wonderful. (And to think the Lutheran churches in this country only offer coffee and doughnuts after their services!) Those of us who could still walk were then given a historical tour of the fortified church. The pastor explained the seating arrangement. In the Middle Ages, it seems, the church was constantly in danger of being attacked. So the older men were seated along the more protected side of the church, the women were seated in the middle of the church, and the younger men were seated near the door so they could take up arms and defend the church if it came under attack. In those days, women carried their babies on their backs, and those who did not have small babies wore a costume that would be damaged by a church pew with a back. Hence the backless pews for women.

This seating arrangement, which once served a purpose, became a tradition—a painful tradition for the female members of that church. Of course, if one grew up with that tradition, one would probably never question it. To an outsider, though, such blind adherence to a tradition that has so obviously ceased to serve a purpose seemed odd.

Joe Dominguez and Vicki Robin, in *Your Money or Your Life*, tell the story of a young girl who observes her mother cutting off both ends of a ham. The girl asks her mother why she has done this. The mother says *her* mother always did it that way. It turned out the grandmother did it that way because *her* mother also always did it that way. When great-grandma is asked why she cut off both ends of the ham, she says, "My pan was too small." Here we have another example of a practice that made perfect sense at one time becoming an unquestioned tradition.

Taking an objective look at our own traditions is important as we enter the holiday season. In a world of two-income families, is it sensible to try to have an elaborate holiday? Are we once again in danger of trying so hard to have a perfect holiday that we are predestined to failure? Try taking this approach: These holidays come only once a year, so to enjoy them, slow down, relax, and stay away from shopping malls. If you must give gifts, give money. And, if Christmas is the holiday you celebrate, take comfort in the fact that the first one was a simple affair celebrated in a stable. Everything else is merely tradition.

HAVE YOURSELF A CHEAP HOLIDAY

We can all save time and money this time of the year by using common sense. Do we need to send Christmas cards to people we see all the time? I don't. Is anyone impressed by expensive cards? I doubt it. I'm much more interested in what the card's senders have to say than I am in the card or the preprinted message. That's true even if my friends say it with a form letter (and some of these are pretty good—my father's annual missives crack people up coast to coast).

If you're sending a bunch of cards with only your name signed (or, worse, printed), I'd suggest culling your list only to those people you care enough about to write to. The only message I get from these impersonal cards is, "I'm still alive." I wonder why people bother to buy a card and use a stamp if they have nothing to say.

If you must give gifts, try to reuse wrapping paper. Who cares if it's slightly wrinkled? If you can't reuse wrapping paper, ask yourself if it's necessary to wrap your gifts—or at least if you need to wrap all of them—in the first place.

One reader wrote that she recycles Christmas cards. She cuts off the front of the cards she received the previous year and makes Christmas postcards out of them.

A friend of mine and I have been exchanging the same (unsigned) card for years. It's been around the world.

And, of course, there are the after-Christmas sales. Immediately after Christmas, prices on Christmas cards, wrapping paper, and other holiday paraphernalia fall to 50 percent off. About a week later, they fall to 75 percent off. That's the time to buy, but buy only what you will use. Remember, if you don't need something, it is not a bargain—even at 75 percent off!

HOLIDAY FOOD HOTLINES

Christmastime for many of us is the first time in months that we cook on a major scale. For those who are not sure about how long to cook meat or who are in need of additional information, help is just a toll-free phone call away:

- **The Butterball Turkey Talk-Line** offers information on thawing, roasting, and carving your turkey and some tips for handling it safely. Their number in the United States and Canada is **800-323-4848**; for the hearing impaired, the number is 800-833-3848. The information is available in English or Spanish.

- The USDA **Meat and Poultry Line** offers recorded messages twenty-four hours a day. During the holiday season, you can speak to a real person weekdays from 10 A.M. to 4 P.M. (EST). Their number is **800-535-4555**. (If you're in the Washington, D.C., area, call 202-720-3333.)

- **The Land O' Lakes Holiday Bakeline** offers general baking assistance. Their number is **800-782-9606**, and they're there from 9 A.M. to 7 P.M. from November 1 through Christmas Eve.

- The **National Turkey Federation** offers the following leaflets: "Safe Handling of Ready-Prepared Holiday Dinners," "Turkey Extra" (what to do with leftovers), and "Roasting a Whole Turkey as Simple as 1-2-3." The last one is available in Spanish as well as English. For these pamphlets, send a business-size, self-addressed, stamped envelope for *each pamphlet* to **National Turkey Federation, 11319 Sunset Hills Rd., Reston, VA 22090**.

GENERAL FOOD SAFETY TIPS

As a person who can't resist buying and cooking a turkey when I can find one for 39¢ a pound or less, I'm always wondering just how long the leftovers will last. Some research led me to some general guidelines. If you keep your leftover turkey in the refrigerator, it should last about four days. Stuffing and gravy will last about two days. Freezing extends the life to about four months for plain turkey, about six months for turkey slices in broth or gravy, and about a month for stuffing and gravy.

Be aware, also, that, if you buy a fresh turkey, you must cook it at once. It will last only a day or two in the refrigerator.

HOLIDAY CONSERVATION

We can all do some recycling during the holiday season. Ribbons, bows, and boxes can all be reused. Wrapping paper from carefully unwrapped gifts can be reused also. A cool iron can resurrect wrinkled wrapping paper.

Holiday cards can be recycled, too. Either use the cover as a post-card or gift tag, or send them to the **Unique Boutique, Sunnyvale Senior Center, 820 W. McKinley Ave., Sunnyvale, CA 94086**, or **St. Jude's Ranch for Children, Box 60100, Boulder City, NV 89006** (St. Jude's prefers only the covers).

I like the idea of buying a living Christmas tree that you plant at the end of the season, but, if you buy a cut tree, you can use its boughs as winter mulch and then as compost for next year's garden. The trunk can be used for firewood. Floral arrangements and holiday plants can also be put in the compost heap. (This may seem disrespectful to those who gave you these, but is throwing them out really any different?)

Elaine St. James's *Simplify Your Life* offers a great approach to gift giving. Ms. St. James, taking her cue from J. R. R. Tolkien's hobbits, gives "mathoms." A mathom is an object of any value for which a use cannot be found but that the owner is not prepared to discard completely. Ms. St. James set up a shelf in her linen closet for mathoms, including vases, trays, decanters, decorative bowls and boxes, and toasters, which she uses for gifts. One source of her mathoms is gifts she can't use. She advises the recipients of her mathoms that they are welcome to pass on (or fob off) the mathom as they see fit.

Ms. St. James's suggestion is both practical and humorous, but it also demonstrates the futility of much of our gift giving. Many of us give gifts the recipient won't use and receive gifts that become fodder for our next garage sales. Perry W. Buffington, Ph.D., writes in a recent *Friendly Exchange* that 40 percent of all gifts given will be *disliked*. Our usual response is, "It's the thought that counts." Why not appreciate the thought and forgo the expense in money, time, and environmental damage of our annual shopping orgy? Dare to be different. Have a frugal holiday, and just say no to wasteful consumption. If you absolutely feel you must give gifts, consider giving money. The recipient can buy what he or she wants, and you can eliminate Christmas shopping.

Last year Jeff Greenfield, a syndicated political and media columnist, suggested that, instead of "becoming one of the hollow-eyed herd swirling up and down the streets of the city, risking coronaries, peptic ulcers, and pre-Christmas Traumatic Stress Disorder," we should consider "diverting what would have been spent on useless, meaningless gifts" into contributions to charity. He suggested giving money directly to organizations that feed people because they are less likely to be "afflicted with questionable or excessive administrative costs." Mr. Greenfield and his family (including his children) have put their money where his mouth is, and, he writes, almost ashamedly, "What was astonishing was how good, from the most selfish perspective imaginable, we felt about this decision."

Speaking of charity, December is a good time to gather together all the stuff you can't use, donate it to charity, and earn a tax deduction.

The December 1993 issue of *Money* (you can probably find this issue at your library) lists typical deductions for twenty common items. Frankly, I was surprised at how high some of these deductions were. A few examples are a blouse, $2.50 to $7.50; men's slacks, $5.00 to $10.50; child's shirt, $2.00 to $4.50, and floor lamp, $7.50 to $25.00. And those deductions are per item. Ten blouses could mean a $75 write-off. Happy housecleaning.

HOLIDAY RESOURCES

Unplug the Christmas Machine, by Jo Robinson and Jean Coppock Staehli (look for this in your library or bookstore, or order it from **William Morrow, 1350 Avenue of the Americas, New York, NY 10019; phone 212-261-6500; the price is $9 plus $1.50 shipping**), gives excellent advice on putting simplicity and joy back in the season. Suggestions range from preparing simple foods to establishing less elaborate family customs. The chapter titled "Inside the Christmas Machine" was perhaps the most revealing of all. In interviews held inside a department store at Christmas, surrounded by shoppers, decorations, and all that goes with our modern version of this religious holiday, people told how sick they felt inside about how the holiday has degenerated into an orgy of materialism.

Simply Christmas (available during holidays in your local bookstore or from **Walker and Company, 720 Fifth Ave., New York, NY 10019—write for current prices**) is revised yearly. It contains more than 200 gift suggestions, including recipes for homemade edibles.

15

IT ISN'T EASY BEING GREEN

It is difficult to know what to believe these days. Is there global warming? Is the destruction of the rain forest deadly? Or is it simply a repeat of what early settlers did in the eastern United States? Everyone wants to do the right thing for the environment. But who knows what that is?

As a result, many of us sometimes feel guilty about such things as using our air conditioners, throwing newspapers out, etc. And preying on our guilt has become, believe it or not, an industry.

The following article was my reaction to some catalogs I received from some purveyors of "green" products.

The frog knew what he was talking about! I have in front of me three catalogs from well-known businesses that sell "ecologically sensitive" products. I also have recent ads from Kmart and Long's, a California drugstore chain.

Since the Sears catalog is no longer free (and modern plumbing probably can't handle the pages, anyway), let's start with something we all need to buy: toilet paper. Kmart offers twenty-four rolls (280 single-ply sheets) of Charmin for $4.97. Long's offers twelve 280-sheet rolls of Nice'nSoft for $2.19. One of the eco-houses offers toilet paper made from recycled paper. They say, "[I]t's very soft and you'll never know the difference." Not until you pay for it, that is. They offer a "sampler pack" of twelve rolls for $8.00. Plus $3.50 shipping. Now, their rolls are

117

500 sheets, so on an apples-to-apples basis, paying $11.50 for their twelve-pack is the same as paying $6.44 for Nice'nSoft at Long's (which is on sale for $2.19). But on an apples-to-apples basis, recycled toilet paper purchased through this eco-house still costs nearly three times Long's sale price for Nice'nSoft!

To help you save your newspapers for recycling, there's "Paper Boy," made from "recycled biodegradable cardboard." It bears a striking resemblance to the biodegradable cardboard boxes I use to save my newspapers for recycling. I get mine free from copy centers, who are pleased to get rid of their empty paper boxes. The Paper Boy costs $6.00 plus shipping and handling.

A final product I want to visit is the Sunfrost refrigerator. Some of you may remember the old refrigerators with the condensers on the top. Most of us have seen them in old movies. This was a very energy-efficient design, and I don't know why the condenser suddenly became something to be ashamed of. At any rate, the condenser is now hidden underneath most refrigerators, where no one ever cleans it, and because its heat rises through the refrigerator, it works harder, using more electricity. Sunfrost, though advertised as a "design breakthrough," is actually a throwback to the simpler top-mounted condenser design. The concept—an energy-efficient refrigerator with fewer working parts—is great. But the end result is a $2,800 (including freight) refrigerator with a one-year warranty.

My electricity costs about $25 per month. If I assume half of that is consumed by my old refrigerator and that the Sunfrost used no electricity and never needed repairs, I would never recoup my investment. Why? Right now, I can buy a U.S. Treasury bond that pays nearly 8 percent interest. My $2,800 would yield $224 per year, or $74 more than the electricity my refrigerator is using. And years from now, I'd still have that $2,800 instead of a used refrigerator.

Every one of these items—recycled paper, a paper saver, and the Sunfrost refrigerator—is a good idea. But I'm put off by their prices as well as the apparent belief of those who sell such items that consumers would, or even worse, *should* pay more for products sold as "green."

It is difficult for me to believe it costs less to cut down a tree, transport that tree to a paper mill, and make paper out of it than it does to make paper out of something that is paper to begin with. I find it difficult to understand the logic of paying three times the cost of a name-brand refrigerator for the Sunfrost, which offers no options and an inferior warranty. I think it's time we asked the obvious question: Are these green sellers relying on consumers' believing their purchases are contributing to a "higher good" and that by paying outrageous prices, these consumers are buying an ecologically clear conscience? As far as I can see, the only way such purchases contribute to the ecology is that these businesses take so much of their customers' money that their customers can't afford anything else, so they won't buy anything harmful to the environment.

A rip-off is a rip-off, even when it is politically correct. Buy your toilet paper cheap. Buy as much of your necessities as you can used. Buy from thrift shops, garage sales, and individuals. That will do more for the environment than paying three times what you have to for a refrigerator. And don't forget to question conventional wisdom. Especially the conventional wisdom of those who stand to gain from the conventional wisdom *du jour*.

16
QUICK TIPS

SHAVING CHEAP

All right, it's confession time. I have never bought shaving cream. And, no, I do not use electricity to shave. For nearly thirty years, I have used plain old soap. I lather it and slap it on my face. And shave. It works. And when I travel, that's one less thing to pack.

READING CHEAP

The best way to read cheap, of course, is to use the library. I have a second-best way. Paperback books at (successful) garage sales rarely exceed 25¢. In most towns, there are used-book stores where you can trade these books once you've read them. Generally, you get about one-fourth of the cover price in trade, and the stores' prices will generally be half the cover price. Let's say you buy a couple of books with a cover price of $4.95 at a garage sale. You read them and trade them in, getting $2.47 credit for them. You find another $4.95 book at the store. It's half price, so you get it in exchange for your credit. You have bought three books with a total cover price of $14.85 for 50¢. And you still have a tradable book that you can read on your own schedule without having to worry about late fines. This is the way I read cheap.

💰 ALTERNATE YOUR FUEL

If your car is like mine (the famous Oldsmobile) and balks and pings at the mere thought of running on regular unleaded, try what I do. I let the fuel run down to half a tank, then I fill the tank alternately with premium and regular unleaded. This approach is not as good as having a car that will run on regular unleaded, but it is a lot better than buying premium unleaded every time!

💰 GETTING BETTER MEALS WHEN YOU TRAVEL BY AIR

If you have had the standard airline meal lately, you are already aware that most airlines have gone cheap as far as food is concerned. If I get a cup of coffee on my regular run to Burbank, I count myself lucky. The afternoon flight that used to offer half a sandwich now offers three-quarters of an ounce of pretzels.

If you wind up on a flight that serves a meal, you can get more for your money by asking for a "special" meal when you make your reservations. Most airlines offer low-cholesterol, vegetarian, and other varieties, almost any of which will be better than the standard meal. There's no extra charge, and you don't even have to be Jewish to ask for the kosher meal.

💰 FREE CREDIT REPORTS

In 1991 TRW promised it would begin giving consumers one free credit report. They have finally come through on this promise. To get yours, write TRW **Consumer Assistance, P.O. Box 2350, Chatsworth, CA 91313-2350.** You'll need to give them your full name (including "Jr.," "Sr.," etc.), your current address, including zip code (and your previous address if you've moved in the last five years), your Social Security number, your year of birth, your spouse's first name (if you are married), and a photocopy of your driver's license, utility bill, or something to let TRW know you are who you claim you are. They're supposed to respond in three weeks.

CLEANING YOUR EYEGLASSES CHEAP

Are you having trouble seeing through your eyeglasses? Take a piece of newspaper, wad it up, unfold it, and use it to clean your glasses. It works as well for me as the Sightsavers tissues. I've used this on both plastic and glass lenses without damage.

HOW I SAVE MONEY BY (SLIGHTLY) LOWERING MY STANDARDS

I saw an article in *Parade* magazine earlier this year that prompted me to experiment with lowering my standards just a bit. The article pointed out that modern conveniences tended to complicate, rather than simplify, our lives. One example discussed was the washing machine.

Our grandparents washed clothes by hand. They washed clothes less frequently, and they wore the same clothes several times between washings.

The standard is now one wearing per wash. That had been my standard even though I change clothes and hang them up immediately when I get home in the evening. I began experimenting with two wearings between washes, and it's working for me. Now, this won't work for everyone, but if you spend your workday indoors in a climate-controlled environment, you might give it a try.

Some advantages of my (slightly) lower standard are (1) I don't do laundry as often, (2) my clothes last longer, (3) I save electricity, soap, softener, and water, and (4) I pollute less.

TIME IS MONEY

Be frugal with your *time* as well as with your money. I recently had to have some work done on the famous Oldsmobile. I go to a shop in my neighborhood that charges reasonable prices and doesn't rip me off (and they've had the opportunity to do so). But there's a trade-off. They're slow as molasses. Knowing that, I save up things to read while I'm waiting for my car. This way I can use the time I have to spend waiting for my car to work on my backlog of unread mail, newspapers, magazines, etc.

I also do this when I travel by air. It helps pass time on the plane, and, if a flight is delayed, I have something to work on. Although I may not be able to control airline schedules, at least I can maintain some control over what I do while I'm delayed. This is a way to make otherwise wasted time productive and less stressful.

CHEAPER HAIR

Save money on haircuts. Get your hair cut a little shorter than normal and then let it grow out a little more than you usually do. That way you can go longer between haircuts.

MORE FROM YOUR BATTERIES

Don't throw out those "dead" AA batteries right away. Remove them from your Walkman, radio, etc. and use them for your quartz clocks. These clocks take such a small amount of power that batteries too weak to run anything else may have enough power to run a clock—for a while.

GROW YOUR OWN PROTEIN

If you're thinking of eating less meat, and if you're planning a garden, check out the **Seeds of Change catalog (621 Old Santa Fe Trail, #10, Santa Fe, NM 87501)**. They'll tell you what to grow to replace the amino acids, enzymes, and protein you would normally get from meat.

 2¢ POSTAGE SCAM

There's a chain letter going around about 2¢ postage. The "secret" to this method is that the people mailing with 2¢ stamps are playing the odds. Some letters will get through without the Postal Service noticing. Many will not, and you'll either wind up getting your letter back (just so you'll know, I don't accept postage-due mail) or the recipient will have to pay 30¢ (plus driving to the post office and standing in line for the privilege if they're not at home when their mail is delivered) to read your letter, which had better be good! First-class postage is 32¢ for the first ounce. Using this scam is not a way to win friends and influence people.

UTILITIES

Watch your thermostat! If your house is empty while you are at work, turn your heat down before you leave. The minimum setting for most home thermostats is 50°F, which is high enough to keep your pipes from freezing. Make this part of your leaving-for-work routine (coffee pot unplugged, stove off, doors locked, thermostat lowered), and it will become automatic.

Also, when you're home in the winter, try to adapt to a lower setting. My thermostat is never above 65°F. This is as good a practice here in California, with our minimal insulation and single-pane windows, as it is in "cold country," where houses are built accordingly.

If you have an electric stove or oven, use it as you would a car. Take advantage of the warm-up time (I have never figured out why so many recipes require that you preheat the oven), and turn the heating elements off just before you're finished cooking in order to take advantage of the still-hot burners. During the summer, try to cook in the evening, when it's cooler, to keep your air conditioner from competing with your stove or oven.

Use your microwave whenever possible. Microwaves use less electricity. On hot days you'll also be glad they contribute much less heat to their surroundings than conventional ovens.

Keep your refrigerator coils clean, and keep your refrigerator full of something, even if it's towels or empty containers. Keep your refrigerator on the lowest setting that does the job. Keeping things colder than necessary wastes electricity and shortens the life of your condenser.

If you are thinking of buying a freezer, consider buying a chest-type freezer rather than an upright one. Cold air stays in the chest-type freezer when you open the door. Uprights lose the cold air when the door is open. If you have a freezer, defrost it regularly and keep it filled.

Use your washing machine and dryer for full loads only. Use the cold-water cycle on your washer whenever possible. In the summer, run your washer and dryer at night, when it's cooler, if they are in your house (as opposed to your garage or basement). This will keep them from heating up your house and running up your air conditioner costs.

Run your dishwasher for full loads only. If your dishwasher has an energy-saving setting, use it. This is another appliance to run only at night to keep it from heating your house.

Your water heater uses a lot of energy just to keep the water in it warm. You can help it do its job by wrapping it with insulation. (Hardware stores sell insulating kits; they cost about $10.) If it's time to think about replacing your water heater, consider a "tankless" unit. A tankless water heater saves you the cost of keeping thirty, forty, or fifty gallons of water warm at all times. And, if you live in earthquake country, take note of the fact these units bolt to the wall, and because they're not filled with water, they're lightweight and will move with the house. (Just so those of you who live on terra firma understand why this is important, water heaters often fall over in an earthquake, and gas water heaters frequently cause the fires that are a common post-earthquake danger.)

Set your central air conditioner at the highest comfortable temperature. Use it with fans; moving air makes the body feel cooler. Remember to turn the fan off when you're not using it. If you plan to live in your house for several years, consider installing good-quality ceiling fans. (I have four Casablancas.)

Finally, fluorescent light bulbs use less energy and contribute less heat to their surroundings than incandescent light bulbs. Consider changing to fluorescent bulbs. Your electric power supplier may even be a good source.

FACING UNEMPLOYMENT

One of the most frustrating things about being laid off is the penalty for using money you have invested in a 401(k) plan or an IRA. You planned to use that money when you retired, but you got "retired" early. If you withdraw the money, you not only pay a 10 percent penalty, you pay taxes on the whole amount, *including the 10 percent penalty*.

Well, there's a way to get at some of your money without paying the penalty. First, if you have a 401(k) plan, set up an IRA (if you don't already have one). After you are laid off, have your employer transfer your 401(k) savings to your IRA. This is the only way to avoid a 20 percent withholding fee. (If you don't immediately replace the 20 percent that the government is withholding, you will trigger the 10 percent penalty on that 20 percent. It is dumb, but it is, alas, true.) Then, under the "annuity exception," you divide the total amount of your IRA by your life expectancy each year, and you can withdraw that amount. For example, if you have $100,000 in your IRA and your age is thirty-five, you can withdraw $2,857. It doesn't sound like much, but it could pay your groceries for a while.

For all the rules and regulations (and there are many—it is a government program, after all), call the IRS at 800-829-1040 (toll-free) and ask for Publication 590, Individual Retirement Accounts.

Health insurance is a major concern for those facing unemployment. Ask your employer about their COBRA plan, under which you are supposed to be able to buy health insurance at group rates for at least eighteen months after you leave. Also, check other health insurance companies. Kaiser Permanente (they operate in California and Oregon), for example, has "no group" plans that start at $123.63 for individuals, $245.26 for those with one dependent, and $325.54 for those with two or more dependents. These rates are monthly. If you have Kaiser coverage with your employer, you can switch at these rates. If not, you'll need to go through the usual application procedure. If you think you may be laid off, please don't wait until the last minute to check on health care.

After you are laid off, the first thing to do is apply for unemployment insurance. The rules vary from state to state. It is possible that, if you received severance or vacation pay, you may have to wait a few weeks for your first week's unemployment compensation (you don't in California). Don't be ashamed to apply for this insurance. While, technically, you didn't pay for it, you can bet your employer calculated it as a cost of having you work for him. And don't take no for an answer if you think you are eligible for unemployment insurance. A family member was rather badly treated by an unemployment counselor on a power trip a few years ago. A letter from the family attorney (at a cost of $20) enabled the counselor to have an attitude adjustment.

In those parts of the country hard-hit by this recession, the unemployed may be eligible for up to fifty-two weeks of payments. Be advised, though, that unemployment insurance became federally taxable as part of the 1986 tax reform act, so budget for this. And state policies vary, so check yours to avoid surprises at tax time.

💰 LONG-DISTANCE PHONE CALLS

Let's look at saving money on our long-distance telephone calls. If you have a lot to say and what you have to say is not all that urgent, write a letter. On the other hand, if you have just a brief message, it may actually be cheaper to call, especially if you're calling from the west to the east. If you can call before 8:00 A.M. (and when it's 8:00 A.M. in California, it's 11:00 A.M. in New York), you can get a heck of a deal. A one-minute call from California to the East Coast is 12¢; two minutes cost 25¢. The peak (most expensive) hours for long-distance calls are 8:00 A.M. to 5:00 P.M. weekdays. Even then, a one-minute call from the West Coast to New York is 24¢. After 5:00 P.M. the rates fall to 14¢ for a one-minute call back East. So, wherever you are, you can probably avoid the peak hours. When it's after 5:00 P.M. in New York, Californians are still hard at work. When it's 7:00 A.M. in Denver, it's 9:00 A.M. in New York, and the cheap rates are still in effect. And when it's 5:30 P.M. in Chicago, you can still do business with California and get the off-peak phone rate. *Note:* The above rates assume you are dialing direct.

Making a long-distance call from a hotel can be very expensive. If you use the hotel's long-distance service, usually an "Alternate Operator Service" (AOS), they will charge a hefty surcharge over and above the charge for the long-distance call. (The AOS shares this surcharge with the hotel, of course.) Once I was on travel, and I was negotiating the purchase of a home. I was staying in a Holiday Inn in New Jersey, and I was trying to use my MCI telephone card. I could not get the toll-free MCI access line from my room. The hotel's AOS had blocked that number. I finally had to find a pay phone, where I could get through to the MCI line to make my call. Of course, it was inconvenient, and I suppose the hotel figured that most people would not want to go to the trouble of finding a pay phone, but I have this odd belief that a hotel should try to make your stay with them as convenient as possible. You're paying for a home away from home, after all, and you don't have to go looking for a pay phone when you're home. I've avoided Holiday Inns since that experience.

I've since learned that some AOS's don't block other carriers' lines, but they charge for your calling your carrier's toll-free number! The only safe bet is to find a pay phone.

If you ever need to call from overseas, check into **Kallback Direct (417 Second Ave. W., Seattle, WA 98119, or call toll-free 800-959-KALL)**. If you have this service, you can call them from anywhere in the world except Cuba and North Korea and get access to a U.S. phone line. If you're calling from, say, Spain to the United States, the rate you will be charged by Kallback Direct is guaranteed to be less than you would have paid AT&T to direct-dial a call from the United States to Spain. For a ten-minute call from Madrid to New York, Kallback Direct charges $9.38; using the Spanish phone system, this same call would cost $30.58. If you want to call from Spain to Tokyo, you pay the direct-dial rates for a call from the United States to Spain plus a call from the United States to Tokyo, the combination of which is cheaper than the charge for a call from Spain to Tokyo. Plus you get the time-of-day discounts, which we discussed earlier, based on Seattle time. If you've ever paid for a call from outside the United States, you can see this is a service that's long been needed. While there are savings available for calls within the United States, Kallback Direct's fees are $10 per month, so their service makes sense primarily for those who need to make calls from outside this country.

Avoid "900" numbers—especially those that don't tell you how much the call will cost. Geri Detwiler of the Bankcard Holders of America in Herndon, Virginia, estimates that 900-number companies bilk Americans out of $40 million annually. If you accidentally get into one of these situations, write or call your phone company. They may take the first "900" call off your bill, although they don't have to. I doubt they'll take more than the first one off, though.

10 NEW YEAR'S RESOLUTIONS

1. Send postcards instead of letters. This saves 34 percent on postage plus the cost of writing paper and envelopes. Buy your postcards at the post office.

2. Don't carry a balance on your credit cards. Pay them in full each month or don't use them. Pay them off even if

you have to take money out of your savings account. Why pay 12 percent (or more) in nondeductible interest when you earn 2 to 3 percent in taxable interest on your savings account?

3. If you smoke, stop. If you're up to a pack a day and you pay $20 for a carton of cigarettes, that's $730 a year. Half a pack a day is $365. And those are after-tax dollars. The monetary savings are short-term gains. I don't want to be a nag, but not smoking could help you avoid health problems, and you may be able to lower your health insurance premiums.

4. Buy your clothing at thrift, resale, and consignment stores. A recent segment I did for CBS was an eye opener for me. I visited one resale shop specializing in children's clothing and found savings that were a whopping 80 percent off retail. And the proprietor had already screened, cleaned, and organized the clothing. Children's resale stores are a particularly good way to save money because children tend to outgrow rather than wear out their clothes.

5. Go through your closets. What you won't or can't wear should go to a consignment store or to charity. (Turn something you can't use into something you can—money or a tax deduction.)

6. Maintain your car. Here's an area where little things mean a lot. Keep up with your lube, oil, and filter changes (I do this every 5,000 miles). Change your transmission fluid periodically (I do this every 10,000 miles). Keep your tire pressure correct and your cooling system maintained. Many people are getting 200,000 miles out of their cars these days merely by maintaining them.

7. To the extent possible, plan your purchases in advance. That way you can look for sales on the specific items you need. If your washing machine is about to go, for example, start looking for a replacement now. You're not

going to be in much of a mood to haggle when the laundry's piling up in the utility room and you can't find any clean clothes to wear.

8. Don't be afraid to ask whether an item will be put on sale in the near future. The worst that can happen is the sales clerk will say no. On the other hand, the answer may be yes—or better yet, the clerk may be willing to reduce the price for an immediate sale. Three years ago I was in the market for a new bed (yes, that's the one thing in my house I bought new). I spent a lot of time looking (as you might imagine), and I finally found the one I wanted. I knew the store that sold the bed had periodic "no sales tax" sales. I told the proprietor I liked the bed, and I asked her when she was going to have another no-tax sale. She snapped, "Are you actually going to buy something?" (I'd been to her store several times.) I said, "If you'll take off the tax, I'll buy it now." She took off an amount equivalent to the tax (saving me 8.25 percent), and I bought the bed.

9. Spread the word. If you're looking for an item, or if you have something to sell, let people know. In the past year I've purchased an office chair ($77.50 delivered) and a nineteen-inch color TV with a remote ($75) as a result of people mentioning they had these items for sale.

10. Don't respond to sweepstakes offers, especially those mailed bulk rate. In the past few months, there have been several news articles about these "sweepstakes mills." One of the articles even warned that calling allegedly toll-free numbers could result in hefty telephone charges. There is no free lunch. If something sounds too good to be true, chances are it is. These sweepstakes mailers belong in the garbage. Put them there and forget them.

☷ IT PAYS TO COMPLAIN

In the past few months, I have received a $50 gift certificate from Hertz, a $30 refund from White Appliances, certificates good for ten free disposable razors and a new product from Gillette, and free repairs to my bed.

Hertz erroneously reported that I rented a car that had been ticketed for parking in a handicapped zone. They straightened things out and gave me the gift certificate.

The heating element in my dryer went bad after eight years. The replacement element went bad after eighteen months. White Appliances paid half the part cost after I wrote them a letter telling them I found this short life unacceptable.

Somehow I wound up with Gillette's pivoting disposable razors. The heads of the first two I used pivoted right off the handle. I wrote to Gillette, and they sent the coupons.

In 1990 I bought a new bed from the Oak and Brass Showcase here in San Jose. I'd had it for more than three years when a man repairing a ceiling fan decided to stand on the bed instead of using his step ladder. The bed, which is well made, was not designed for that much stress, and the side rail gave out. I telephoned the Oak and Brass Showcase, and I told them the truth about what happened. I thought I'd have to buy a new side rail. They told me to bring the side rail in, and they'd see what they could do. They reglued it and drilled new screw holes at no cost. It's actually stronger than it was before it was damaged. Now, *that's* customer service!

It does pay to complain. And here's how to do it effectively.

First, remain calm. People are scared by those of us who can remain calm when it is obvious someone's neck needs wringing. A recent example was another car rental situation I had with Hertz. I had reserved a compact car. Hertz was out of compact cars, and the clerk at the counter offered a full-size car for $1 more per day. I was going to do a lot of driving, so I agreed. When I got to the car lot, the manager there told me I was not entitled to a full-size car for the rate I paid, and he reissued the contract for a smaller car. I very calmly told him what had happened at the check-in counter, and I very calmly but also very obviously wrote down the name of the car lot manager (the implication here being that when—not if—I complained, I'd be able to tell *who* as well as what the problem was). I got the full-size car I'd paid for.

Second, when possible, write, don't call. A letter demands an answer. A telephone conversation is your word against someone else's. If you decide to telephone, get the name of the person with whom you are speaking. If they won't give it to you, don't waste your time. A perfect example was the situation with White Appliances. I called the toll-free number of their Customer Relations Center and spoke with a most uninformed young person who kept saying, "What can I do for you?" It seemed to me she should know what she had the authority to do. The letter I subsequently sent worked much better.

Now, where to get the addresses to write to? That answer is easy and almost free! Write the **Consumer Information Center, P.O. Box 100, Pueblo, CO 81002, enclose $1 for postage, and ask for their** *Consumer's Resource Handbook*. It gives you the addresses, phone numbers (often toll-free), and usually a specific person to contact at most major American companies.

EFFECTIVE BITCHING WORKS OVERSEAS, TOO!

After ten days in the Hotel Gellert, I was more than ready to leave. As always, I examined my bill, and I found a 2,200-florint ($27.50) charge I could not understand. When I found out the charge was for a concert ticket I had not been given, I asked that the charge be removed. The clerk simply said it was part of the package. I said I'd never even been offered a ticket. And then I was presented with the kind of response guaranteed to raise my blood pressure: "But, sir, you didn't ask for the ticket." In other words, it's my fault I didn't get something to which I was entitled because I didn't demand it.

After explaining to the hotel clerk that I would contest this charge on my Visa bill (which, by the way, is an excellent reason to use a charge card), I got a 1,500-florint refund. I'm still out 700 florints, but that's better than being out the whole amount.

IT MAY PAY TO BE COMPLIMENTARY

As I've said, it can pay to complain. I recently learned it may also pay to be complimentary. I was in New Jersey in January when a surprise snowstorm plowed through the area. I had reservations on TWA, but they couldn't get me out of Newark in time to meet my connecting flight in St. Louis. Without even asking if I'd take a later flight, TWA put me on another airline.

This was quite a contrast to the way most airlines treat their cattle—er, I mean passengers. Ten years ago, under similar circumstances, Continental assured me (falsely) I'd make a connection. I spent half a day at the Houston airport waiting for the next Continental flight to my destination. It is no accident that I have not flown Continental since 1984.

I wrote TWA, telling them what a refreshing surprise this treatment was. They thanked me for my letter and sent a coupon good for $25 off my next flight.

YOUR ANSWERING MACHINE COULD BE COSTING YOU MONEY!

I recently found a charge for a collect call on my phone bill. Since I don't accept collect calls, and since no one was home when the charge occurred, I phoned AT&T, who almost too readily agreed to remove the charge. When I pressed them to explain how a collect call no one was home to accept got billed to me, they admitted there is a glitch in their technology. Their "robot operators" interpret the beep on many answering machines as accepting incoming collect calls. After they explained this, I said, "This will make an interesting article." The representative got all flustered and asked me not to write about the situation "because that would encourage a lot of people to call." Well, for heaven's sake. If anyone should be able to handle phone calls, AT&T should! The bottom line here is, examine your phone bill and question any collect calls you did not accept.

LETTERS, WE GET LETTERS

Bill Robinson writes that he was in a thrift shop and saw a card table for $1, but its cardboard surface was so soiled it hardly seemed worth taking home. Out of curiosity, Bill checked the legs and noticed all four snapped out perfectly. There were no mechanical defects, so he bought the table, took it home, and stripped the cardboard off. He cut a square top of quarter-inch plywood, attached it to the table frame, and finished it with several coats of spar varnish. He says, "We now have a sturdy, attractive card table that serves many purposes and stores easily."

In fact, Bill says, he found two more similarly soiled tables, which he bought. He fixed both and sold one at a flea market for $12. He concludes, "Check the price on new card tables and you'll see why this is a real money-maker for those willing to do a fairly simple job of repair and improvement. More of Bill's tips follow:

"Some people, several times a year, get a horribly itching infectious type of dandruff. I'm one of them. Go to the doctor, and he prescribes a shampoo that includes a very expensive Selsun Blue. Our pharmacist pointed out you can buy the same nonprescription shampoo, which contains about half the active ingredients and use twice as much (it costs a lot less than half the price of the prescription variety). I've found something that works better and faster—*for me*. My wife watches the sales and buys plastic bottles of hydrogen peroxide disinfectant at an average price of 49¢. Before I enter the shower, I place a bottle in a sink of warm water. When I'm ready to wash my hair, I take the now-warm hydrogen peroxide and empty it over my head, rubbing it in vigorously. Unlike rubbing alcohol, it does not sting. I then rinse with water and use regular shampoo. One application does it. Expensive, prescription-strength Selsun Blue takes several applications." (Bill emphasizes that he cannot promise this will work for everyone.)

💵 GETTING RID OF STUFF

I've spent the last few months going through my stuff, trying to decide what to keep and what to toss. In the past, I'd simply put the discards out and called the Salvation Army. Problem solved. Not this time. I discovered that both the Salvation Army and Goodwill have become quite selective about what they're willing to accept as donations. I had a functional 1970s hide-a-bed that was deemed unacceptable by both charities. I think its only crime was it was an earth tone color. It wasn't ripped or anything; it just was out of fashion. I checked the cost of having it hauled to the dump, but I really didn't want to do that because hauling the hide-a-bed to the dump was expensive, and the hide-a-bed was still usable.

I discovered that the local daily newspaper has ads that cost $1.50 per line for five days. I advertised the hide-a-bed as a free item. I had nearly fifty calls. The couple who wound up with the hide-a-bed live in a tony suburb of San Jose, have children, and say they don't want to spend money on good furniture until their children are old enough not to tear it up. (To paraphrase Ernest Hemingway's response to F. Scott Fitzgerald's statement "The rich are different from you and me," I'd have to say, "Yes. They know how to hold on to their money.")

Shortly after that experience, my washing machine breathed its last. After a repairman confirmed that fixing the machine would cost more than replacing it, I figured there were repairpeople out there who could use the parts, so I spent another $1.50 with the local daily. Sure enough, an appliance repairman took me up on my offer.

This was a win-win approach all around. The people who took the items got things they could use. I got rid of things I didn't want to move. The items were recycled and, thus, saved from early trips to the local landfill, and, heck, the *San Jose Mercury News* made $3 off the deals.

💰 CHEAPER CHECKS

Regarding check-printing companies, I've noticed that prices are all over the place. Some companies give discounts for additional orders, but some charge even more for additional orders than for initial orders. This is amazing to me. These places have already incurred the nonrecurring (fixed-cost) setup charges to print your order, so printing additional sets should be cheaper, not more expensive. I'd advise my readers not to patronize check printers that charge more for the second order than they do for the first. These companies are not thinking clearly, and there are plenty of check printers who, as they should, discount the second order.

Of the check-printing companies I'm aware of, current prices run as follows:

- Designer (P.O. Box 12966, Birmingham, AL 35202) offers the first box of 200 for $4.95. Additional boxes are $3.95 plus $1 shipping per box. Designer is currently offering free address labels with check orders.

- Artistic (One Artistic Plaza, P.O. Box 1501, Elmira, NY 14902-1501) offers the same deal as Designer without the free address labels.

- Custom Direct (P.O. Box 145439, Cincinnati, OH 45250-5439) has the same basic deal, except the maximum number of checks they offered was 400.

- Checks in the Mail (5314 N. Irwindale Ave., Irwindale, CA 91706) is one of those that offer the first box for $4.95 and additional boxes for $6.95; what a deal!

- The Check Store (P.O. Box 5145, Denver, CO 80217-5145) offers the same deal as Checks in the Mail except that their shipping costs are a flat $1 (but their reorder prices are a healthy $6.95 per box).

- Current (P.O. Box 19000, Colorado Springs, CO 80935-9000) has a "limited time" offer of the first 200 checks for $4.95 and the second for $4.95. This is for new customers only; their reorder price is $6.95, and their shipping charges are $1 per box.

As you can see, there are many variables in these offers. So read the ads carefully, look at the price of the first box and subsequent boxes, reorder prices, shipping costs, tea leaves, and goat entrails. And maybe you'll get the best deal. Good luck. Given the alternatives listed, I'd say either Designer or Artistic currently offers the best value.

MOVING

A couple of people have asked me how I moved. Reading between the lines, I have the feeling that many people pictured me tossing my things in a rented truck with a car carrier and driving off with the dogs and me in the cab. Well, I hate to disillusion you, but . . .

In 1970, two friends and I helped move one of our college professors from Edmond, Oklahoma, to Huntington, West Virginia. It was fun, but I decided then and there that was going to be a once-in-a-lifetime experience. Even then, I didn't believe my professor had saved much money on his move (especially when he had three starving, jobless college grads to feed).

An important part of frugality is knowing your limitations. And my limitations include driving long distances in trucks with car carriers. But

I did an analysis, and the approach I took was not a great deal more expensive.

I had the advantage of knowing I was moving several months in advance. So I began scrounging boxes. I wound up buying some boxes I couldn't scrounge (mirror boxes and a wardrobe). I was shocked at how expensive boxes are—even used ones.

I don't mind packing. In fact, I found it somewhat cathartic as I discovered many things I didn't know I had and could, therefore, live without. I did all my packing, which saved a bundle. (I learned movers charge $30 to pack one mirror box.)

I invited four moving companies to bid on my move. Their bids (for the same move) were $2,500, $2,800, $3,400, and $3,600. And all of these were either not-to-exceed or firm prices. I chose the low bidder, American Red Ball, a company that had moved me once before. (No surprise here—as many times as I have moved, I've probably used most major carriers at least once.) Besides being the low bidder, American Red Ball's agent asked for no irrelevant information (such as why I was moving, what I was going to do in Kansas City, etc.). To their credit, both American Red Ball and Mayflower (the second-lowest bidder) advised how I could save money on the move. The American Red Ball agent told me where I could buy used moving boxes.

I did a price comparison on a do-it-yourself move. Renting a twenty-foot Ryder truck with a car carrier would have cost $1,674, which included a 15 percent discount. Add to that the cost of fuel for the trip (Ryder estimated seven miles per gallon), which would have come to an additional $320 (at $1 per gallon), and the difference between having American Red Ball move me and moving myself came to $526. And for that $526, American Red Ball did the loading and unloading. And I did not have to worry about having twenty feet of truck, six-plus thousand pounds of stuff, and a car behind me as I drove more than halfway across the country.

Those of you who move yourselves have my admiration. But, if you're thinking of a move, I would suggest you at least have a moving company (or four) give you an estimate. You may decide the extra hassle is not worth the savings.

The *New York Times* recently had an article on **MovePower**, a Connecticut company that can get commercial rates for individual moves. I did not use MovePower, in part because I was pressed for time, but also because they offer a lot of things I did not need (discounts on real estate commissions, destination information, access to mortgage companies) in their $49.95 (plus $3.45 shipping fees) package. And I was satisfied with the price of my move. Nevertheless, if MovePower sounds like something you'd like to know more about, call them at **800-692-3786**.

YOUR TAXES

For the past several years, I've begun and ended a check register with the tax year. I file that register with the backup information for my tax forms. That way, if I have to locate a check I wrote that year to substantiate a deduction, I can find it in the register.

Should you have trouble with the IRS, first remember that they are people, too, relying on computer data that may have been erroneously entered. I once had an employer enter my W-2 information twice, doubling my income. It happens. If you cannot reach a resolution with the front-line folks, ask to speak with the Problem Resolution Office. These people can do wonders when the IRS or an employer or a bank has made a mistake.

Now is a good time to take a look at just how much your mortgage is saving you in income taxes. I suggest you figure your federal and state income taxes with and without your mortgage interest deduction. That net difference is the amount of taxes you didn't pay because of the deductible interest you paid on your mortgage. Now take a look at how much interest you paid. If you also pay a premium for private mortgage insurance or FHA or VA mortgage insurance, add that to the amount of interest you paid. (It's not deductible, but you still paid it because you had a mortgage.) Compare the amount of interest you paid with the amount of money you saved on your taxes. Did you really save on your taxes because of your home loan? Be aware, also, that the deduction for home mortgage interest is becoming increasingly a target for tax reformers bent on reducing the federal deficit. A mortgage is a way to buy a home. Don't keep your mortgage just to save taxes.

CHEAP CLASSES

Check out the local adult education programs in your area. Quite frequently they offer classes on how to save money, complete with recommendations on where to buy what you need cheap. The University of Missouri at Kansas City (UMKC) offers just such a course through its Communiversity program. The two-day, three-hour class, which cost $9, was taught by two local cheapskates, running partners David Biersmith and David Sechrest. Here are some of their recommendations:

- Save fuel by organizing your trips to avoid driving extra miles. Also, pump your own gas instead of paying more at a full-service station.

- Add extra rice or noodles and extra water to packaged rice mixes. This reduces the fat and sodium content per serving.

- Reuse grocery bags at stores that give a discount for doing so. When the bags start wearing out, use them for garbage.

- Buy nonperishable items in quantity when they are on sale. Name-brand bathroom tissue, paper towels, detergents, etc. can usually be bought as cheaply as generic products this way.

- Take a senior citizen shopping. And take advantage of his or her discount. (All right, you don't *have* to do this if you find it dishonest.)

- Reduce or eliminate meat portions in meals. Replace meat with lower-cost vegetable and grain products. This may have health benefits, too.

- Plan after-holiday celebrations. Does it really mean you care any less for your loved one if you celebrate Valentine's Day on February 15 and take advantage of the half-price sales?

- Eat cereal instead of fast food. It is cheaper and usually healthier.

- After using your oven in cold weather (and turning it off), leave it open to let heat out into the room. In summer, try to avoid using appliances that add heat to the room during the hottest part of the day.

- If you buy the dryer sheet softeners, cut them in half to double the value of each box.

- Don't throw out small pieces of bar soap. Wet the small piece and the new bar and stick them together.

- Add water to your shampoo to get more uses.

- Reuse plastic bread bags, produce bags, and newspaper containers. These can substitute for trash bags, sandwich bags, and plastic gloves. You can dispose of diapers in bread bags, use newspaper containers for handling bug sprays, and bread bags and newspaper containers come in handy for a variety of dirty jobs. *(I've used recycled plastic bags for years to pick up dog poop. I do the dirty job, pull the bag over my find of the day, and then tie a knot in the bag, thus sealing it from flies and other curious insects.)*

- Change oil in your auto frequently (about every 5,000 miles) to prolong the life of your car. Shop around if changing your own oil is not feasible.

- Drive defensively and observe speed limits. Avoid the high cost of accidents, speeding tickets, and the resulting increases in insurance rates.

- Pay your auto insurance premiums annually instead of every six months. You'll get a lower rate and avoid midyear rate increases.

- If you're in the market for a house, check out bank- and S&L-owned foreclosures. Also check out "company-owned" real estate that employers in your area buy as part of their employees' relocation packages.

- Never buy artificially sweetened soft drinks past their expiration date. They go flat very quickly. *(I'd recommend not buying soft drinks at all—drink water instead.)*

- In the event of a terminal illness, put assets in an irrevocable trust for your children or heirs. This will enable you to qualify for Medicaid and avoid depleting your assets, but it must be done before you enter a nursing home. *(I'd recommend discussing this with an attorney first.)*

- If you do not have medical insurance and if you cannot afford health care, be aware there are alternatives. Find out about free clinics in your area. And be aware of medical schools, which may offer cheap if not free care.

- Consider dental schools for your dental needs. True, you'll have a student working on you, but your student's teacher will be supervising the work. You get two dentists for less than the normal price of one!

💰 DEALING WITH FLEAS

Ola Kaufman sent a copy of her 41-page manual, *Flea-Away: Controlling Fleas the Natural Way* **($6.45 postpaid from The Harvola Company, Box 403, Dept. LC, 14846 Sutton St., Sherman Oaks, CA 91403**). There are some interesting facts in this book that explain why flea control is a challenge (for example, a flea can be frozen for a year and survive). The manual suggests the use of such things as diatomaceous earth, planting garlic and wax myrtle, a light bulb over a pan of soapy water, cedar chips, citrus peel, herbal flea collars, etc.

In San Jose, fleas were a year-round problem. And I tried several of the suggestions, including citrus treatment and the light over the soapy water. The citrus treatment Ms. Kaufman suggested (boiling lemons and using the results on your animal) made my dog smell better, but it didn't solve the flea problem. The light over the water managed to catch a couple of fleas per night, but that didn't really put a dent in my flea populaton. In short, I have my doubts about being able to control today's fleas by natural means.

Ms. Kaufman's guide does offer some excellent advice, which is to groom your animal—the comb will rid him or her of fleas. She also offers a use for the part of the flea collar you cut off to fit the collar to your 'mal—put the remaining part of the collar in your vacuum cleaner bag.

It will kill the fleas that wind up in the bag when you vacuum. There are a lot of suggestions in this book. I haven't tried them all. And some may work better in different areas of the country than others. But the bottom line for me is this: I was not able to win the flea war using natural remedies.

Amazingly, I had success with a suggestion made by Elaine St. James in her book *Simplify Your Life: 100 Ways to Slow Down and Enjoy the Things That Really Matter* (**Hyperion, 1992**). "Way" number 16, "Pets Simplified," recommended Flea Busters' treatment, which is environmentally safe, simple, and nontoxic. Its active ingredient is orthoboric acid, and it is a powdery substance that is applied to carpets, rugs, and parts of furniture. When fleas come into contact with it, they start drying up. I was very happy—actually, I was ecstatic—with the results in San Jose. Flea Busters' treatment is not cheap (expect to pay around $200), but the treatment is guaranteed for a year. Be advised the first five weeks can be rough, as the dehydrating fleas do become a bit frenetic, but once they're gone, your house is essentially flea free. For your local **Flea Busters**, look in the phone book or call **800-759-FLEA.**

I had wondered why something like the Arm & Hammer powdered carpet deodorant couldn't be developed for flea control, and I've finally seen something like it at pet stores. You put it on your carpet and vacuum it up. I understand the same active ingredient that Flea Busters' uses, orthoboric acid, is in some of these treatments, but I don't know if the concentration is as high (Flea Busters' is 64 percent). You may want to try this do-it-yourself approach before calling in Flea Busters.

I've read about a new monthly flea control pill for pets. It's called Program. Its price depends on the weight of your animal (as I write this, the price for a 50-pound dog is around $65 per year). It works by entering your pet's blood, which is the flea's food. It causes the flea's eggs not to hatch, so each flea that ingests blood treated with Program becomes infertile. This pill provides a lot of advantages, and, while it is currently expensive, it is a lot less expensive than many other approaches. (Fogging my house in San Jose used to run around $50 each time I did it, and that was when I could find the foggers on sale.)

The pill is only available from veterinarians, and demand for it currently far exceeds the supply. Once the pill is more readily available, I would expect the price will come down a bit. Even at current prices, though, and assuming Program works, if you have fewer than three pets,

Program is going to be less expensive than Flea Busters. If Program works, I would imagine Flea Busters' prices will come down.

CHILDREN AND MONEY

The Spring 1995 NCFE *Motivator, published by the National Center for Financial Education, offered some good suggestions in response to the question, How do we get our children to appreciate the value of a dollar? The following are* NCFE's *suggestions and are reprinted with permission:*

A properly managed allowance is, of course, the basis for doing so. The Philip Johnson family of Phoenix, Arizona, have some good ideas. Here are a few of them:

- **Assign basic household chores.** Even a four-year-old can make his or her bed and pick up playthings. Have a list of "little jobs" that small hands can do to earn a dime or a quarter. Also, provide a piggy bank for savings.

- **Don't buy toys on demand.** Help your children look forward to birthdays and holidays for special items.

- **Let children learn about actions and consequences.** Having possessions brings responsibilities. Don't be so eager to bail them out of a difficult situation.

For NCFE's catalog, **"The Money Bookstore,"** and for a copy of their brochure, **"18 Ways to Teach Your Children or Grandchildren the Value of Money,"** send **$1** to NCFE at **P.O. Box 34070, San Diego, CA 92163-4070**.

THE INTERNET

You can reach me on the Internet by using the address livcheap@aol.com. I signed up with America OnLine (AOL), which offered the first month free and also gave me ten free hours. I now pay $9.95 per month, which

includes five hours' usage. I've been a bit disappointed with many of
AOL's services as well as the maturity level of some of the people in AOL's
"rooms," but I like the E-mail feature. It is nice to be able to send
E-mail anywhere in the world for a basic monthly fee. On the downside,
AOL has its own way of "gaming" the system. It's always "adding new
artwork," "adding new features," etc. *on its customers' time*! The present artwork is just fine. I'd just as soon not have my five hours eaten
up by the system adding new stuff!

But E-mail alternatives are coming! The September issue of
SmartMoney tells of two new free (that is, paid for by advertisers, rather
like television) E-mail services that are coming soon. Unfortunately for
those of us who use Macintoshes, they won't be coming soon for us, but
if you have a PC, you might want to get in touch with **FreeMark at
617-492-6600 or Juno at 800-654-5866** and get on their mailing list.

NINE WAYS TO SAVE TIME, MONEY, AND YOUR SANITY

Every winter people make all sorts of lists—shopping lists, New Year's
resolutions, etc. Here is my list of ways to make the New Year your best
year (so far!):

- **If you don't like your job, don't do it.** This sounds
  simplistic, I know. But I've just lost an acquaintance to
  cancer. This man hated his job. He hated the people he
  worked with. He dripped venom wherever he went. And
  this was the third case like this I'd seen—a former boss,
  a coworker early in my career, and this man. All hated
  their jobs, all of them kept working because they knew
  that "one day" they'd be able to retire and live the life
  they wanted to live, and all of them died of cancer before
  they were old enough to retire. Tragic? Certainly. But let
  their tragedies be a lesson to us all. Some of us were not
  born to spend our lives in a corporation. We are square
  pegs trying to force ourselves into round holes, and we
  can't do it without losing a part of ourselves. It is noth-

ing to be ashamed of, but it is certainly something we need to face up to!

- **Turn the television off.** I have two friends who are rearing their children without television. Both sets of children have discovered books and are excelling in school. Two families are not enough to prove a correlation, I know. But it is just possible that television and low performance in school go together.

- **Learn to do without.** Or at least to do with less. We all have our weaknesses. Mine are books and records. Quite frequently I'll find myself buying more while asking myself why I'm not home enjoying the ones I already have!

- **Learn to savor silence.** I love quiet. That's one reason I'm leaving my townhouse. There's always noise here, whether it's the background sound of Interstate 280, one of the three visits our trash collectors make every Tuesday, or the twice-weekly serenade of our gardeners' leaf blowers. When I can enjoy silence, I savor it. I let my mind enjoy the frivolities of fiction. I've been known to pig out on a 600-page book in one day. And relish that day for several more. Silence is golden.

- **Use your television set to watch good movies on tape.** I'll let you define what's "good." I've recently seen ads for five movies for five days for $5. Considering the cost of first-run movies, movie rentals are truly one of the bargains of our time.

- **Use your library.** Libraries are one of the best bargains of all time. You can read books free (but get them back on time!), browse through magazines and out-of-state newspapers, and take advantage of any number of reference materials. Also, many libraries have ongoing or periodic "Friends of the Library" sales where you can buy books at bargain prices.

- **Find yourself a good doctor.** If your doctor won't listen to you, if he or she dismisses your complaints as insignificant or automatically attributes them to stress, depression, boredom, or "nerves," or if your doctor treats you as subservient (remember, *you're* the customer), find a doctor who treats you as an equal, who will explain what he or she suggests you do as well as what the options are. I know how difficult it is to leave a doctor you've been going to for years, no matter how awful he or she is. I put off changing doctors for five years, even though I knew mine was no prize. Only after I discovered by accident that the fatigue I was suffering was the result of diabetes (not boredom) did I realize how dangerous it is to stay with a bad doctor out of habit.

- **Make your life and your mind clutter-free.** Clutter is stuff that you get no use from, yet it takes up space in your home and your life. Get rid of stuff you can't or won't use. Less stuff can make a small living area seem larger. And clutter is not limited to the physical. Try to let go of mental clutter as well. Let go of guilt from the past. Let go of concern about the media circus *du jour*. (Did the outcome of the O. J. Simpson trial, for example, *really* have an impact on your life?)

- **Think for yourself.** Don't let the media, your friends, your family, or me tell you what to do. If something doesn't make sense to you, don't do it. Only you know what's right for you, and only you will suffer the consequences if you follow bad advice.

17
HOW I MADE MORE TIME IN MY LIFE

I was watching too much television. But there was so much to watch! Television was ruling my life. My schedule revolved around television.

Years ago I had read *Walden*. Thoreau said, "And I am sure that I never read any memorable news in a newspaper. If we read of one man robbed, or murdered, or killed by accident, or one house burned, or one vessel wrecked, or one steamboat blown up, or one cow run over on the Western Railroad, or one mad dog killed, or one lot of grasshoppers in the winter—we never need read of another. One is enough. If you are acquainted with the principle, what do you care for a myriad instances and applications? To a philosopher, all *news*, as it is called, is gossip." But Thoreau seemed irrelevant in our electronic age.

Suddenly I tired of television. I think my fill came during Iraq's invasion of Kuwait and the subsequent Gulf War, when the same stories ran over and over again, and my television began to seem more like a purveyor of propaganda than a source of information.

I had traveled to Romania, where there is one station. My hotel charged an extra $5 a day for television. I just said no, even though many programs were in English with Romanian subtitles. I went out more than I would have otherwise, into a society where most people travel without automobiles, where hot water is not always available, and where food shortages are the norm rather than the exception. But the people were friendly and open. They weren't cocooning. They were interdependent. They didn't ignore or fight with their neighbors. They needed their help.

When I got home, I tried cutting back on my television viewing. It didn't work. I realized that, for me, it was all or nothing. On August 18, 1991, I pulled the plug and began reading one of the books I'd bought over the years to read "someday." This one was about the Bonus Army Protest that took place in 1932. As I was reading this book, I was transported back to my grandmother's house, where I spent many of my childhood summers. She had told me of that summer of 1932 and of the Bonus March. I remembered the languid summers of my youth when this woman who had seen so much entertained me, not by turning on the television, but by telling me the story of her life. Her childhood in Sweden, her emigration the same year the *Titanic* sank, Ellis Island, New York at the time of the First World War, her marriage, her move to Fort Riley, homesteading in Colorado, the dust bowl, the final move to Oklahoma City, the Second World War, and the vacation trip to Montana that ended in tragedy on a Kansas highway, leaving her widowed and crippled.

I realized that if my grandmother had taken the easy way out—propped me in front of her television set and turned it on—my life would have been much poorer. I have always felt a connectedness with history, and I think she gave that to me.

History continues, and August 19, 1991, nearly sent me back to CNN as I awoke to the announcement of the coup in the USSR. I resisted temptation and relied on National Public Radio. Frankly, I think they do a better job than CNN. NPR analyzes the news. CNN, in its rush to be first, uses a shotgun approach. You get it all. The good. The bad. But more often than not, the insignificant. The gossip. Thoreau, you see, wrote for our time, too.

I wonder how many children growing up today will feel a connectedness with history. Or with society. Everything they know they learned from television, from *Sesame Street* to *Teenage Mutant Ninja Turtles*. Perhaps that's the reason so many young people don't know when the Civil War was fought and can't locate where they live on a map of the United States.

And perhaps television is the reason so many adults have so little time. The average person watches six hours of television per day. Add to that eight hours on a job, commute time, and lunch hour. It's a wonder anything gets done!

When I gave up television, I expected to feel at least some sense of deprivation. What I felt instead was a sense of liberation. I was taking back that part of my life that had been given over to television. Suddenly, I had the time to do the things I was going to do "someday."

My life became more my own.

18

OUR JOBS: EXPECTATIONS AND REALITY

A reader submitted the following story to be considered for the "Dumb Idea of the Month":

"Company X," while enjoying record profits and increasing its dividend, has been laying off employees and giving one-time bonuses to employees eligible to retire. Also, for the first time since a close encounter with bankruptcy twenty years ago, the company decided not to give its lower-level employees a pay raise, instead giving "bonuses" (averaging 2 percent) to some "high performers." This policy did not apply to upper management, where it's "business as usual."

One young employee wrote to the president of Company X, explaining this policy was shortsighted and especially unfair to younger employees. As is usually the case in large companies, the responsibility for responding to the employee was delegated down several levels, winding up in the "Human Resources" Department, which in essence told the employee to put up or find "an employer more in keeping with your theories." My reader asked if I didn't agree this was dumb.

Well, in the context of our modern world of euphemisms and double-talk, the response probably was dumb. But it was, at least, refreshingly honest.

What is dumb is the belief of the employee who wrote the letter that he is part of a "team" and that he evidently relies on his job for a sense of identity. In this one slip of the pen, Company X has let this employee know he is merely a commodity, that he has no say in the direction of Company X, and that, if he doesn't like that arrangement, he can leave. Does this employee (and millions like him) need a ton of bricks to fall on his head to get his attention?

No matter how "professional" one is, it boils down to this: If you work for someone else, you do your job. Your reward is your paycheck. Period. Labor for money. Got it?

Companies have, especially recently, been deluding or frightening employees into contributing more of their own time to the company. Many employees play along, believing that if they help out, they'll be rewarded. Usually their reward is a lower hourly pay (taking into account the contributed time), less time with their families, and more work.

These employees justify their actions by telling themselves (and their families) that they are needed by the "team." That it's "just for a while." And someday things will come together. However, "just for a while" becomes a career, and "someday" never comes. In the process they let their jobs become their lives, and, when their employers act like what they are—employers—they feel betrayed. It's as if a family member has suddenly turned disloyal. I'm reminded of the Johnny Rivers song in which a woman picks up a sick snake, nurses it back to health, and is shocked when it bites her. The snake tells the woman that she knew he was a snake when she took him in.

These people have given the best years of their lives to an entity that, like the snake, has suddenly turned on them. Their feelings, in the context of their contributions, are normal. But along the way they've forgotten an important part of being human: a job is just that. It is a job. It is a way to make money. It is not a life. And perhaps now that the young man who wrote to the president of Company X knows his true value to his employer, he can get on with his real life.

In *Your Money or Your Life*, one of the best books I've read in a long time, authors Joe Dominguez and Vicki Robin say, in a paragraph that should be etched in stone and placed in the offices of all of us who let, have let, or are in danger of letting our jobs become more than they should be:

Our jobs are also called upon to provide the exhilaration
of romance and the depths of love. It's as though we believed

that there is a Job Charming out there—like the Prince Charming in fairy tales—that will fill our needs and inspire us to greatness. We've come to believe that, through this job, we would somehow have it all: status, meaning, adventure, travel, luxury, respect, power, tough challenges and fantastic rewards. All we need is to find Mr. or Ms. Right—Mr. or Ms. Right Job. Perhaps what keeps some of us stuck in the home/freeway/office loop is this very Job Charming illusion. We're like the princess who keeps kissing toads, hoping one day to find herself hugging a handsome prince. Our jobs are our toads.

💰 RESOURCE REVIEW

Viking sent me a copy of *Your Money or Your Life*, by Joe Dominguez and Vicki Robin. This book should be in bookstores as well as in your local library. As you know, I usually recommend you use your library instead of buying books. But not this time. At $11.95 (or less—I've seen copies for $6 in used-book stores), this book could be one of the best investments you will ever make, for both your money and your life. And it's a book you should keep readily accessible.

And Dominguez and Robin know what they are talking about; each has lived on $6,000 per year for more than twenty years. The book shows how inflation (which seems to be a fear that keeps a lot of people I know stuck in their routines) is a hobgoblin that for many products does not exist and for others can be confronted effectively by increasing awareness, or consciousness, of what we buy and how. The book gives a concrete nine-step plan (handily summarized in the Epilogue) for determining how much you need to live, how to achieve that level of income (and a little more) through sound, worry-free investments, and how to start working on your life instead of for your money. The book is full of humor, insight, and examples of real people who have followed the program. Once I picked the book up, I couldn't put it down.

19
RUNNING AWAY

California has certainly had its share of troubles lately. Riots, fires, floods, mudslides, and earthquakes. Now our own version of the plague of locusts, the state legislature, is considering a series of "temporary" taxes to repair damage caused by the Northridge earthquake. Forgive my cynicism, but the last "temporary" sales tax increase—the one put in place to repair the damage from the 1989 Loma Prieta earthquake—is still with us. It's called something else, of course, but it's no longer temporary. As I recall, the rationale for renaming it and making it permanent was something along the lines that people were used to paying it. So I guess we will have to get used to paying the new taxes, too.

An awful lot of Californians are fed up with the trials and tribulations of life in the Golden State. And a lot of them are leaving. Bill Seavey of the Greener Pastures Institute has made a career of helping unhappy Californians relocate. (For more on Greener Pastures, see the discussion of resources later in this chapter.) And if people want to move, well, that's what made this country what it is—right? But wait a minute.

Our previous migrations have pretty much been in search of a better future. Or at least better land, cheaper land, or a better climate. Usually people who liked where they were moved somewhere they thought they would like better, as the songs they left us prove. ("Across the Wide Missouri" is a good example.) Past migrations have been made by people moving *to* something—not by people running away from something. (One exception to this rule was the mass movement to Texas of people fleeing their debts—Texas's bankruptcy law remains among the most liberal in the nation as a result.)

Today's migrants are different. They're running away. Often they are running away from a problem of their own making. And often the problems may not be all that serious.

I've lived in eight cities in seven states, some of which I've liked more than others. One of the few times I ran into trouble was when I tried to transplant my city-bred self to rural New Hampshire. It didn't work. And I know I am not alone. Say what you will about cities—it's all true. But there are those of us who won't live anywhere else. Where else can you, in the space of a few short blocks, see people from India, Vietnam, Russia, Iran, and Ethiopia, to name but a few sources of our recent immigration, living peacefully among us born-in-the-USA hybrids?

It is possible that those running away from California won't miss the diversity this state has to offer. It is possible they will find happiness in the confining intimacy of some homogeneous small town. But I suggest they declare a time out before they start packing and think about what they'll be missing. Maybe they should reflect on what brought them to California in the first place. And they should know that Californians are not universally welcome in communities that, surprisingly, have survived without us for a hundred years or more.

A recent *Wall Street Journal* article about Californians moving to the town of St. George, Utah, explores some of the reasons. Many Californians, forgetting what they thought they were trying to get away from, try to turn their new communities into mini-Californias. This is not the way to win friends and influence your new neighbors. It is also not a good idea to build a $400,000 mansion in an area where the median home costs $35,000, in spite of the fact you sold your hovel in Manhattan Beach for that much. (Pay the capital gains tax and buy a more modest home that's appropriate for your neighborhood—you'll still come out ahead financially, and your neighbors will speak to you.) St. George is only one of many examples. Enough Californians have moved to Seattle and the state of Oregon to foster a "pull up the drawbridge" mentality among natives. I encountered this mentality for the first time when I moved from

Los Angeles to Austin, Texas, in 1984. Being unwelcome in your new community is no fun.

I'm not making a lifetime commitment to California. (In fact, don't be surprised if, very soon, LCN has a new address.) I'm on a month-to-month basis now, but I know there are a lot of things I'll miss when I leave. Does anyone know a good Muslim Chinese restaurant in Kansas City?

One thing I can say for certain is: When I leave, I won't be running away.

RESOURCES FOR THOSE THINKING OF A LIFE IN THE COUNTRY

Bill Seavey's **Greener Pastures Institute (P.O. Box 2190, Pahrump, NV 89041)** is involved in helping urban dwellers relocate to smaller cities. He is offering his *Eden Seeker's Catalog* free if you will send him a self-addressed stamped envelope (SASE). If you're considering a move to the country, there are some good resources available through Greener Pastures Institute, and they offer discounts of 15 percent to 25 percent, depending on the size of your order.

Lisa Shaw, a Brooklyn native, moved, not to the Midwest, but to rural New Hampshire. She is so happy about her move that she began *Sticks*, an objective bimonthly newsletter designed to help others decide whether a move from the city to the country is for them, and *Sticks* even lists help-wanted ads primarily for Maine, New Hampshire, and Vermont, but a few for Texas, Montana, and Massachusetts sneaked their way into the issue I saw. *Sticks* is 10 pages, and a subscription is **$36 per year from William Hill Publishing, R.R. 1, Box 1234, Grafton, NH 03240.** For a sample issue and a list of other publications available from *Sticks*, send $5.

If you're thinking of leaving the big city for something more bucolic, there are a couple of ways to get a handle on prices in various parts of the country. The first is *Rural Property Bulletin* **($16 per year from P.O. Box 37, Sparks, NE 69220—mention that you're an** LCN **subscriber and you can get it for $12 per year),** which lists properties and businesses for sale (primarily) by owner. **United National Real Estate (1600 N. Corrington Ave., Kansas City, MO 64120 or 800-999-1020)** publishes a quarterly 200-plus-page catalog of sample listings across the country for $4.95 postpaid.

Once you find your paradise, how do you make a living there? One alternative might be a home-based business. Oklahoma is at the forefront of the home-based business movement by recognizing that home-based entrepreneurs do not demand the tax concessions, property tax exemptions, etc. that large companies look for when they move into an area. Home-based entrepreneurs quietly go about their business, pay their taxes, and contribute to their community. And Oklahoma is interested in attracting these folks. If you're interested in what Oklahoma has to offer, write **Dr. Marilyn Barnes, Home-Based Business Specialist, Oklahoma State University, Central Office for Home-Based Entrepreneurship, HES 135, Stillwater, OK 74078, or call 405-744-5776.**

Another option might be the flea market business. Jordan L. Cooper's *Shadow Merchants: Successful Retailing Without a Storefront* tells how to get into the business. The author, who now lives in the "best part" of an unspecified town, began with $43.75. He tells how you can follow in his footsteps. **The book is $12.95 plus $4 shipping from Loompanics Unlimited, P.O. Box 1197, Port Townsend, WA 98368 (Washington residents add 7.8 percent sales tax)**. With every order Loompanics will send their $5 catalog of literature, much of which will be of dubious value.

A few really determined ex-urbanites have decided to live temporarily or permanently "off the grid"—without electricity. This life off the grid is a lifelong reality for many Americans, notably the Amish, who live without electricity out of religious principle. How they manage in today's world is explained in *Living Without Electricity* by Stephen Scott and Kenneth Pellman (**$5.95 plus $2.50 shipping from Good Books, P.O. Box 419, Intercourse, PA 17534-0419, or toll-free 800-762-7171**).

If you're curious about where the Amish buy their appliances and tools, one source is **Lehmann's (P.O. Box 41, Kidron, OH 44636)**, who offer their *Non-Electric Catalog* for $2. Some of the prices in this catalog are pretty steep, which probably explains why there were so many Amish at a farm auction I once attended in Lancaster County, Pennsylvania.

For others who might be interested in living with electricity but off the grid, there's *Home Power*, a slick, bimonthly magazine full of articles on and sources for renewable energy. It's **$22.50 per year from P.O. Box 520, Ashland, OR 97520**.

For the self-sufficient country life, **Happy Hovel Foods and Country Store (P.O. Box 781, Yelm, WA 98597)** offers their *Food Storage and Self Sufficiency Handbook and Catalog* for $7.

Countryside **($18 per year—six issues—from W11564 Highway 64, Withee, WI 54498)** is a charming magazine by and for those who live in a rural environment. It is easy to see how this jewel has been around since 1917.

The Caretaker Gazette **($24 per year—six issues—from 2380 NE Ellis Way, Suite C16Q, Pullman, WA 99163)** is a good way for those whose approach to country life might be "try it before you buy it." The newsletter helps landowners and caretakers find each other. In the issue I saw, there were caretaker jobs advertised throughout the country as well as Puerto Rico and the West Indies.

READERS RESPOND

I had some thought-provoking letters as a result of the article "Running Away" back in Issue 26. Bill Robinson of Bandon, Oregon, writes:

You nailed it exactly like it is. I do not speak from any high Oregon moral ground, because I spent twenty years in San Diego. But these younger Californians! It's enough to make an Oregonian out of you! They are ruining small towns like Burns. And they possess another characteristic—one that not many have written about but which amuses me. So many of these transplants leave here in winter. Some neighborhoods become ghost towns. These people have it backwards! The Oregon summers are rough. But the winters! No tourists, quiet roads, cheap hotel and resort rates, a cozy book by the fire . . .

Laura Martin-Buhler, who edits The Gentle Survivalist *(Box 4004, St. George, UT 84770), writes, regarding the influx of people to her area:*

Many people who grew up here and left to go to work are moving back from Southern California and Nevada. They want a peaceful place to raise their children, so they are giving up high-paid jobs to return here. There are also many retirees moving from colder areas all over the country. This has created a building boom here, and such booms always attract a transient population of service trade people, some of whom are a little fringy and take advantage of friendly folks. An example is a sprinkler setter who didn't do a quality job for me. He charged a high price, and I later found out he had been sent to the state penitentiary for stealing from his employer.

Then there are many people who move here for the stability of the community, but they don't participate in the activities that make it stable and peaceful. They take, but they do not contribute. These people are usually from the larger cities, and they often bring with them children who have been influenced by gang activities. Sadly, it's often too late for these children. They don't fit in with the local kids who are involved in the Scouts and service activities. They fall into gangs of kids who are also from bigger cities and are more comfortable riding around in flashy cars, playing boom boxes, wearing baggies, sporting extreme haircuts, and affecting a cold rudeness. Drugs and alcohol are also part of the act. The kids here don't shun these children; they simply go off by themselves because they think the kids here are boring.

Some adults from the big cities are much the same. They complain there aren't enough bars here, they run to the Nevada state line to gamble and visit porno shops. It really is a strange polarity, and the rising crime rate is sending many long-time residents to smaller towns for a little peace.

And water is a big issue. A historical Native American gathering place is in danger of being destroyed for its water. It is still beautiful here, but it will never be the same with houses being built in the hills and filling the green fields.

20
ALTERNATIVES

"I can't believe this," said the young woman through clenched teeth as she put the first of four quarters in the vending machine. "They're charging a *dollar* for orange juice!"

I was in the vending area of one of Silicon Valley's more progressive employers. In other areas of the facility I had seen refrigerators and microwave ovens, and the company provided hot and cold bottled water free to its employees.

So why was the angry young woman patronizing the overpriced vending machines? Evidently she couldn't see the alternatives that were all around her.

If she wanted orange juice, she could have brought some from home and put it in one of the company-provided refrigerators. If she merely wanted something to drink, there was the free bottled water. No one forced her to feed the overpriced vending machine.

Quite often we overlook our alternatives. We may forget we have ground beef and cheese in the refrigerator as we drive to McDonald's to wait in line for a cheeseburger. We may stay stuck in a job, a relationship, or a routine that we don't like because we're unaware of—or worse, afraid of—the alternatives.

How many people do we know who constantly complain about their jobs but aren't doing anything about finding something else? How many people do we know who put their brains on hold the minute they get home from work by turning the television set on? These are probably the same people who complain they never have time to do anything. How many people claim they just can't save any money? (You may have noticed I skipped right over the relationship thing.)

Back in the late 1970s, a friend of mine and his new (second) wife visited me in Kansas City. They were impressed with the job I had done furnishing my house. My friend's wife asked where I had found certain pieces, and I would usually have to answer "at a garage sale," "at an auction," or "this belonged to my grandmother." I sensed a mounting frustration in my friend's new wife. Finally, she blurted out, "Don't you ever get anything the normal way?" When I asked her what she meant, she said, "You know, go to a furniture store and buy it there." I explained that to do it her way was much more expensive and, frankly, not as much fun as the alternatives that were out there. I might as well have been speaking in a foreign language. My friend's wife was a harbinger of the eighties. After their divorce in 1984, she married higher on the corporate ladder, leaving my friend with debts he and his third wife are just now paying off (oops—there's that pesky relationship thing again!).

Last year, San Jose adopted a new garbage collection system. The city now provides trash containers, and I was left with a garbage can that was of no use to me. Early this year, a friend of mine told me she was going to get rid of some lamps that reminded her of her last husband—the one who made her swear off marriage for good (oops—there it is again!). She lives in a different town, and I offered to swap my garbage can, which she can still use, for her lamps. She agreed, and now we each have something we can use at no cost. Had we done things the "normal" way, my friend and I would each have thrown out what we couldn't use and bought what we needed new.

There are alternatives in almost any situation. In October 1993, for example, the *San Jose Mercury News* ran an article about a couple who managed to buy a 2,500-square-foot home for $100,000 (comparable homes here are easily $400,000). How did they do it? They moved the house from a lot in the way of a commercial development to another lot. A lot of work, yes. But the savings were substantial. As you might imagine, the couple say 75 percent of their furnishings are from garage sales!

In my book *Living Cheap: THE Survival Guide for the Nineties*, I likened the person who cannot imagine what he will do in retirement to a person who walks down 88th Street in New York City every day. One day 88th Street is closed, and he is immobilized. There are alternatives all around him, but he cannot see them. The same is true of almost any situation. Don't automatically do things the "normal" way. Look for alternatives. And share them with me. I'd love to hear about new ways you've found to save money.

21

RETIRE?
YES YOU CAN!

I skimmed Gail Sheehy's new bestseller, *New Passages* (Random House, 1995), which has some interesting ideas about how people are living longer, becoming old later, and redefining life stages. Unfortunately, Ms. Sheehy engages in a certain amount of the gratuitous male bashing that now seems de rigueur among bestselling female authors. While the male bashing was unfortunate, the fatal flaw in this book for me was Ms. Sheehy's assertion that, because a sixty-five-year old couple will need $483,460 to retire with a conventional pension or $660,070 without one, retirement among the present generation is unlikely because "nobody can really save this much." I was surprised neither Ms. Sheehy nor her Random House editor were aware of the existence of compound interest tables, IRAs, Keoghs, or 401(k), plans, all of which allow accumulating the stated amounts to be eminently doable by the time a couple reaches age sixty-five if they start early enough.

The book retails for $24.50, but I have seen it at warehouse stores for $15. I'd recommend getting it at your library. I saw nothing in the book that won't keep a while, and I doubt that many of us will consider this book something we would want for our home libraries.

THE FACTS ABOUT SAVING

Ms. Sheehy's statement that no one can save enough to retire was only the latest I'd seen in what seems to have become a campaign to convince Americans they will never be able to retire. I suppose the corollary to this defeatism is we should spend our money now without thinking about a tomorrow we can't do anything about anyway. The conventional wisdom of the 1990s seems to be that Americans will have to stay at their jobs until they die. Just as they did in the 1890s. The irony is that this baloney could well become a self-fulfilling prophecy if we buy into it and take no control of our own future.

I urge everyone out there who has a computer to get a program that calculates the amount of regular deposits a person needs to make to accumulate enough to retire. These programs are available cheap if not free. I received The Best of Uptime as a freebie for trying a magazine. If you do not have access to a computer, I suggest you look at an amortization table. Instead of looking at it as paying off a loan, look at it in terms of how much you can earn by a constant savings program. Later in this chapter, I show some examples of just how doable it is to save the amount Gail Sheehy says we need to retire.

First, though, let me go into another aspect of the retirement defeatism that's being bandied about these days. Conventional wisdom says we need 80 percent of our preretirement income to live on when we retire. For some people that may be true. For others it's just so much hot air. If you live in San Francisco, Los Angeles, New York, or Boston and move to a less expensive area when you retire, will you still need 80 percent of your income? If you're paying $2,000 a month in rent or on a mortgage and move to a paid-for home somewhere else, will you still need 80 percent of that $2,000? Before you begin figuring out whether you will be able to retire, ignore what everyone else tells you and figure out for yourself what income you will need. And then go for it.

To figure out how much you'll need, you'll have to figure out how much you're spending now and how much of your current spending will continue when you retire. The only way I know to do that is write down everything you buy, how much it cost, and whether that is something you'll buy once you retire. I'd recommend you do this for two years because, once you start, you'll find many things you won't want to continue doing. One woman, for example, said on a recent talk show that her daily stop at a gourmet coffee shop resulted in a $700-a-year habit that she eliminated.

When you're examining your spending habits, do sweat the small stuff. There are three keys to accumulating a retirement nest egg. One is time. One is the rate of return your money will earn you. The last is keeping at it. It is true, as Gail Sheehy says, that a sixty-five-year-old couple will not be able to save $660,070 if, on the day before their sixty-fifth birthdays, they have saved nothing. However, if a couple—two people—at the age of twenty-five squeeze a mere $6.98 a day ($3.49 each) out of their budget and invest that money at 8 percent until they are sixty-five, they will have the amount Gail Sheehy says they need to retire. They will have saved $101,919.20 over forty years, or less than $7 a day. But the money they invested will have earned them an additional $515,150.80 in interest.

Again, this formula has three variables—the amount of money you save, how long you save it, and what rate of return you can get. Of these, the most important is the second. Just as an example, if a thirty-five-year old couple want to accumulate $660,070 by the time they are sixty-five, they will have to invest $15.96 per day at 8 percent. This is still probably doable at less than $8 per person, but it is more than twice the amount the twenty-five-year-olds must save. A forty-five-year-old couple would have to save $39.52 per day, and a fifty-five-year-old couple would have to save a daunting $124.83 every day to match what the twenty-five-year-olds can do with less than $7 per day.

So I hope you can see that getting with it on your retirement savings program is much more important than thinking about it, reading about it, and listening to the defeatist conventional wisdom of our times. The best advice I can give you is in the ad for Nike. Just do it.

💰 RETIREMENT CHART

The following chart shows how much you need to save to have the $660,070 Gail Sheehy says you would need to retire at sixty-five. Keep in mind that these figures are for a couple.

Age When Program Began	Savings Per Day	Savings Per Year	Interest Rate	Couple's Total Contribution	Total Interest Earned
25	$11.69	$4,265.07	6.0%	$170,603	$489,467
25	$10.30	$3,758.26	6.5%	$150,330	$509,740
25	$ 9.06	$3,306.38	7.0%	$132,255	$527,815
25	$ 7.96	$2,904.52	7.5%	$116,181	$543,889
25	$ 6.98	$2,547.98	8.0%	$101,919	$558,151
35	$22.87	$8,349.17	6.0%	$250,475	$409,595
35	$20.94	$7,641.92	6.5%	$229,258	$430,812
35	$19.14	$6,987.77	7.0%	$209,633	$450,437
35	$17.49	$6,383.69	7.5%	$191,511	$468,559
35	$15.96	$5,826.72	8.0%	$174,802	$485,268
45	$49.16	$17,943.71	6.0%	$358,874	$301,196
45	$46.58	$17,001.02	6.5%	$340,020	$320,050
45	$44.11	$16,101.04	7.0%	$322,021	$338,049
45	$41.76	$15,242.46	7.5%	$304,849	$355,221
45	$39.52	$14,423.99	8.0%	$288,480	$371,590
55	$137.20	$50,078.16	6.0%	$500,782	$159,288
55	$134.01	$48,914.28	6.5%	$489,143	$170,927
55	$130.89	$47,774.22	7.0%	$477,742	$182,328
55	$127.83	$46,657.66	7.5%	$466,577	$193,493
55	$124.83	$45,564.29	8.0%	$455,643	$204,427

As you can see from the chart, the twenty-five-year-olds who get a return of 8 percent don't have to save $660,070. They only have to save $101,919 over forty years. The rest of the work is done by the money they save.

22

WHEN IT DOESN'T PAY TO BE CHEAP

I know you can't believe I'm saying it doesn't always pay to be cheap. But I am.

My friend Steve was telling me about the extensive remodeling job he was having done to his kitchen. "What do you think about getting a trash compactor?" he asked. Actually I hadn't given it much thought at all, but I advised Steve that, since he was already spending a good deal of money to get his kitchen redone, now was the time to get a trash compactor if he wanted one.

He bought the trash compactor, and it actually turned out to be a good investment. The town in which he lives changed the way it charges for garbage pickup. The fewer containers Steve puts out, the less he pays in garbage bills. The trash compactor paid for itself after just a few months.

When I visited the Peter and Paul Fortress in St. Petersburg, Russia, I met some good jazz musicians who were selling cassettes of their music. The cassettes were $3.99, and I really enjoy jazz. But at that time the average Russian made the ruble equivalent of $10 a month. I had been in Russia long enough to adjust to their economy. I could not convince myself that one cassette should cost 40 percent of a month's income, and my host was aghast at the fact I even considered paying that much for a cassette. So I didn't. But I've regretted it ever since. A cassette for $3.99 would be a bargain here. And, given that I'd spent a couple of thousand dollars to travel to Russia, I was foolish not to go the extra $3.99 for a souvenir I would have enjoyed.

A few years ago, when I lived in Texas, one of the state's oldest home builders began a new housing development. My parents built their house in 1958. I still remember some of the problems they encountered during the six months of construction (and the fun we all had turning the bare, red Oklahoma clay into a lawn after the house was finished). Nevertheless, my parents had been able to get the house built the way they wanted. And they still live in it. I liked one of the Texas home builders' plans, and I asked them to make one simple change—build the house with double-pane windows. The salesman told me he'd have to take it up with the builder, who refused. The builder told me I could always add storm windows after the house was built. Instead I added storm windows to the house I was already living in. The builder went bankrupt shortly afterward. His company hadn't become one of the state's oldest home builders by being so cheap and inflexible with its customers. Evidently, by the time the builder found out people don't buy houses the way they buy the hamburgers you can't have your way, it was too late. It didn't pay him to be so cheap.

I've seen many articles lately about the negative effects of "downsizing" in the corporate world. It seems that shedding employees is not the way to increase productivity. One local company, once one of the major employers in the Silicon Valley, is sapping its employees' morale in as many ways as possible. Just before Christmas, it laid off about 1,400 people, many of whom were senior employees earning good salaries. Those who remained discovered they were in for many unpleasant changes in the new year. Besides picking up the work of those who were let go, they faced a new sick leave policy in which those prone to short-term illnesses would be using their vacation time for sick leave or sacrificing pay when they were ill. It didn't matter if a person had months of sick leave saved up—those months of sick leave were not available for short-term illnesses anymore. Additionally, some genius decided to cross-train employees (on the employees' own time) so they would become "generalists" instead of specialists. In other words, instead of groups of people who produce a good, specialized product, everyone was now expected to be able to produce any number of mediocre products.

This company then announced it was going to lay off another 1,200 people in 1994. The company's expectation was that its employees would work hard so they would not be laid off. Instead, productivity plummeted as people realized they might need a job, but they didn't necessarily need a job with that company. The company has incurred severance costs for 2,600 people and will probably have to defend itself in court against several class-action suits. Its productivity is down, its employee morale is nonexistent, and its profitability is probably in decline as well.

Take it from the cheap guy. Whether you're a consumer, a tourist, a businessperson, or an employer, it doesn't *always* pay to be cheap!

23

THE IMMIGRANT'S TRUNK

When I first mentioned my grandmother in some detail in LCN, the response was overwhelming. Readers wanted to know more about her. She was a remarkable woman, although she would probably simply say she lived in remarkable times. The following is a brief biography.

Astrid Naemi Englund was born May 7, 1897, in Misterhult, a small community on the east coast of Sweden. She was the ninth of eleven children. At the age of ten she was "farmed out" as a housekeeper because her family could not afford to keep her. In June 1912, the month after she turned fifteen, she immigrated to America. She first went to Omaha, where her sister, who had arrived in 1911, lived. She got a job as a maid with a family associated with the Union Pacific Railroad. As their fortune increased in those days of no income taxes, they decided to move to New York. My grandmother moved with them.

She met her future husband in Omaha before the move to New York, but her father had made her promise not to marry before she reached the age of twenty. In 1917 she moved to Kansas, where my grandfather was stationed during World War I. They married that August.

After the war they moved to Colorado, where my grandfather homesteaded a farm. From the stories she told me, I gathered her time on the farm was the happiest time of her life. It was also the most difficult. I don't think the farm was ever self-sufficient. My father was born there in 1920; his brother and only sibling was born in 1921. In the mid-1920s the family was back in Omaha to earn some money for a second go at farming. In the late 1920s they were back on the farm. In the early 1930s my grandfather worked in Oklahoma City to support the farm, which had grown to 960 acres and which my grandmother ran by herself. The dust bowl finally killed her dream of living on the farm. Even if she could have held on financially, the health risks of living through daily dust storms were too severe. "Dust pneumonia" had killed too many of her friends. She didn't want to lose her children to it.

In 1935 she joined my grandfather in Oklahoma City. On Thanksgiving Day, the family moved into a home they bought from a bank that had foreclosed on it. They bought the entire contents of another house for $100 from a family who was leaving Oklahoma. I still use some of that furniture.

They rented rooms, both my grandmother and grandfather worked, and eventually they were, for their times, financially comfortable. They sold the farm in the 1950s and bought a small retirement farm in southeastern Oklahoma, where they planned to move when my grandfather retired in January 1956. But even that was not to be.

In July 1955, two days after they left Oklahoma City on a vacation trip to Montana, their car crashed head-on into a semi-trailer truck in Kansas. My grandfather died in the accident. My grandmother was badly injured with both legs and several ribs broken. She never fully recovered from the leg injuries.

On November 30, 1974, after suffering two strokes in two months, she died.

More than twenty years later, I still miss her.

MY GRANDMOTHER'S TRUNK

As I packed box after box for my move to Kansas City, my thoughts often came back to the small wooden trunk my Swedish great-grandfather made for his daughter's trip to America in 1912. The trunk, which made the move with me, measures thirty inches wide by eighteen inches deep by eighteen inches high. That's a little over five and a half cubic feet. My grandmother often said, "All I brought with me to America fit in that trunk."

Of course, she meant all the material things she brought with her fit in the trunk. The stamina, stubbornness, and grit she would need to get through two world wars, the Depression, the dust bowl, and other obstacles that faced people of her generation could not fit in any trunk. Once, when I was very young, during a howling winter storm that brought back memories of the dust bowl to her, she said, "Would you believe in those days the dust was so fine we had to hang wet sheets over the windows? And still the dust came into the house."

But I often wonder what she packed in her immigrant's trunk. What filled that five and a half cubic feet of permanent separation from her past? I know she brought a Swedish Bible, her Catechism, her school records, and some family photographs. But I can only surmise the rest. Some clothes, of course, but what else? I have no way of knowing, so I ask myself what I would pack. As I packed box after box of pared-down household goods, the idea of fitting all of my possessions into a small trunk became alternately an impossible dream and a pleasant-sounding option.

Finally, I realized that my grandmother probably did not look on her limitation of five and a half cubic feet as a hardship, but rather as simply something that had to be. Her mother believed a war was imminent, and, if my grandmother were to emigrate, she should do it soon. War did, in fact, erupt two years later. Although Sweden remained neutral, sea travel was not safe, as passengers on the *Lusitania* would discover.

When her brother decided to leave for America, she decided to go with him. They were originally scheduled on a June sailing of the *Titanic*. After that ship sank in April, they were rescheduled on its sister ship, the *Olympic*. They arrived in Liverpool to discover the *Olympic* was not going anywhere for a while. (The *Olympic* had the same flaws in its "watertight compartments" the Titanic had, and it was undergoing renovation.) They wound up getting a $90 refund and a trip on the smaller and older *California* (which had earned a place in the history books because it was close enough to the *Titanic* to have helped, but its crew had turned off the radio and was not aware anything had happened—it did pick up survivors the next day).

My grandmother arrived at Ellis Island July 7, 1912, three days after a raucous Fourth of July celebration she did not understand. After Ellis Island she and her brother bought a bag of groceries for 25¢, and they boarded a train for Omaha. The bag of groceries included tomatoes, which many immigrants had never tasted and did not like. (Try to imagine biting into a tomato for the first time!) My normally frugal grandmother amused herself by throwing her tomatoes at telegraph poles the train passed on the trip to Omaha.

The trunk went with her to New York, Kansas, Colorado, and Oklahoma. And, once again, the eighty-three-year-old trunk has made a move, this time as one item of a household of six to seven thousand pounds. Once again it is an immigrant's trunk.

I think of our times and of hers. I think of people who feel deprived if they cannot have the latest fashion, the latest automobile, the latest fad. And I think of children who feel their world will end if they cannot have the latest Power Rangers toy or Mortal Kombat computer game. Then I think of her five and a half cubic feet of possessions, and I realize most of us do not know the meaning of the word *deprivation*. At least not in the material sense.

If you have ancestors who survived hard times and thrived without an abundance of material possessions, you might consider introducing them to your children through stories. Make use of those old photograph albums: "That's your great-grandmother. She came to this farm with only a mule and . . . ." Odds are your children (or grandchildren) will want to know more.

THE DUGOUT

The first and last time I saw the dugout was in 1968. I would imagine it is gone by now. It was in bad condition when I saw it. For my older sister's high school graduation present, my father took us on a trip to Colorado, where he was born. My grandparents had homesteaded in Southeastern Colorado, and they, like most homesteaders, had made do with the materials available. When homesteaders had first broken the ground in Kansas, they found inches of sod, and they made their first homes out of this sod. In that barren part of Colorado, most people built their first homes by digging into the ground.

This is what my grandparents had done. The dugout grew over the years to a three-room shack. It was, at least when I saw it, uninsulated.

In fact, only one board separated the inside from the outside in the parts that were above ground. It was heated by an iron stove, and the fuel in that treeless land had been cow chips (no, those were not precursors of microchips).

My grandmother's dream was to own a farm, and she decided she would only marry a farmer. My grandfather, who was born in a large city in Europe and had lived only in cities in this country, eventually agreed to become a farmer. When the government offered 160 acres of land free to those who would live on it, the deal sounded too good to be true. Time would reveal it was just that.

They moved to the farm after World War I and lived there a few years, long enough to get their "patent," or ownership, and long enough to buy out some of their neighbors. Their 160 acres eventually grew to 960, but when the farm depression of the 1920s caught up with them, they moved to Omaha to work and save some money for a second try at farming.

The next move, I believe, was to Oklahoma City in 1927, but later in the decade, they were back on the farm. Their land produced good wheat as long as the rains came. The rains stopped in the early 1930s. At first, believing this was a one-season fluke, they agreed my grandfather would return to Oklahoma City, work, and send money to the farm, which he did. For several years my grandmother ran the farm and raised her two children herself. She planted, negotiated with and fed the combine crews during harvest time, raised cattle, and raised chickens.

The dry season lasted for years, and then came the winds and the dust bowl. In 1935 she left the farm for good after seeing many of her friends lose everything, some even their lives to dust pneumonia. Their farm was debt-free. They sold it twenty years later.

As I was growing up, I heard many stories about the farm and the dugout. I believe, in spite of all the hardship involved, the years she spent trying to make her dream of owning a farm and living on it come true were the happiest of her life. Although her dream did not come true, she had done everything she could to make it happen.

Many of us live safe, insulated lives working at safe, insulated jobs and living in safe, insulated homes. But I think the most common complaint of the 1990s could be summed up by the title of the old Peggy Lee song "Is That All There Is?" Perhaps some of us need to shake up our lives to find out what we really want. I recently received a letter from a reader who wrote, "I've received notice I'll soon be without a job, which has totally revitalized me mentally and emotionally, and I am looking forward to exploring new pursuits."

Elaine St. James, in her new book *Inner Simplicity: 100 Ways to Regain Peace and to Nourish Your Soul*, describes the process this reader is going through in "way" number 50: "Do the things you fear." She suggests that we make a list of things we would like to do but haven't done because of fear. Ms. St. James suggests these things may well be the things we should be doing. Our dreams, like those of my grandmother, may not come true if we pursue them. They certainly won't happen if we let fear keep us from trying.

24

THE "*LCN* GOES TO . . ." SERIES

For years friends had asked me when I planned to visit the Soviet Union. I really never planned to visit the place, so I simply said I'd get around to it if they changed the name of Leningrad back to St. Petersburg. I never thought that would happen, but in 1991 the Soviet Union fell apart, and once again the beautiful city on the Neva was named St. Petersburg. I went to Russia and Hungary in 1992. The following articles are my observations.

LCN GOES TO MOSCOW

The good news about a trip to Russia these days is that anything you can buy with rubles is incredibly cheap. I damaged my shoes in a fall off a bus at London's Heathrow Airport (I've fallen in many of the world's great cities), and it cost 200 rubles to get new heels put on them in Moscow. At the then-current exchange rate, that was less than 50¢. The bad news is that a lot of Muscovites like Americans so well they want green souvenirs of our visits there. You will find people whose sole English vocabulary consists of "ten dollars." Admittedly that gives them a better command of English than I have of Russian.

My first encounter with this on an official level was at the Kremlin. My Russian host, Viola, had purchased ruble tickets (costing about 12¢ each) to a Faberge exhibit and the Armory. When I presented my ticket at the Faberge exhibit, a woman with all the charm of a concentration camp guard threw it back at me and snarled, "Ten dollars for *you*." I pointed out that this ticket was for the exhibit. She shook her head and snarled more loudly, "Ten dollars for *you*." To illustrate the absurdity of this price, it is approximately what the average Russian earns in a *month*. The refusal at the Armory, where, I understand, jewels, weapons, and other artifacts from the czarist era are on display, was more polite but just as firm, even though my ticket was for that date and time.

Unless some low-level official arbitrarily decided to gouge foreigners, one must expect that such unrealistic pricing will become part of the "new" Russia, which may cause some of us cheapskates to think twice about a trip there. While I could understand charging foreigners more, $10 is too much. I cannot recall ever paying $10 to see an exhibit, and I didn't in Moscow either.

Now, I don't want you to get the impression that Muscovites are unpleasant (the woman at the Faberge exhibit was by far the exception rather than the rule) or heartless. Often, while riding the Metro (their subway), I saw people get up and tell a story about why they needed money. The first such person I saw was an elderly woman who pointed out, among other things, her worn boots. As she walked through the car after her speech, most people gave her money. On the other hand, if the stories were not convincing, contributions were few and far between.

Moscow had an unusually severe cold snap the first two days I was there, but that didn't stop me from taking the Metro to Ismaylovsky Park, on the east edge of the city, where every Sunday there is a big flea market. The best prices for typical souvenirs are here. Small wooden doll sets start at $2.50 (which, while cheap, is one-fourth of the average monthly income in Russia). Dollars are preferred over rubles, and you can get a fair rate here if you want to change dollars into rubles (but don't change too much—I had excess rubles at the end of my trip, and I had changed only a total of $20). During the week, many of the same vendors can be found on Arbat Street, an open-air bazaar, but prices are higher there.

I enjoyed (free, since I was there anyway) the often whimsical 1930s Metro stations. At Mayakovskaya, near where I stayed, the ceiling is decorated with colorful mosaics designed to reflect scenes one would see while looking at the sky—airplanes, skyscrapers, and so on.

More mosaics are in the Novokuznetskaya station, but these are from the perspective of looking up through manhole covers. (Many of the people in these seem to be looking at you, asking with their eyes, "What are you doing down there?") More serious but just as impressive are the larger-than-life bronzes at Revolution Square and the stained glass at the Novoslobodskaya station. The price of a ride on the Metro went from one ruble to three on December 1, but that's still less than a penny, and you can go anywhere on the very extensive system for those three rubles.

On a day trip to the town of Sergiev Posad, about fifty miles outside Moscow, I saw Russian dachas, which I'd heard so much about, for the first time. It was a disillusioning experience—the dachas are small (two or three rooms—they reminded me of a lot of lake cabins I have seen) and anything but elegant. Most looked like a larger version of the types of storage sheds sold at stores like Sears. However, as I will discuss later, these dachas, once simply weekend cottages, have become a major means of survival for post-Soviet Russians.

LCN GOES TO ST. PETERSBURG

The man seated next to me on the comfortable five-hour train ride to St. Petersburg noticed I was reading an English-language book and asked, "Is this your first trip to St. Petersburg?" I told him it was. He then said, "You will love St. Petersburg. It is a city; Moscow is a big village." He was right. Moscow is interesting, but St. Petersburg is easy to love. Because it is built on a series of islands, it has been called the Venice of the North.

The city's architecture, stunning as it is on the outside, is clearly reflective of a people who spend a lot of their lives indoors. The insides of the theaters, opera houses, museums, and the justifiably famous Winter Palace are beyond belief. If you decide to see the Winter Palace, go early. Even in winter, long lines form for latecomers. And be advised the two-tier pricing is in effect here, but foreigners still pay only about $1 (more if you take a camera or video recorder) to see this unique palace and the art displayed inside.

Among the best bargains I found were the symphony, opera, and ballet. The most expensive tickets are currently 100 rubles—about 25¢.

But buy early. Local "businessmen" are buying up these ruble tickets and scalping them outside the theaters. (I overheard an American bragging about his great 1,000-ruble ticket; he had paid a scalper ten times the going rate.)

Northeast of downtown is a grim reminder of the city's 900-day siege during World War II. An estimated 490,000 people are buried in a series of mass graves marked only with the year of burial. Two small buildings at the entrance of the cemetery tell the history of the siege (in Russian). There's no charge to see this moving monument, and don't be alarmed by the soldiers there. The previously unguarded cemetery recently became a gathering place for young skinheads, and the guards are there to prevent these people from defacing monuments.

It was in St. Petersburg that I learned how important dacha gardens are to today's Russians. My hosts, Igor, Ilona, and their eight-year-old son, Sevre, are dependent on Ilona's parents' dacha garden in which they grow almost all their produce. Carrots, beets, potatoes, berries, etc. are preserved for winter use, as are mushrooms Igor forages in local forests. This winter, Ilona has only had to purchase cabbage, meat, bread, and dairy products, all of which (except cabbage) are used sparingly. This in itself is amazing. Even more surprising is the fact that Ilona also works six days a week as a supervisory psychiatrist at a facility for troubled children. (She jokes that she turns into a kitchen machine when she gets home.) Igor writes and teaches English in a St. Petersburg university.

Their reasons for growing and preserving their own food are both economic and health related. Russia's governmental breakdown has led to de facto deregulation of health standards. According to Igor, early last year many people became ill and one child died as a result of excess nitrates in watermelons. Many Russians now completely avoid commercially grown produce.

Igor and Ilona told me the story of their charming prerevolutionary apartment. When they first moved to it in 1978, it was a "communal" apartment. One room was theirs; the room I used belonged to a woman who had lived there since 1928, and the room now occupied by Sevre was a "communal" room. At that time there was no bathroom (the nearest one was at a sauna a block and a half away), and the kitchen was strictly partitioned by the other tenant, who cleaned only her half of the stove, her table, etc. When the other tenant died a few years ago, she was not replaced, and Igor installed a bathroom and water heater, giving him an advantage most Russians don't have—control over his hot water. In most postrevolutionary areas, heat and hot water are central, and one boiler may serve several blocks. Getting more heat is not a matter of adjusting a thermostat; it is, rather, a matter of adding another layer of clothing. And when there's no hot water, you won't get any sympathy from your neighbors—they don't have any either!

The Russian government is now giving apartments to tenants who will agree to accept the responsibility for maintaining them. Igor and Ilona have not yet decided whether they will accept this deal. Their view is that their apartment is old, and they are wary of accepting gifts from a government that has been less than honest with its citizens in the past.

LCN GOES TO BUDAPEST

If something sounds too good to be true, it probably is. Good advice. I should have taken it.

I'd looked forward to my stay at the famous Gellert Hotel, facing the Danube, in Budapest. The brochure looked appealing—the use of the famous thermal baths, four massages, two meals a day, and an opera or concert in a $524 seven-day package. Unfortunately, airline schedules in Europe being what they are, I wound up having ten days in Budapest. At the last minute a scheduled home stay fell apart, and the hotel "generously" agreed to extend my stay (but not the special) at a daily rate of $75 (which is half their published rate).

What the brochure didn't say was that the free massages were for ten minutes (value $1.20 each), the concert or opera will only appear on your bill unless you insist on attending, and, while the hotel may face the Danube, your room (twin bed, no desk) certainly won't. And although the breakfast was a buffet and was hassle-free, the evening meal vouchers are a story in themselves.

Those vouchers could be redeemed only after 7 P.M. and only in one specific restaurant. While the limit of 1,200 florints (about $15 at the time of my visit) should have been more than adequate, at this restaurant the prices were exorbitant. (I'd read that meals at Budapest's best restaurants rarely exceeded $15, including drinks and dessert, and this restaurant is not in danger of being named one of Budapest's best.) The dark, tomblike restaurant, with its appropriately embalmed and condescending waiters, had very few customers. When it was reserved one night for a private party, I discovered the reason. One floor down was a friendly, brightly lit cafe (our substitute restaurant for that evening) serving the *same* food! But it was much cheaper. Upstairs, goulash was 350 florints (about $4.35). Downstairs, it was 90 florints ($1.15). A side salad upstairs was 300 florints ($3.75); downstairs it was 140 florints ($1.75) and much fresher.

Even more amusing was the fact that all the people I had seen upstairs were in this cafe that evening. Evidently the only customers who used the upstairs restaurant were those who had a "special" that included vouchers redeemable only in that restaurant. We were captive diners! After this, I made a habit of going to the downstairs restaurant and asking if I could use my vouchers there. I was never refused.

It amazes me that, with the dollar so strong in Hungary (and it's even stronger now), the hotel would be so petty, gaming every detail of their special. But they were. And, while I certainly can't recommend the Gellert, I did enjoy Budapest.

Budapest is much more expensive than Russia, but it's cheaper than, say, London. Vaci utca, near Elisabeth Bridge, is the place to shop for souvenirs (and I'd recommend the Folkart Centrum for quality goods at decent prices). The metro at eighteen florints (about 23¢) is a bargain, but I never could figure out how anyone knew whether you actually paid. Commercial tours of Budapest are expensive. A three-hour Grey Line tour is about $16, and a tour to the artist's village of Szentendre is about $50 (you can go there on the train for $2.40 round-trip), so, if you go, see Budapest on your own. But get a new map. Streets, parks, etc. are being renamed at an unbelievable pace as Budapest tries to erase its communist past.

When it comes to public rest rooms, Budapest is a city of palms. You'll find an open one nearly everywhere, and the charge will range from five to ten florints (about 6¢ to 12¢). The upside to this is that the rest rooms are usually clean, and the attendant will have toilet paper available for you. In Russia, the rest rooms are free, but I guarantee you'll gag (and I was there in the winter—I don't even want to think about what they're like in warm weather).

By our standards, food in shops is a bargain. I bought cheese, rolls, yogurt, and pastries at a shop near the hotel and was able to eat for about $1.20 per meal. Many Hungarian wines are less than $1 per bottle, making them cheaper in Budapest than soft drinks.

For the person looking for something different, but not quite as spartan as Russia, Budapest might be a good compromise. It offers beautiful scenery, interesting architecture, a generally favorable exchange rate (if you get away from the touristy areas), friendly people, many of whom speak English (although more speak German), and a convertible currency.

25

THE BEST OF "DUMB IDEAS OF THE MONTH"

From the most popular column in Living Cheap News, *here is a sample of ideas, products, and businesses that merit a special something:*

From the November 1991 promotional flyer: Our first selection is a new product: recipes on videotape. Now, isn't this an idea the world has been waiting for? Instead of receiving recipes in written form, you get them on videotape. This means you either get to use electricity to run both your TV and VCR while you write the recipe from the videotape, or you get to try to make the recipe while watching the videotape. How much flour, sugar, and eggs can a remote control take, anyway? This is definitely a case of trying to force electronics into a niche where it doesn't belong. Buy a used recipe book. Forget the movie.

February 1992: On a recent trip, I rented a 1992 Oldsmobile Cutlass Ciera ($18 per weekend day and no mileage charge from Avis). This was a great little car (although Avis alleges it is "full size"), but it had a feature that drove me up the wall. When you put the car in gear, the doors locked automatically. But the reverse didn't happen. When I'd park the car and try to get out of it, I had to unlock the door manually. Frankly, I resent General Motors making the decision to lock me into their car. If they are going to force this on me, the least they could do is make the thing unlock the doors when the car is in Park. The Cadillacs have this reverse feature.

Why put half the option in the smaller cars? Actually, why put the option in at all? If you're in an accident—or if you have a heart attack with the windows up, the only option for your rescuers is to break the window. At best, this means you have one more thing to fix when you repair your car; at worst, breaking the window could take precious time away from your rescue. This feature is dangerous *and* dumb.

When I look for my next car, I would certainly consider a Ciera, but I wouldn't buy one if this feature is standard. Why can't American car makers concentrate on making their products better and forget about dumbing them up?

March 1992: The dumb idea of the month goes to George Bush's plan to reduce the amount of federal tax withholding. He's not reducing taxes, just the amount withheld to pay taxes. People will have more money to spend this (election) year, but the bill still comes due in 1993. Isn't this a little like borrowing money from voters to buy their votes? This is cynical as well as dumb.

And it didn't work!

September 1992: The dumb idea of the month—perhaps even of the last quarter century—is call waiting. Not only is call waiting inherently rude, allowing people to jump to the head of the line, you actually pay to do something (telling someone you're on another line) that you could have done free via the old, reliable busy signal. If you have this option, get rid of it. Save money and friendships!

November 1992: I recently rented a Buick Skylark. I'm beginning to think General Motors' designers are trying to see just how much stupidity the American public will tolerate. The windshield wiper controls are on a lever mounted on the steering column right in front of the gearshift lever! You have to reach around the wiper lever to shift gears. I was constantly turning the wipers on with my wrist when I shifted from Drive to Reverse or Park. I think some engineer must have asked himself where the most inconvenient place for these controls would be. His boss wouldn't let him put them in the back seat, so he put them in front of the gearshift. C'mon, GM! Put the windshield wiper controls and the light switches back on the dash. They're out of the way there, and you don't have to take the steering column off when something goes wrong with these switches.

April 1993: This month the makers of Banquet frozen chicken get the award. What had been a 28-ounce package was now 24 ounces. Without increasing the price, Banquet has made its chicken 14 percent more expensive.

Other companies are doing this as well. For example, the formerly 6½-ounce can of tuna is now 6¼ ounces (nearly a 4 percent price increase). But 14 percent? On something I can easily live without? Give me a break.

November 1993: The prize this month goes to Kal Kan, the makers of Pedigree dog food. These folks are putting our pets on a diet behind our backs! What had until recently been a 23-ounce can of Fido food is now down to 22 ounces. The 14-ounce can is now 13.2 ounces. Without changing the price, Kal Kan's making 4.3 percent more on the larger can and 5.7 percent more on the smaller can. Is dog food such a precious commodity that Kal Kan is going to make a fortune by shorting us an ounce or less a can?

Pet owners of America, unite! Send a postcard to: Consumer Affairs, Kal Kan Foods, Inc., Vernon, CA 90058. Let them know you think this move is shoddy.

December 1993: This one is so bad I thought it was a joke when I first heard about it earlier this year. The Treasury Historical Association (Box 2818, Washington, DC 20038) is selling a Christmas tree ornament to commemorate the eightieth anniversary of the Internal Revenue Service. The ornament is 3¼ inches by 3½ inches, gold colored, and it depicts the 1913 IRS tax return. This is the last thing I'd want to see on my Christmas tree (after all, the real thing will be here in January), but if you're interested, they're $10 postpaid.

February 1994: My favorite ideas are those that take something that is free or nearly free and make the most of it. Now there is a product that takes something that is usually incredibly cheap and makes it expensive. The dumb idea this month is bottled iced tea. I wound up buying some at a restaurant, thinking I was getting iced tea (something that is usually served unsweetened in restaurants). The waiter slapped a bottle of "all natural" Snapple in front of me. A look at the ingredients in this stuff reveals that it's more than meets the eye; it's made with filtered water, sugar and/or high fructose corn syrup, natural tea, citric acid, and natural lemon flavor with "other natural flavors." It is important to note that "sugar and/or high fructose corn syrup" is listed ahead of tea. This stuff has more sweetener in it than tea! Make your own healthier tea, save money, and help the environment by eliminating all the bottles and cans used to package this stuff.

March 1994: This month the prize goes to the Campbell Soup Company (Camden, NJ 08103-1701), makers of Swanson chicken broth, whose formerly 15-ounce can is now 14½ ounces, nearly 4 percent smaller. Really, Campbell's! Is chicken broth something so rare, exotic, or difficult to make that it justifies new cans and labels to save half an ounce per can?

April 1994: The coveted prize has to be split between two winners this month. Yes Entertainment's TV Teddy ($70) and Toby Terrier ($50), made by Tiger Electronics, are two stuffed toys that encourage children to do just what *everyone*, and I mean everyone, says they shouldn't be doing: watching more television. TV Teddy picks up signals off a transmitter that connects to the television, so he can become "interactive" with broadcast shows. Toby Terrier can only "interact" with videotapes. Forget these toys. Turn the TV off and send the children outside to "interact" with a real terrier or, better yet, other children.

June–July 1994: The award this month goes to talk shows. I spent some time at Wright Patterson Air Force Base in the early 1970s, when Phil Donahue was first starting in the business. I watched his show, which was then local. It was all right. As we all know, he moved on to Chicago and then New York. Over the years I've seen about ten of his shows, and, sad to say, many dealt with topics I could have lived without knowing much about. I watched a recent Oprah Winfrey show about the minutiae of a stupid family's long-running squabble. I sat through about ten minutes of a Sally Jessy Raphael show that was beyond dumb. And then there's the ever-lovable Maury Povich (Mr. Connie Chung), who not only has one of the tackiest shows this side of Geraldo, but also the nerve to say that if it weren't for people in Texas, Florida, and California, he wouldn't have a show. (If you live in one of those states and would like to let Mr. Povich know just how much you appreciate that remark, the show's toll-free number is 800-436-2879.)

Now, I know it's tough to put on a good show every day, fifty-two weeks a year, but I have also seen a talk show up close. There is very little planning or organization involved. Guests are sabotaged and embarrassed for the sake of "entertainment." All in all, I find the current concept of a "talk show" triply amazing. I'm amazed anyone would want to produce such tripe, I'm aghast at some of the incredibly personal things people are willing to discuss about themselves in front of the entire nation, and the most amazing aspect of all is there are people in this country with nothing better to do than watch this trash. At times like these, I think of Groucho Marx, who said, "I find television very educational. Whenever someone turns it on, I go in another room and read a book."

August 1994: It seems that the packers of Masters Touch tomatoes had a problem. How would people know that the tomatoes they were buying were genuine Masters Touch tomatoes? Their environmentally conscious, user-friendly, dumber-than-dirt solution? To put a label on each tomato. I am not making this up. I recently bought some of these on sale for 10¢ each. Not only are these labels difficult and time-consuming to remove, they leave the tomatoes discolored, and you're lucky to get the label off without breaking the tomato's skin.

How dumb is this idea? Let me count the ways: First, someone (who costs money) has to put the labels (which cost money) on each tomato. Second, the consumer has to remove and dispose of these non-biodegradable things. Designer labels are dumb enough on jeans, folks. Let's keep them off our food.

December 1994: If you have someone on your shopping list who has a computer and who was really caught up in the O. J. Simpson story, or if you have someone on your list who has no life but who does have a computer, Turner Home Entertainment has a deal for you! For about $19 at just about any computer store, you can buy a CD-ROM titled, *The People vs. O. J. Simpson*. And it comes in either a Windows or a Macintosh format! Wow! The coveted prize goes to Ted Turner this month for coming up with a new way to make money from old CNN news clips and the public's lack of taste.

If this CD-ROM is successful, we're told, there'll be more. And I'll bet it will be successful. The general public seems to crave what has become known as tabloid journalism. But the only way I'd want this under my tree is outdoors. In the garden. As compost.

March 1995: The coveted award for this month, as well as the Ebenezer Scrooge Holiday Work Schedule Award for 1994, goes to the Thrifty Drug Store chain for not only staying open on Christmas, but also running an ad that made fun of businesses that had the nerve not to follow suit. Among the clever (?) lines in the ad was a phone message from an imaginary competitor that said, "We appreciate your patronage, but not enough that we'd stay open on Christmas Day."

Having shopped at Thrifty a (very) few times, I can understand why they would want to stay open on a day when people would have nowhere else to go. But I also believe that, at least one day a year, business should take a back seat to families. And that should be the rule, not the exception, as implied in this ad. Thrifty? Bah! Humbug!

August 1995: This month's award is a tie between the Michigan Bulb Company for not being able to decide whether they are a nursery or a sweepstakes mill and me for ordering something from them. They had a pretty good price on some berry plants, so I naively sent in my order. I have been treated to weekly sweepstakes mailings ever since. What's worse is that Michigan Bulb Company has so little regard for their customers that they sell their customers' names to nearly every other sweepstakes mill in the country.

I will admit I did win a "prize" in their sweepstakes. Some company that provides planting guide cards similar to recipe cards would, if I merely claimed my "prize," send me ten of those cards valued (by them) at $29.95. That was the bad news. The worse news was that, by claiming my "prize," I'd be enrolling in a subscription to these cards. Oh joy! Imagine the sucker lists I'd get on by claiming that "prize"!

I've learned from this experience to shop for plants locally. I've seen local ads for berry bushes that were less expensive and didn't involve shipping charges. If I pay for them anonymously with cash, I'll never get any sweepstakes mailers as a result of my purchase!

November 1995: Deceptive coupon ads get the award this month. You've seen them. They're the ones that say, for example, "$9.99 with $1.50 mail-in offer." First, the item will cost you, in this case, $11.49 plus tax. Then, to get the $1.50 back, you'll spend another 32¢. So, assuming an 8 percent sales tax, your total cost is $12.41. Your net refund is $1.18. Your cost is not $9.99. It's $11.23, or a full 12.4 percent more than the advertised price!

I was recently in Oklahoma City, which has one of the highest sales taxes I've ever seen: 8.375 percent on everything, including food. While I was there, a store advertised Peter Pan peanut butter for 99¢ with a 40¢-off coupon (which was on each jar). It turned out the price of the peanut butter was $1.39. Sales tax was charged on that amount. Then the 40¢ was deducted. The net price of the peanut butter was $1.11, or 12 percent more than the advertised price. If manufacturers really want to save us money, why don't they just lower their prices instead of making us pay sales tax on money we never see?

December 1995: The award goes to those retailers who are overly anxious to start our annual holiday shopping orgy. My first Christmas catalog, from Miles Kimball of Oshkosh, Wisconsin, complete with pictures of snow scenes and warmly dressed children, arrived during an August heat wave and was promptly discarded. The shopping season, which used to seem long even when it started the day after Thanksgiving, is now being stretched to four months, or one-third of a year! Merchants of America, give us a break! No one is interested in doing his or her Christmas shopping at the same time back-to-school sales are going on!

February 1996: The coveted award this month goes to those truly "off-brand" telephone services that are flooding our mailboxes with deceptive advertising. The latest (as I write this) is **DimeLine (800-544-1510)**, which claims in big print to give you a flat rate of 10¢ per minute "anytime, any day, to anywhere in the U.S." Only by getting out your magnifying glass and examining the nearly microscopic print do you discover DimeLine charges a $5 per month access fee (equivalent to 50 of those 10¢ minutes), and the minimum charge is for a three-minute call (in other words, no call will cost you less than 30¢ plus the access fee)! This is about the worst deal I've seen for those of us who make a few short long-distance calls each month. (The first call would run at least $5.30 figuring the access fee plus the minimum charge.) And the advertising is incredibly disingenuous.

26
SELECTED
LETTERS

One of the nice things about writing a newsletter is hearing from readers. Sometimes they like what I'm doing. Sometimes they don't. At any rate, few are shy about stating their opinions!

From a Santa Clara, California, reader of my book Living Cheap*:*

> As a frugal working woman, I appreciated your spirit and the hints in *Living Cheap*.
>
> However, I was offended by your statement (on page 57) ". . . finding a good real estate agent is like finding an honest whore." Prostitutes offer a service for money like any business person. Please don't insult honest prostitutes by comparing them to deceptive real estate agents.

From Patricia Green of Key West, Florida:

> I make my typewriter ribbon last by taking one drop of machine oil (like Three-in-One) and lightly pushing it with my fingers along the entire ribbon. I let it sit a while, and then I manually push the ribbon back and forth slowly a few times. My finger comes out of this slightly smudged, but I've used the same ribbon for nearly ten years. *(While this may be a good*

way to extend the life of ribbons for manual typewriters, it WILL NOT work on electric typewriter ribbons.)

Every once in a while I get a letter from a reader who could give me lessons in frugality. Here is such a letter from Mrs. Ruth Glicker of Hallandale, Florida:

I use vinegar to get rid of tiny ants around my sink. If you don't have vinegar, use your dish detergent and leave it on the sink in a thin layer.

To keep fleas off my dog, I use Avon Skin-So-Soft on her underside.

To kill aphids, put dish detergent, a little Pine-Sol, and water in a spray bottle and spray. This also works on ants. Save all your spray bottles.

When leaving your house in hot climates, put some bay leaves in your closets to prevent that "musty" odor from building up. Also put some charcoal in your closets to prevent mold.

Wash and reuse your aluminum foil and your plastic bags.

Buy the items that are reduced at the produce counter if they're a good buy. I recently bought six big Delicious apples for 39¢. We don't mind cutting off a little bruise.

Spread borax powder (like Twenty Mule Team) around your house to eliminate fleas.

When you send a get-well card to a friend in the hospital, put the friend's return address on the envelope. That way, if the friend has left the hospital, the card will be forwarded to him or her, not to you!

Mrs. Glicker was right! I had never had a problem with ants, but last summer produced a bumper crop of ants in Northern California. I had an invasion, as did everyone I know. The ants went after my dogs' food, which until then I had left out all day in the kitchen. I got rid of the ants I saw and washed the kitchen floor with vinegar. I found a nest nearby and put vinegar around it. I haven't seen ant one in the house since.

From Kimberly Balkoski of San Francisco:

You've just paid for my subscription about fifteen-fold with your blurb on GM cars. About two weeks ago our 1987 Oldsmobile Delta 88 started to break down, the engine stopping on the highway repeatedly, and our car picked Yosemite National Park to start these maneuvers! Although mechanics in Oakhurst and Merced, California, gave it a crack, we broke down yet again and had to be towed 150 miles home at a cost of $200. My home dealer fixed the car free (he cited some warranty gobbledy goop). When I later read issue 4 [of LCN], I understood this was not just my problem, and I understood why my dealer didn't elaborate on the absence of a charge. I called the GM "800" number you gave, and a few days later my dealer called to say he thinks he can refund the $150 I shelled out in Oakhurst and the $150 I shelled out in Merced, both to GM dealers. He says it doesn't look good on recouping the towing charges, but I'll still try. If I hadn't known to make that phone call (thanks!), no one would have reimbursed me that $300.

And I like the way your newsletter is taking shape. Keep it up!

I. Barnes of Sunnyvale, California, writes:

I enjoy reading your LCN and have made use of a couple of items. Speaking of jam *(I mentioned a place to buy jam in an earlier LCN),* Safeway Stores' jam has won state fair prizes, and every so often, the jam goes on sale for 99¢ for an 18-ounce jar. They have six or seven different flavors, all delicious. Also, many of Safeway's house brands are the equal of highly advertised national brands at two-thirds of the price.

And, no, I don't work for Safeway. I'm just a customer who's been satisfied since 1960.

Steve Halpern of New Orleans says:

> I don't reuse envelopes (except the padded kind), but I do use return envelopes (non-postpaid only) that only require a label. *(He sent me a sample—he puts the label over the address on the envelope.)* They cost an infinitesimal fraction of a cent each. I obliterate the bar code with a felt-tipped pen.

Diane Sterling Switzer of Mission Viejo, California, writes:

> I stretch my tuna salad with coleslaw or leftover macaroni salad. You get your protein and veggies all in one dish that way. *(Sounds good!)*

Marie Sternburger of Sunnyvale, California, telephoned me with some great ideas. When her shampoo bottle is nearly empty, she sloshes a little water in it—she can always get at least one more shampoo out of it that way (and you mix shampoo with water when you wash your hair, anyway).

She advises that small women can wear boys' clothes, such as windbreakers. They're cheaper and wear better, she says. The same is true of boys' socks for women with small feet.

She has a credit card but always gets the annual fee removed by threatening to cancel the card. She asks for a discount if she pays cash instead of using her credit card. She advises shopping at thrift stores for a reason I would never have thought of: she says they're a good place to get out-of-stock patterns, such as Corning's older ones.

She recommends Birkenstock shoes. She's worn the same ones for nearly twenty years (they've been resoled, of course). To help them wear better, she puts Barge cement on the cork parts of her soles.

She recommends buying good-quality unfinished furniture and staining it yourself.

Saving the best for last, she told me that community colleges are a great place to find people to work for you. She recommends calling the placement office, which will post your notice. If you're looking for someone to do something complex, she says to get references.

Joan Hollingsworth, of Santa Clara, California, says:

I tried your recipe for fish salad *(mixing a can of mackerel into your regular tuna salad)*, and it was delicious. My cats went crazy, so I gave them some, too. They loved it. Later, it occurred to me that your recipe is cheaper than cat food! *(I won't swear my fish salad is good for cats. But I like it.)*

Julie Summers of Philomath, Oregon, writes regarding my mentioning that cereal purchased from bulk bins is cheaper and that I buy bran and wheat germ that way:

Whole grains contain bran and germ and cost a fraction of what you're paying for them separately. Also, once milled, the germ is highly perishable. Thus, the germ you are eating may be detracting from rather than adding to your health. I buy whole grain in 50-pound sacks and grind it by hand right before use.

Fifty pounds might seem like a lot, but if kept reasonably cool, whole grains retain their freshness (ability to sprout) for years, even decades. (I've gotten 99 percent sprouting from ten-year-old wheat.) Thus, you needn't worry about using it up fast.

My favorite breakfast for the past few months has been whole-wheat pancakes. I mix water, yeast, and flour the night before, set the batter in a cool place (near the floor), and in the morning the batter is bubbly and ready to beat and pour on my Teflon pan. (Keeping the batter cool overnight prevents souring; if it were left for a shorter time, it could take a higher temperature without souring.) That's a healthful, delicious, stick-to-the-ribs breakfast for 10¢ a pound (20¢ if organic) for the main ingredient.

One of the negative aspects of living in an urban area is often the lack of storage space. On the other hand, in an urban area it is often not difficult to find friends who will go together and purchase in bulk. Two people buying a 50-pound bag of whole wheat would entitle each to 25 pounds. That's still a lot of wheat to store. Five people going together would result in each one getting ten pounds. Now that is manageable. And, at 10¢ a pound, that's a buck apiece for a lot of cereal. Just think of it as Nineties Networking.

From Harry Shubart of Evanston, Illinois:

A "small" way to live cheap is to buy a car with good fuel mileage, low maintenance, and one that will last. I have a 1979 Rabbit Diesel that when last checked was getting forty-eight miles per gallon. It has had very low maintenance, and it still reliably goes from Point A to Point B. The saving of a minimum $4,000 a year for those who now buy a new car every two or three years is in zero depreciation, low maintenance, and fuel economy. *(Also, older cars are usually cheaper to insure.)*

Another way to live cheap and at the same time provide yourself with healthy heart-lung exercise (while helping the environment) is to cut your grass with a machete, as I do, to the local legal height limit of eight inches. This avoids fume and noise pollution and saves the cost of purchasing and operating a power mower.

Dick Bojack of Burlingame, California, wrote to say:

There's a way to beat even discount brokers' commissions on some stock purchases. Buy one share of the stock from a broker and have the broker register the stock in your name and address. When you receive the share and the accompanying information from the company, take advantage of the "Direct Stock Purchase Plan" that most utilities and many large companies offer. You can purchase additional shares directly from the company and save 100 percent of the brokers' fees.

Martha Spragins of Oxford, Mississippi, writes:

I've got a cheap trick for anyone who cooks at home on a regular basis. Save the wrappers from the outside of sticks of margarine or butter in a resealable plastic bag in the freezer. Whenever you need to grease a pan or casserole dish, use one of the wrappers. A single wrapper contains enough butter or margarine to grease a 9″ × 12″ or larger pan, a cookie sheet, or a casserole.

Also, if you are at a loss to solve a problem in your home cheaply, call a home economist in your area. They are usually listed in the phone book as Home Extension Officers. They can solve everything from ant invasion (with vinegar painted in the area they are in) to loaning you canners for home canning. You will find they have thousands of ideas for cheap living. They can also put you in contact with other people in your area with whom you can share ideas for saving money. I'm studying to be a home economist at the University of Mississippi in Oxford.

Mrs. Fred Baue, of Tucson, Arizona, writes:

I'm surprised that a penny-pincher like you would still be buying cleaning supplies at the grocery store. Since reading Don Aslett's book *Is There Life After Housework?*, I started buying cleaning supplies at a janitorial supply company (which Madison Avenue knows nothing about). Products sold at the grocery store are mostly water. Janitorial cleaners are usually concentrates to which you add the water. A gallon of solution for general cleaning has lasted me over four years (I don't mop every week), and it cost less than $10. A pint bottle of window cleaner concentrate (the blue stuff) cost $9.95 but has lasted five years. I use it every day.

Sometimes the homemade solution isn't always the best. I haven't used newspaper to clean my windows in ten years. I use a squeegee, which is what the professionals use.

Aslett has many money- and time-saving ideas. Your readers might like to get hold of his books. He also has videos available on home management. He is also quite an engaging and funny writer. Here's to cleaning cheap.

Thanks for the great advice. The tenth anniversary edition of **Is There Life After Housework?** *is* **$10.95 plus $3 shipping from Writer's Digest, 1507 Dana Ave., Cincinnati, OH 45207 (or toll-free 800-289-0963).**

Joan Hollingsworth of Santa Clara, California, wrote again to say she loves almost any kind of beans, and she doesn't waste the water she cooks the beans in, either. She makes minestrone as follows:

> To the water I've cooked my beans in I add pasta, vegetables, tomato sauce, and Italian seasoning to taste. I also add Parmesan cheese. This makes a great minestrone.

Helen G. Burrie of San Diego writes:

> A few months ago, I began cooking one day a month, freezing the meals. It's an efficient use of time and energy, and it encourages less waste of produce items, which often spoil before all of them are used.
>
> An excellent book to help a person get started with this project is *Once-a-Month Cooking*, by Mimi Wilson and Beth Aagerborg. It offers two two-week plans and two one-month plans, including a menu calendar, grocery shopping list, containers needed, cooking day assembly order, and, of course, the recipes!
>
> It can be ordered for $9 from 1-800-A-FAMILY or found at Christian bookstores.
>
> *Thank you very much for this information. This sounds like an excellent way to make more time in your life for your family.*

Marge Chambers of Spring Valley, California, writes about a problem that's been frustrating her:

> From time to time I try to take advantage of rebate offers. The first problem I encounter is that all of the rebate offers want the entire sales receipt. If you are trying for several rebates on one shopping trip, how are you supposed to get a sales receipt for each one? Stores pretty much refuse to ring up each item

separately. I'm not interested in standing in line three or four times. In fact, I'm not real happy to stand in line once. Then, if you do manage to have the sales receipt, the scanner thing from the box, the form properly filled out, and all the other required stuff that must be completed perfectly, you spend a 32¢ stamp and send that sucker off.

Well, guess what. Most of the time it just never comes. They just do not send anything back in the mail. So there you are, feeling like a fool. You went to a lot of trouble, wasted a stamp, and received nothing. Can you think of anything that can be done about this?

Yes, I have some suggestions. First, if the clerks at the check-out stands refuse to ring up an item separately, ask to speak to their manager. Explain to the manager why you need the item rung up separately. Unless he or she is a complete dolt, you should have no problem getting him or her to see the light. You are, after all, the customer, and, even better, as far as the store manager is concerned, you are taking advantage of a discount that doesn't cost the store anything.

Regarding not receiving the rebate, keep records. *If possible,* keep copies! *Most fulfillment houses are not affiliated with the manufacturers offering the rebates; they are working under contract, and they won't be able to keep those contracts if they make the manufacturers' customers unhappy. If you don't get a rebate you've sent in for, write the manufacturer, giving details on the rebate you sent in for as well as the date you sent in for it and the address to which you sent your request. Good luck.*

In the November 1993 LCN *I said, "If anyone knows how to make use of turkey bones, I'd sure like to hear from you!" Hear from you I did. Joan Hollingsworth, Patricia Green of Key West, Florida, and K. C. Duerig of King Hill, Idaho, all said that, since bone meal is good fertilizer, the turkey bones should be dried, crushed with a hammer, and used as fertilizer. Gail Bedard of Bedard, Illinois, writes:*

We have always saved, dried, and glitter-sprayed the wishbones. We use them as Christmas ornaments. Hung on their red ribbons, they are symbols of all the holiday dinners we have shared and all the wishes we had come true. We throw the carcass way out back for the wild animals to enjoy. It always disappears.

Beth Hartford-DeRoos of Tracy, California, writes:

I love your publication and almost always stop to read each new issue promptly. I have yet to be disappointed in any of the books, etc. you have noted, and, in fact, I usually attempt to purchase them at cost for my local library. Coming at life from a Quaker/Buddhist viewpoint, I believe that, by donating such books as well as sharing your excellent newsletter, we are walking softer upon the earth and living in harmony, body, mind, and spirit. It is true as you noted *[in issue 27]* in your remarks about the book *Downscaling* that some authors write from a religious, usually a Christian, perspective. The book *Voluntary Simplicity*, which you noted in a past issue, brings in a Quaker or even Buddhist way of thinking. I appreciate learning how other cultures and religions are encouraging responsibility.

Living in California and being home schoolers, we always look for cheap or, better yet, free activities and have discovered the joy in visiting cemeteries. Did you know there are a number of people from the Donner Party buried in the old St. Raymond's cemetery in Dublin? We also found it very educational to visit the Hindu temple in Livermore, the Islamic mosque in Berkeley, and the Mormon temple in Oakland. How many Californians have visited any of the old missions in their area? Another free activity that is really rewarding is volunteering with Habitat for Humanity or a local food bank. We urge people who can to plant extra tomatoes, beans, etc. to give to those in their neighborhood who are on fixed income by choice or by accident. It is a great way to make new friends.

Finally, have you ever tried the horse shampoo found in pet and livestock stores? It's great!

Thank you for your comments. I have not yet tried the horse shampoo, but I see no reason it wouldn't work on people as well as horses. After all, udder balm (for us city folk, that's a cream made for cows) is supposed to be a good hand cream.

I do want to report that some of my readers have written to say they have subscribed to some of the newsletters I've reviewed only to have the newsletters go out of business without sending refunds. I was very disappointed with one newsletter that I recommended highly in 1992. I subscribed and didn't get any more issues. I wrote the editor, who said, "Oh, I had other priorities, so I stopped doing the newsletter." She sent a refund, but only after I had written her. I wondered how many of my readers had subscribed, not complained, and lost their money. If you subscribe to anything and you don't get what you pay for, invest in a postcard. Perhaps you can at least get some of your money back.

Finally, Ms. Hartford-DeRoos is doing her community a great favor by investing in books for her local library. While I usually give ordering information for books I recommend, I urge my readers to use and support your local libraries. What better way is there to practice frugality than to learn more about it free?

Mercedes Herman of New York writes:

I enjoy your paper and have found several ways to save money—especially in buying a home. I had been looking at a more expensive home—buying more home than I needed. I took your advice and bought a smaller house, and I got one new and reasonably priced.

Simone Silverstein of New York writes:

I just had my fourth child and was shocked at what the hospital charged. The total was $7,217.15, of which $4,673 was for me and $2,624.15 was for the baby. This is a charge for a twenty-four-hour stay. The hospital (thank God) did not do anything—really! My baby was in my room, not in the nursery. This is a lot of money to charge for what women have been doing for thousands of years! Should I have my next one at home? My doctor, whom I loved and is the only one who actually did something—catch the baby—charged an additional

$4,560. This means in the first twenty-four hours of my son's life, he cost me $11,857.15. I love my son and would pay anything for him, but I feel these prices are a little crazy. I will protest the bill, and I will let you know the outcome.

By the way, a tip for your readers is *breast-feeding.* I've nursed my kids until they could walk and talk and ask for real food themselves. I have never bought a bottle of formula or jar of baby food. When they are ready, they can eat off my plate.

First, as to whether you should have the next baby at home, I'm going to ask my readers for their advice on that one. I have heard of midwives who come to homes and deliver there. And, as you pointed out, women have been having babies for quite a while.

I am absolutely no expert on children, so I don't know whether the hospital bill was out of line. It does seem high for the services you received, but hospitals have enormous overheads these days. As I pointed out in issue number 16, if a doctor or a hospital performs a service for someone who cannot pay, the costs of those services are paid for by those of us who can pay. One alternative to having your next child at home might be a trip to Canada, where you may be able to take advantage of their "socialized medicine."

Bill Robinson, of Bandon, Oregon, sent something from the Sunday San Francisco Chronicle *that may be of interest to you:*

Department of Agriculture researchers calculate that a child born in 1993 can be expected to cost its parents $231,140 by the time said offspring is seventeen years old.

Trish McElhiney, of Safety Harbor, Florida, wrote the following in response to Simone Silverstein's letter:

Thanks so much for your newsletter. While I don't always practice what you (or I, for that matter) preach, I do hold these philosophies close to my heart and am gratified when I run across someone who feels as I do. Anyway, I wanted to share with you my experience when my last child was born in 1993. My husband and I were pretty disgusted with the manner in which our first child came into the world (in a hospital—all the bells and whistles and interventions—yuk!), so, when our second child was born, we looked into a birthing center, and that was a more positive experience. We really didn't give much thought to what it cost to have the first two children. When we found out we were having number three, we wanted to accomplish two things: have more control over the pregnancy and birth and be as cost-efficient as possible without compromising the care the baby and I would receive.

We found our answer in our midwife and friend Karin Kearns, a licensed midwife (*not* a certified nurse midwife—they are subject to MDs; our LM was not). She charged $2,700 for the entire process, which included house calls (!) and classes and everything related to the birth, which was in the comfort and privacy of our home. I had to wrangle with my insurance company to cover her services (at 70 percent, since she was not affiliated with the PPO network I'm in), so our total cost was about $800, which we paid in installments over the course of the pregnancy.

I breast-fed my daughter exclusively for six months, then she started on mashed table food. For the first three months, I used cloth diapers with diaper covers bought used (but spotlessly clean) from a diaper service—3½ dozen diapers and a dozen covers for about $25. Friends loaned clothes, and she slept with me. Now I know babies don't have to cost that much at all. Oh, yes, the delivery was the easiest I'd had.

A reader from Augusta, Michigan, who requested not to be identified, writes:

You said you couldn't understand why so many recipes require you to preheat the oven. For you and others who may not know, it is so your food will bake evenly. If you are baking a roast or potatoes it may not be a big deal. However, if you try baking desserts such as a cake, muffins, pies, etc. and don't preheat, the results will make you sorry you even began.

Thanks for your letter. As many of those who have tasted the results (including some canine companions) can attest, many of my forays into the world of cooking have made me sorry I even began! I'll try preheating next time.

Sally S. Miller of Flemington, New Jersey, writes:

Every morning I think of you, so I finally decided to sit down and write. Concerning shampoo, coffee, and moving.

A year ago, after surgery on my neck, I was told to wash my neck and shoulder area with Dial (an antibacterial soap). I decided I might as well do the rest of me, so I just washed top to bottom with Dial. I have continued to use Dial the whole year and find it convenient and inexpensive. The reason you shampoo twice: the first round is to loosen up the scalp stuff, rinsing it off, then washing the hair more carefully the second time. I find the bar soap just fine for this. Then I read about the hydrogen peroxide, and wow! How did you know about my scalp thingies? *(Actually, I can't take credit for this; Bill Robinson of Bandon, Oregon, suggested it.)* I used it in between shampooing and got rid of them in two days. I passed the word on to a friend who also had this minor scalp condition (both of us for the first time in our lives). Does this say something about the Earth and her creatures, stress, and taking care of ourselves?

Several years ago, after a doctor mentioned cutting down my coffee after he found lumps in my breasts, I gradually started mixing in decaf (amazingly, the lumps got smaller!), then started using less and less of my mixture until I was using one-quarter scoop of regular coffee plus one-quarter scoop of decaf to twelve cups of fresh well water (which I now serve to guests, calling it "coffee tea"). Then I read in LCN about reusing the grounds for the next day, so I started doing that. What a savings over a few years ago, when I drank nine cups a day of regular coffee! And how much better for my health!

I moved six times in two years, and the least traumatic was when I had a long-distance carrier selected ahead of time, knew exactly what each of us was packing, drove on ahead, and did the packing and unpacking slowly. I used paper boxes from my local print shop. I agree that it was worth the money and cheaper than a rental truck.

I suspect the best ways to move are to either get rid of all your stuff or carry it with you all the time (I know several people who live in their vans or cars). Since I am still attached to my three rooms of possessions, I'm trying to stay in the same place a little longer so I won't have to deal with moving. But if I should have to, I think I'd like to store my stuff, go on the road with my new (old) Mac, and visit some of the people I've been corresponding with—maybe help put out an issue, share information.

Ms. Miller reports she's working on a book, The Prairie Revolution. *I'll let you know when it's done.*

Ruthann DeMan of Bel Air, Maryland, writes:

I enjoy your newsletter so much! I have found many cost-saving ideas and I look forward to receiving your publication each and every month. I am writing to you because as a single parent I feel there is a great need to address the needs of divorced moms (and dads) who have the children and face the high cost of living each day. I try to implement your suggestions as best I can, but I would also appreciate more ideas geared toward a one-income family. It would be wonderful if you could devote some ideas each month to benefit those of us who are raising children alone and struggle with child support (or lack thereof), teenagers' wants and needs, how to save on a single income, etc. Please see if there might be some way you can incorporate topics for single parents with children into your newsletter.

I've never been a single parent, but a close friend of mine lost his wife to cancer a few years ago. At the time he had a seven-year-old son, and the thing I remember most about those times was that my friend simply had no time for himself. The lack of time to do things the most economical way is a major challenge for a single parent. So sometimes it is best to settle for doing things the second most economical way. For example, a single parent will probably not have time to spend weekends going to garage sales. But he or she might find time to go to a few thrift, resale, or consignment shops to look for clothes. Unfortunately, some children may not want to wear used clothes. The next most economical approach to clothing would be to shop department stores' outlet, or clearance, stores. Buying out of season is another approach. Shop for summer clothes at the end of summer, for example. You and your children will be wearing styles a year old, but who notices these days?

A single parent will have to enlist his or her children's cooperation. A divorced acquaintance told me that, after a few years of trying to give her children everything, she held a family conference and told them she just couldn't continue to cater to their every whim. She laid out a list of either/ors. Either they could move to a smaller house, or the children would have to give up their private school. Either they could make their clothes do for another year, or they would have to give up their summer vacation. My friend told me she was amazed at how mature her preteen daughters turned out to be. Once they realized the situation and were made a part of the decision-making process, they were happy to do their part.

Warren Mullison of Culver City, California, writes:

I spent twenty-two years with Sears in their catalog order operations. When the catalog closed, I was out on the street. I know I'm not alone. There must be thousands of men and women aged fifty to sixty who gave so many years of their lives to corporate America and are now "downsized" out of a career. To find a new job one must fight these three obstacles: age discrimination, being "overqualified," and having outdated computer skills. I now work as a waiter. Fortunately my house and car are paid for, and I have no credit card debt. This is part of America 1995. Who will write our story?

To me, the corporate mentality of people as disposable assets is the shame of America 1995. I can't help but wonder who will be able to buy what downsized companies produce when no one has a job. Our only defense is to prepare ourselves to live without our jobs.

And finally, my favorite letter:

Joanne Goleman of Minden, Louisiana, writes:
I enjoy your newsletter. Being a curious soul, I subscribed to several newsletters when I became interested in the New Frugality movement. I felt there must be more to it than learning fifty-three more things to do with soap slivers, and I was right. Yours is the most thought-provoking newsletter by far. Thank you for keeping it interesting.

27
ADDITIONAL
RESOURCES

The following resources are those I have reviewed in *Living Cheap News*. First, although when appropriate I have provided ordering information, I do not recommend that you go out and buy all of these publications. In the case of books, most libraries will either have them or be able to get them for you through the Interlibrary Loan Program. In some cases there will be a charge for this service, but it will be far less than the price of the book.

In the case of newsletters, I have generally provided the subscription price and, when available, the sample policy. Please do not expect the publishers of these newsletters to send you a sample issue at their expense. First, remember these newsletters are usually one-person or one-family businesses. Postage is expensive. (Fully half the cost of publishing *Living Cheap News* goes to postage, one stamp at a time.) Furthermore, writing addresses in the volume we receive sample requests is unreasonably time-consuming for our limited human resources. When in doubt, enclose $1 and a *stamped*, self-addressed business-size envelope. If you enclose neither, don't be surprised if you don't get a response.

No list of New Frugality publications would be complete without a mention of the mother of them all. Amy Dacyczyn's **The Tightwad Gazette ($12 per year from R.R. 1 Box 3570, Leeds, ME 04263)** remains by far the best known. Although the newsletter will cease publication in December 1996, earlier issues have been turned into two books that share the newsletter's name.

My local newspaper quoted from ***The Banker's Secret Bulletin*** **(for a sample copy, send $1 to Good Advice Press, Box 78, Elizaville, NY 12523)**. I sent for the sample copy and got more than a dollar's worth of information on credit cards. I may have to rethink my approach. Not only do I use a credit card, I pay $50 a year for mine. I do get one frequent-flyer mile for each dollar I charge, and I pay the bill in full each month. (I've never paid interest on a credit card.) An upcoming issue will explore renting versus buying your home. *The Banker's Secret* questions conventional wisdom, and I like that!

The folks at ***The Banker's Secret Bulletin*** have come up with an issue so good they're getting a fourth mention in *LCN*. Issue 8 discusses creating an "ace in the hole." It's not about poker; it's about starting a sideline business for fun, profit, and, not incidentally in these times of mass layoffs, something to fall back on if you find a pink slip in your pay envelope. Marc Eisenson and his brother are also starting "Ace in the Hole" seminars.

If you buy books (and, let's face it, not all of us have a flexible enough schedule to use the library and get the books back in time to avoid a fine), about the best discount bookseller I've found is **Edward R. Hamilton, Falls Village, CT 06031-5000**. Their catalog is free. In the last catalog, for example, Rodale's *Cut Your Bills in Half*, which was published in 1989 and retailed for $24.95, could be had for $3.95. Edward R. Hamilton does not have a toll-free number and does not accept credit cards, but they pass on to their customers the savings from not having these services. They do not charge sales tax (a major consideration for those living in states with high sales taxes), and their shipping charge on all orders is currently a flat $3. If you order something they're out of, often they will send you a check that, if used for full or partial payment on your next order, will allow you to have that order shipped free.

One of the best books I've read in a long time is one I recently purchased from Edward R. Hamilton, ***Cashing In on the American Dream***, by Paul Terhorst. It was published in 1988 at $16.95, and Edward R. Hamilton offered it for $2.95. Terhorst retired at age thirty-five, and he shows how just about anyone can do it. He recommends selling your house (of course, that was a lot easier a few years ago) and, if possible, doing without a car. After just having paid my property taxes, home-owners' insurance, and auto insurance, the combination of which was enough to support a large family in Eastern Europe for a few years, I can understand Terhorst's assertion that, in many cases, we are working to support our possessions. Though he owns an apartment in Brazil (purchased for $20,000), he takes advantage of being footloose by living all over the world—primarily in Third World countries, where the currency exchange rates really let him live cheap. This book not only questions conventional wisdom, it gives answers to questions most of us would never think to ask. If you're tired of the rat race, I can't recommend this book highly enough.

If you're a student or a teacher, **American Educational Services, 419 Lentz Court, Lansing, MI 48917 (800-748-0039)**, sells magazines cheap. Through them, *The Wall Street Journal* is $79.50 per year, and *Money* is $18.75. Each year, as your subscriptions get close to renewal time, you'll hear from the publisher. Wait to renew until you hear from American Educational Services—or give them a call.

Publishers Marketing Service (3 Oak Leaf Dr., Waretown, NJ 08758) offers discounted prices on a wide variety of magazines. Frankly, their prices are good, but, in many cases, I've seen better. Their selection, however, is excellent. You can even get foreign magazines. Send them a postcard and ask to see their brochure.

If you're in the market for magazines, **Below Wholesale Magazines (1909 Prosperity, Reno, NV 89502, or 800-800-0062)** offers some of the best prices I've seen, especially if you have a business card. For example, *The New Yorker*, an excellent weekly magazine, is available for less than $10 a year (that's 52 issues) for those who have business cards.

I recently tossed an eighteen-year-old Westbend coffeemaker that was good except for one key part: a lid through which the water ran. Too bad I didn't know about **Culinary Parts Unlimited**. Their number is **800-543-7549**. If you know what part you need, have the model number of your appliance, and are willing to use a credit card, they'll send you the part.

Recently I was having trouble locating a pair of my favorite tennis shoes, the made-in-the-U.S.A. Converse All Star low-tops. I've been wearing these since 1970 (no, not the same pair). I find them comfortable, unpretentious, and—best of all—cheap. I telephoned all around town. No luck. Finally, I pressed one of the local stores for Converse's phone number. I simply couldn't believe they'd stopped making my favorite tennis shoe. Luckily, the phone number is toll-free (800-428-2667; if that doesn't work, try 800-648-5620), and even more fortunate is the fact you can find out whether there is a Converse outlet store near you. Even if there isn't, don't fret. You can telephone the one nearest you and order from them. I did and paid $18.99 for my pair.

A reader sent me a copy of ***Geri Cook's Best Bargains in L.A. and Orange Counties* (P.O. Box 67989, Los Angeles, CA 90067, phone 310-203-9233)**. At $30 a year, it's a bit pricey, but it's got something for everyone. The first article in the issue I have is about shopping in Thailand and Hong Kong. I almost didn't go any further—if I ever make it to Asia, it won't be to shop. But the same issue also has articles about resale stores for men's clothes, bakery outlets, and "noteworthy sales." If you live in the Los Angeles area, you might find this useful.

Walker and Company sent me a copy of Erica Barkemeyer's ***80+ Great Ideas for Making Money at Home***. This book has some interesting suggestions. Two I liked were pet-sitting and house-sitting. (I once knew a woman who did this in exchange for rent. Erica says you can actually get paid for staying in someone's house while they're away.) Nowadays, with even the biggest corporations announcing massive layoffs, it might not be a bad idea to consider starting a sideline business of your own. Even if you're not in danger of losing your job, there are many tax advantages available to the home-based entrepreneur. The thing I liked best about this book is that the author gives you an overview of each idea and then recommends sources for further reading. The book should be available through your local bookstore or, even better, your library. If not, you can order it from **Walker and Company, 720 Fifth Ave., New York, NY 10019 (the toll-free number is 800-289-2553)**. The paperback edition is $14.95, and Walker tacks on $3 for handling. They also add sales tax for residents of New York and California.

The Frugal Shopper, by Ralph Nader and Wesley J. Smith, was a long time coming (I ordered mine March 2 and received it April 16), and the constant change in type styles is a strain on my eyes. But it covers a host of topics, including lawyers, automobiles, insurance, and doctors. It is **$10 from The Frugal Shopper, P.O. Box 19367, Washington, DC 20036**.

I read about ***The Green Commuter***, by Joel Makower, in my local newspaper. He tells how to drive environmentally consciously. **The book is $12.45** and should be available in bookstores or, even better, your library. If not, you can order it from **Tilden Press, 1526 Connecticut Ave., Washington, DC 20036 (or toll-free 800-955-GREEN for credit card orders)**.

Philip Slater's ***Wealth Addiction***, a book on tape, starts off slow and stays slow. It contains endless stories of miserable misers and their unhappy offspring (all right, there *is* an end, but you'll be wondering after the first hour)—right up to the last fifteen minutes. Then it's as if the author finally remembers he has a message and is running out of time to spit it out. And what a message! He, like Paul Terhorst, lives simply. He says he lives on one-fourth of what he lived on twenty years ago. (This is impressive if he lived on $20,000 twenty years ago; it's hardly relevant if he lived on $200,000 back then—the exact figure remains a mystery.) He ends with an incisive observation: Most Americans are fighting for a first-class cabin on the *Titanic*.

Another book on tape is Jerrold Mundis's ***How to Get Out of Debt, Stay Out of Debt & Live Prosperously***. Mundis offers concrete solutions to getting control of debt. I've never been inclined to go overboard in this regard, so it's difficult for me to relate to some of the advice. I recently met another newsletter editor who at one time had accumulated $100,000 in consumer debt. Still, some of Mundis's statements struck me as peculiar. For example, he does not consider a mortgage a debt. When I had a mortgage, I certainly felt in debt. He is adamantly opposed to credit cards. I find mine convenient, and I save fuel by shopping from home using my credit card (and I get frequent-flyer miles when I use it). One of the most disappointing aspects of this book is Mr. Mundis's belief that saving 10 percent is all it takes to be frugal. It seems to me that someone making $100,000 a year might be able to save a lot more than 10 percent, while someone living on minimum wage would do well to save anything. This book was not written for me, but if you have uncontrollable urges "to debt"—Mr. Mundis uses *debt* as a verb (all right, I know I use *cheap* as an adverb), this book may be for you.

Rhonda Barfield, who feeds her family of six on $50 a week (the national average for a family of four is $136, according to the St. Charles, Missouri, *Journal*), has written ***Thrifty Business: 111 Money Saving***

Tips. This 32-page booklet is available for **$4 postpaid from her at 407 Lilac, St. Charles, MO 63303**.

I have recently become aware of some "back to the land" publications. The first is ***Backwoods Home* magazine ($17.95 per year from 1257 Siskiyou Blvd., #213, Ashland, OR 97520)**. Self-dubbed "the magazine *The Mother Earth News* should have been," this bimonthly offering does remind me of the old TMEN. I stopped subscribing to TMEN in 1984, when it embraced the Grace Commission's recommendations, including reducing pay and benefits for civil servants. (J. Peter Grace, incidentally, was recently named one of the country's most overpaid CEOS by compensation consultant Graef S. Crystal.) I had just left civil service that year for better pay and benefits, so I knew the Grace Commission was full of it on at least that recommendation. Similarly, *Backwoods Home* magazine's politics are, well, pretty far right. On the other hand, they have a section on self-sufficiency that has some great suggestions. I'd suggest holding your nose on the editorial and enjoying the rest of the magazine. (If you don't want to spring for $17.95, most libraries will subscribe to magazines if they get enough requests.)

Making *Backwoods Home* magazine seem downright tame is ***Living Free* ($9 for six issues from Jim Stumm, Box 29, Hiller Branch, Buffalo, NY 14223)**. At first I thought it was going *Living Cheap News* one better (living free versus merely living cheap), but it turned out to be more of a Libertarian type of free. With a good deal of paranoia thrown in. I can't really recommend this one, but if you're looking for something truly different, this might be it.

At the other end of the survivalist spectrum is Laura D. Martin-Buhler's ***The Gentle Survivalist* ($22 per year from Box 4004, St. George, UT 84770)**. Mixing a little New Age philosophy with down-to-earth money-saving and health tips, Ms. Martin-Buhler has come up with a gentle, interesting approach to frugality, which I found appealing. If you would like to sample *The Gentle Survivalist* before subscribing, send $1 for a sample copy.

The Book Peddlers sent me a copy of Vicky Lansky's ***Another Use for 101 Common Household Items* ($6.95 plus $2.25 postage and handling from The Book Peddlers, 18326 Minnetonka Blvd., Deephaven, MN 55391, or toll-free 800-255-3379)**. This book is 143 pages of just what it says it is. Who ever would have thought of keeping a pair of pantyhose in your car to use to tie down the lid of the trunk if you have something bulky to haul? Ms. Lansky is the "Help!" columnist for *Family Circle* magazine, and it's obvious from this book that she knows her job well!

A good mailing list to get on is that of **Career Press (P.O. Box 34, Hawthorne, NJ 07507; toll-free 800-CAREER-1)**. The good news is they publish some good books, and they'll give you a discount (and sometimes a free book) if you order directly from them. The bad news is their shipping charges are high ($3.50 for the first book; $1 for each additional book to $8.50).

I read about Bernice Lifton's ***Bug Busters: Poison-Free Pest Controls for Your House & Garden*** in the *Los Angeles Times* a few months ago. Ms. Lifton was forced to research this subject because her son was allergic to commercial pest controls. While the book gives good advice on keeping your home pest-free (Ms. Lifton repeatedly suggests keeping your house clean), she dwells a bit too much on the reasons for getting rid of pests for my tastes (fleas carry plague, mosquitoes carry malaria and encephalitis, etc.). The fact that they're in my house is enough of a reason for me. The nice thing about natural pest control is it is often cheaper than using commercial products. For example, Ms. Lifton says grated citrus peel kills fleas. Simmer lemons for forty-five minutes, cool, strain, and wet your pet thoroughly with the mixture. You get dead fleas and a lemon-scented animal! This book should be available in your library or your local bookstore. If not, it is available for **$9.95 plus $3 shipping from Avery Publishing Group, Inc., 120 Old Broadway, Garden City Park, NY 11040**. New York residents should add sales tax.

Thinking of leaving the big city? Whatever put that idea into my— I mean your—head? First, though, read ***Country Bound!*™ *Trade Your Business Suit Blues for Blue Jean Dreams*™ ($19.95, plus $3 shipping and $1.40 sales tax if you live in Colorado, from Communication Creativity, P.O. Box 909, Dept. CB, Buena Vista, CO 81211, or toll-free 800-331-8355—if you mention *LCN*, you can get a 10 percent discount on the book)**. I was a little skeptical about ordering this one, but once I started reading it, I couldn't put it down. It is well organized and quite objective. If you are thinking of a move to a smaller town, this book will be one of your best investments. They made all the wrong choices at first (even moving to a town they found they didn't like—they call it "First Try" in their book). I had always thought when I moved to a smaller area, I'd take a year off and read and recuperate. A big mistake, say the Rosses. People will think you're aloof. Turn down a few invitations, and soon you won't have any to turn down! They are now happily settled in Buena Vista, and, through their efforts, anyone who wants to follow in their footsteps can avoid his or her own "First Try."

Dwelling Portably, the ultimate in cheap-housing magazines, is for those who want to live in tents, often by squatting ("surreptitious homesteading"). While this lifestyle may be too rugged for many of us, if you're into camping as a hobby, some of the ideas you'll read here may be applicable to you. **It's $1 per issue from P.O. Box 190, Philomath, OR 97370.**

In most areas it's getting to be time to think about putting in that garden. But where to buy the seeds? A company I've dealt with for more than ten years is **Le Jardin du Gourmet, St. Johnsbury Center, VT 05863.** They offer an amazing variety of seeds and plants. Best of all for us urban folk, they have 25¢ seed packets that, though marketed as samples, will probably be more than enough for a city garden. Send them a postcard and ask for their catalog.

John Howells's ***Retirement on a Shoestring*** (**$6.95 plus $1.75 shipping—California residents add 8.25 percent sales tax—from Gateway Books, 13 Bedford Cove, San Rafael, CA 94901**) tells how to live cheap after you leave your job. From living in a foreign country (like Mexico) to living in a motor home (and he tells about "Slab City," an abandoned—and demolished except for the concrete slab building foundations—World War II military base near Niland, California, where one person interviewed lives well on $350 a month), to being a single retiree, Mr. Howells writes about ways to live after work. His book ends by listing his favorite retirement spots in the United States.

If you find magazine articles long on gossip and short on substance, Michael Rozek has a newsletter for you. ***Rozek's*** (**$10 per year for six issues from 3424 10th Ave. West, Seattle, WA 98119**) carries one article, about one person, per eight-page issue. If you are into in-depth articles, this may be for you.

Over age fifty? Check out (of your library if possible) Sue Goldstein's ***Great Buys for People Over 50: How to Save Money on Every-***

thing. Published by Penguin, this $10 book should be pretty generally available in bookstores. At 476 pages, it appears to live up to its subtitle. It covers a wide range of consumer goods and services, and it has several sections on travel.

If you find yourself put off by your doctor, **People's Medical Society (462 Walnut St., Allentown, PA 18102, or phone toll-free 800-624-8773)** may be of interest to you. For $20 a year, you get their bimonthly newsletter and their periodic catalog of publications, which includes books as well as various health bulletins.

Wayne Lackner sent a copy of his *Health Insurance: Understanding It and Medicare*. **(It's normally $9.95 plus $2 shipping from Fee Publishing Company, P.O. Box 681N, Kent, OH 44240, but if you mention you saw it here, he'll pay the shipping.)** My first reaction was a groan. I couldn't imagine reading 150 pages about such a dull topic, but I was pleasantly surprised. The book is well written, informative, and especially helpful for those who have no insurance or who are facing the loss of their health insurance as a result of layoffs.

Matthew Lesko has written several books on government benefits. His new book, *What to Do When You Can't Afford Health Care* **($24.95 plus $4.50 shipping from Information USA, 1100-D N. Quincy St., Arlington, VA 22201, or phone toll-free 800-862-5372)**, is a telephone-book-sized guide to about 5,000 sources of help available to Americans with serious health problems. The sources are handily indexed alphabetically by disease. I would suggest that, while this book is a must for your public library, it may be overkill for the individual reader.

For a list of free and cheap publications available through the courtesy of Uncle Sam and your tax dollars, send a postcard to **S. James, Consumer Information Center-3B, P.O. Box 100, Pueblo, CO 81002**, and ask for their *Consumer Information Catalog*. Topics include cars, children, employment and education, federal programs, food and nutrition, health, travel, small business, and money. Here's a way to get some benefit from your tax dollars.

Gustave Berle's *Retiring to Your Own Business* **($14.95 plus $2 shipping and handling from Puma Publishing, 1670 Coral Dr., Santa Maria, CA 93454, or toll-free 800-255-5730, ext. 110)** discusses the advantages of starting something you want to do after you retire, perhaps the most important of which is the increased life spans of today's retirees. Dr. Berle tells how to determine whether you are a likely entrepreneur, how to find a loan, the pros and cons of a home office, and relocation—including relocation to "acceptable" foreign countries.

For those not ready to retire, Kate Wendleton's ***Through the Brick Wall: How to Job-Hunt in a Tight Market* (published by Villard, this book should be available in your library or from your local bookstore for $13)** discusses an approach that she says is often overlooked by job hunters, who concentrate only on trying to get an interview and doing well in the interview. She recommends assessing what you want to do, planning a campaign for the job targets you are actually interested in, interviewing, and then, perhaps most important, following up on your job interviews.

Surviving Unemployment: A Family Handbook for Weathering Hard Times, by Cathy Beyer, Doris Pike, and Loretta McGovern **(published by Henry Holt and Company, this book should be available in your library or from your local bookstore for $10.95)**, gives a firsthand account of how Ms. Beyer survived the Texas recession, which preceded the national downturn by a few years, and how, with a little planning and a lot of family support (she, her husband, their daughter, and their pets wound up living with his parents for a few months), others can follow the path she blazed. From discussing how to live well on less to prioritizing creditors and what to do about medical expenses, this book provides useful advice for those who may find themselves joining the unemployed before we see the light at the end of the tunnel again.

Steven Woodham is giving away his secrets. Steve's a barber/stylist, and he's written ***Cut Hair at Home Like a Pro* ($9.95 postpaid from Steve's Haircuts, c/o Anadat Publications, 41187 Via Cedro, Murrieta, CA 92562-2093)**. Bill Clinton, take note: Do it yourself and save $200.

Andrew Feinberg's ***Downsize Your Debt* (published by Penguin Books, this book should be available in your library or from your local bookstore for $10)** is a revealing book. Mr. Feinberg tells how to get out of an uncomfortable debt situation, and what your rights are if you find you're in over your head. His thirty-three-question "Debt Quiz" is an eye-opener even to those of us who consider ourselves in control of our finances. This is a serious book about a serious problem.

Our nation's leaders should be required to read this book as they work on the federal budget.

If you're like I am, you make all sorts of New Year's resolutions, and one of them might be to stick to a budget. Last year, I began keeping track of where every penny went. At the end of each month, I tally up the income and the outgo. Dr. George R. Hancock sent me his ***Balance Your Budget*** (**$4 postpaid from P.O. Box 308, Westville, OK 74965**), which is essentially a set of twelve monthly balance sheets to take you through the year. You could make your own, of course—someday—but his are bound, his price is certainly not outrageous, and you don't have to wait for "someday." I've found them helpful.

One of the best little books I've seen in a long time is the Green Group's ***101 Ways to Save Money and Our Planet*** (**$5.95 plus $1.75 shipping and handling from Paper Chase, Inc., 5721 Magazine St., Suite 152, New Orleans, LA 70115—they will give a 40 percent discount if you order five or more books**). Each of the 101 tips lists its money-saving benefits, planet-saving benefits, and where to get the product.

Patricia C. Gallagher's ***Raising Happy Kids on a Reasonable Budget*** tells how to raise children without going broke. She covers various subjects from financial aid to sickness prevention. Published by Betterway Books, this 132-page book should be available in your library or from bookstores **for $10.95 or you can order it by calling toll-free 800-289-0963**. Ms. Gallagher also offers a pamphlet, **"100 Ways to Save Money While Raising a Family," for $1 from P. Gallagher, Box 555, Worcester, PA 19490**.

Another way to save money on children is not to have them. ***ChildFree*** (**$24 per year or $45 for two years from The ChildFree Network, 7777 Sunrise Blvd., Suite 1800, Citrus Heights, CA 95610**) is a newsletter for those who are without children "by choice or by chance." While I believe this is a much-needed publication, it tends to be a tad on the defensive side, constantly and a bit stridently defending a decision that, bottom line, is no one's business.

One of the most thought-provoking books I've read in a long time, ***Ain't Nobody's Business if You Do***, by Peter McWilliams (**$22.95 postpaid from Prelude Press, 8159 Santa Monica Blvd., Los Angeles, CA 90046, or toll-free 800-543-3101**), presents a well-researched 788-

page argument for legalization of "consensual crimes"—crimes that do not harm the person or property of others. Mr. McWilliams shows how the United States could quickly eliminate the *entire national debt* by not spending the money we now invest in arresting and prosecuting the four million people accused of violating laws against consensual crimes every year. McWilliams frequently uses Biblical references (often in the original Greek or Hebrew) and documents how some laws came into being (for instance, the prohibition of marijuana—even the word *marijuana*—seems to have been the result of a 1930s campaign by the DuPont Corporation and William Randolph Hearst to keep cheap hemp from competing with their wood-based paper-manufacturing processes). In this way, he shows that, though we may on a personal level disagree with certain consensual crimes, requiring our government to force our morality on others is both a dangerous and expensive proposition.

After six years of drought in California, I received from Santa Barbara, one of the areas hardest hit, ***How to Get Water Smart*** (**$9.95 plus $2 shipping and California sales tax, if applicable, from Terra Firma Publishing, 1216 State St., Suite 607, Santa Barbara, CA 93101**). The book gives ways to save money with existing fixtures. It also describes products designed to save water. The goal of these products is admirable, but many are so expensive that you'd have to save an awful lot of water to justify buying them. For example, there's the $840 Contempra faucet with an infrared sensor and the $1,614 AEG Favorit dishwasher, "attractive for its frugality with water." I didn't know frugality could be so expensive!

Ken Scholen's ***Retirement Income on the House*** (**$24.95 plus $4.50 shipping from NCHEC—Suite 300, 1210 E. College Dr., Marshall, MN 56258, or toll-free 800-247-6553**) is *the* source of information about reverse mortgages. Reverse mortgages let senior citizens turn the equity in their homes into income, and they continue to live in their homes. This 340-page paperback takes the reader through the basic questions, including the big one: Do you really need additional income? This book is probably in your library. I'd suggest you examine it there, and, if you find it is something you might need to keep handy, then you can order it.

Barbara J. Winter's ***Making a Living Without a Job*** is an excellent book on living outside a corporation. Ms. Winter relocated and began her business (in that order), which has expanded to include activities as varied as catering English teas and conducting career seminars. Ms. Winter is at her best when advocating, at times a bit too stridently, that her readers leave their jobs. With that one caveat, I recommend this book, which may be ordered from **Good Advice Press, Box 78, Elizaville, NY 12523 for $13.95 postpaid**. Good Advice Press has also updated its $3 booklet, *Stop Junk Mail Forever*. This 20-page booklet tells how to stop junk mail you don't want while remaining on mailing lists you might find useful. I was surprised to find how accessible mailing information is and that the Postal Service even sells change-of-address data to direct mailers! Perhaps the Postal Service should concentrate on delivering the mail.

Charles Long's *How to Survive Without a Salary* (**US$12.95 plus US$.90 shipping from Firefly Books Ltd., 250 Sparks Ave., Willowdale, Ontario, Canada M5H 2S4, or toll-free 800-387-5085 for credit card orders**) gives the author's philosophical reasons for leaving the corporate world and tells how he survives without a salary. Mr. Long is Canadian, and his explanations of U.S. tax laws are sometimes shaky—especially on early IRA and Keogh withdrawals (he may have gotten his information from the IRS's help line), but his understanding of how to live cheap is definitely worth the price of the book (especially if you, as he recommends, get it from your library). I got a kick out of his description of his clothes cycle: Shirts are worn until the elbows go, and then they become short-sleeve shirts. Long trousers become shorts. When clothes are beyond repair, they become work clothes. Then they become rags. I thought I was the only person who did that! On a more serious level, he describes, almost poetically, the loss to the world when useless things are produced: "The plastic box around the pet rock has spent the potential of the oil that made it—forever. That loss is universal, eternal, and irreversible."

Mike and Carolyn Russell's *How to Build Almost Anything Starting with Practically Nothing* (**US$18.95 plus US$.90 from Firefly Books Ltd.**) is pretty much what it purports to be. In 170 pages, this 8½″ × 11″ paperback shows how, if you can be flexible, you can use scrap wood to build whatever you need. Starting with the basics (what tools you'll need and how to use them), they discuss building various items from shelves to sheds.

A year ago I gave one of my strongest recommendations to Joe Dominguez's and Vicki Robin's book *Your Money or Your Life*. If you haven't read it, you should. It is now available in paperback for $11, and many bookstores, Crown among them, offer discounts to that price. Joe and Vicki's group, the New Road Map Foundation, now offers a couple of booklets. The first is the 23-page ***All-Consuming Passion: Waking Up from the American Dream***, which is full of anecdotes that should give even the most fervent advocates of rampant consumerism pause for thought. My favorite: Total energy consumed in producing a 12-ounce can of diet soda: 2,200 calories; total food energy in a 12-ounce can of diet soda: 1 calorie. The second booklet is ***How Earth-Friendly Are You?*** This pamphlet is a questionnaire to help you determine the impact of your lifestyle on the environment. If environmental concern is your reason for being frugal, this pamphlet may be for you. (**Each booklet is $2 postpaid from Q.T.S., P.O. Box 15352, Seattle, WA 98115; they offer quantity discounts, and their phone number is 206-527-0437.**)

The New Road Map Foundation also sent a copy of their new ***Network to Reduce Overconsumption*** (**$10 postpaid from them at P.O. Box 15981, Seattle, WA 98115**). This directory of organizations and leaders involved in the New Frugality movement was compiled to provide resources for such things as finding speakers for conferences, providing frugality "partners" (the book is arranged geographically), and as a conversation piece.

The Context Institute sent Issue 37 of their magazine, ***In Context*** (**$24 per year—four issues—from P.O. Box 11470, Bainbridge Island, WA 98110**). This issue's focus, "It's About Time," contains thirteen articles examining different aspects of the hectic lives we lead. "The Pursuit of Happiness" is an in-depth study of the Kellogg experiment with a shorter workweek.

The Seattle area seems to have become a hotbed of the frugality movement. Also hailing from there, ***Out of the Rat Race*** (**$12 per year—ten issues—from Box 95341, Seattle, WA 98145; for a sample issue, send a** SASE), edited by Susan Gregory, is a newsletter that seems to be based on the teachings of the New Road Map Foundation. It's well written, intelligent, and full of helpful suggestions for getting out of the rat race.

Hyperion Press sent a review copy of Elaine St. James's *Simplify Your Life: 100 Ways to Slow Down Your Life and Enjoy the Things That Really Matter*. **This 250-page $6.95 book should be available in your bookstore or library.** The author and her husband were typical eighties folks who had it all—all except what they really wanted. They were not living where they wanted to live, they didn't have time or energy for a life, and they generally discovered that, in spite of all their things, they were miserable. Unlike most people, who just complain about these situations, Ms. St. James decided to do something. She and her husband got rid of all the stuff they didn't use, moved to where they wanted to live, and drastically reduced their need for things. In a well-organized and concise style, Ms. St. James offers advice on what to do if you don't enjoy the holidays, a *very* interesting approach to gift giving, and what to do if you don't like what you do for a living. She also offers some suggestions that are refreshing, such as cancel your newspaper (I canceled one of mine after considering how little use it was), don't answer the phone (or the doorbell) just because it is ringing, and stop the busywork. Some of her most sage advice is that we stop trying to change people. I know how frustrating it is when people ask for advice and then ignore it. What people are really asking for, advises Ms. St. James, is a supportive ear. In the end people do what they want to do. This book gets a highly recommended rating from the Cheap Guy.

Elaine St. James has written another winner. Hyperion sent a galley of her new book, *Inner Simplicity: 100 Ways to Regain Peace and to Nourish Your Soul*, which I found quite timely. Now, I must advise you this book is written from a New Age perspective. Although it leaves room for you to define your higher power as "God," "the universe," or whatever, some of you will find some of the suggestions offensive. One, number 92, suggests consulting tarot cards, the I Ching, or a Ouija board. Number 85 suggests consulting a psychic. I suggest that if you find these particular suggestions offensive, you should ignore them. However, I would also suggest you not reject the entire book because you do not agree with a few suggestions. (I cannot see myself following number 66, which calls for getting rid of your anger by beating up on your pillows.) There are enough good ideas in here to compensate for the few questionable ones. I found number 44, "Reduce your need to be in the know," helpful. Ms. St. James asks, "Do you really want to spend your time and energy immersing yourself in bad news so you can seem knowledgeable to someone you probably don't even care about?" If the world would follow suggestion number 65, "Stop judging others" (advice also proffered by Christ, by the way), much of the bad news would go away.

My sister, the overachiever of the family, is an executive who frequently burns the midnight (literally) oil in her office. She told me about a man her boss telephoned, who said, "You'll have to make this fast. I'm leaving in fifteen minutes." My sister's boss said to her, with an amazed look on his face, "Why, he only works forty hours a week!" What a concept! Amy Saltzman tells a similar story in her book *Downshifting: Reinventing Success on a Slower Track*. (Unfortunately, this 1991 book is out of print, so look for it in your library or in used-book stores.) After describing typical "fast track" lives, Ms. Saltzman describes alternatives and interviews people who chose "the roads less traveled." The alternatives addressed include plateauing, backtracking, shifting careers, self-employment, and moving from the larger cities to less developed and less expensive areas.

In the old-friends-revisited category, I found Harry Browne's 1973 book *How I Found Freedom in an Unfree World* at a Friends of the Library sale. I would certainly recommend this book to anyone who feels trapped in an unpleasant situation. Mr. Browne advises that there is no trap one cannot escape if one is willing to pay the price. And he should know. He wanted out of his marriage. The price was that he not have any contact with his daughter. He paid the price, believing it was better for all concerned to end what he says was an unbearable situation. The book is good and thought provoking, with descriptions of the many "traps" we allow to limit our freedom. On the other hand, Mr. Browne's approach to life could become a totally self-centered one.

Todd Temple's 1993 book, *52 Ways to Make This Your Best Year Yet* **($9.94 including shipping from Melton Book Company, P.O. Box 140990, Nashville, TN 37214)**, is now old enough to be in your community's library. Although the book is written for a Christian audience, it has things to offer people of any faith.

Elrena Parton sent a copy of her book *Recycle Using Everyday Items* **($8 postpaid from her at 1183 Pleasant View Rd., Woodbury, TN 37190)**. While this book has about twice as many commas as it needs, I found it refreshing because, while most books on recycling concern themselves with how best to throw things away, Ms. Parton suggests instead that we find alternative uses for these things, and she provides 62 pages of suggestions.

I was very happy to receive Jonni Stivers McCoy's *Miserly Moms: Living on One Income in a Two Income Economy* (**$5.95 postpaid from** *LCN*). The 60-page book tells how Ms. Stivers managed to stop working when she became a mother and, by cutting costs, how she essentially maintained the same standard of living she and her husband had enjoyed as a two-income couple in San Jose, which she describes accurately as "one of the most expensive areas in America." She shares her methods, tips, and some eye-opening research with her readers. (People who swear by warehouse stores should find her analysis of warehouse prices versus other store prices interesting.) In many instances, Ms. Stivers takes the approach I like best: instead of automatically trying to find a way to buy something cheaper, she questions whether one needs to buy the item at all.

An excellent read is Alan Durning's *How Much Is Enough?: The Consumer Society and the Future of the Earth* (**$8.95 plus sales tax if you live in California, Pennsylvania, New York, or Illinois from W. W. Norton, 500 Fifth Ave., New York, NY 10110, or toll-free 800-223-2584**). Starting with the observation that Minnesota's Mall of America is expected to attract more visitors annually than the Vatican or Mecca, Mr. Durning examines in 150 pages how environmentally and personally destructive our culture of consumption is. He discusses the myth of "consume or decline," providing an answer to those who like to say, "If everyone were as frugal as you, our economy would suffer." He describes how advertising cultivates needs where none exist, suggests how we can build a culture of permanence, and concludes with a resource section.

For 365 ways to save, Jackie Iglehart publishes a great annual wall calendar. **It's $6.95 from The Penny Pincher, 2 Hilltop Rd., Mendham, NJ 07945-1215.**

I never thought much of Paladin Press, but they recently sent a catalog that, along with their usual categories—weapons, combat shooting, silencers, etc.—has a section on financial freedom. Some of the books look interesting. (Keep in mind that I haven't read these.) Among them are John Green's *Free Stuff*, Edward H. Romney's *Living Well on Practically Nothing*, and Bob Hammond's *Life After Debt*. Write P.O. Box 1307, Boulder, CO 80306 for Paladin's free catalog.

I recently received a copy of ***Out of Bounds* ($14 per year—four issues—from P.O. Box 5108, Arlington, VA 22205)**. If you're politically conservative and want to stay that way, this magazine is probably not for you. And what does it have to do with frugality? Nothing. But any magazine that's this well written and thought provoking is going to get raves from me. In Issue 2, 74 pages in length, there's an article on how we have become observers rather than doers, an article on feminism that reflects the viewpoint that women today have fewer options because of the economy (where have I heard that before?), and an admittedly obnoxiously titled article on how communities and police departments are using asset-forfeiture laws for revenue enhancement.

I recently read about Cal-A-Co, an anonymous newsletter editor who occasionally provides small grants to worthy projects. Now, this sounded like someone I'd like to know more about! Cal-A-Co's newsletter, ***Another Look, Unlimited® News* ($15 per year—12 issues—from P.O. Box 220, Dept. N, Holts Summit, MO 65043)**, is quite a collection. The emphasis is on reuse of discards (but no Dumpster diving), but there are also articles about shopping for gifts at thrift stores, recipes, and the editor's philosophy. For a sample issue, send $1 and a self-addressed, stamped envelope.

Walker and Company sent a copy of their new paperback edition of Elizabeth Lewin's ***Kiss the Rat Race Goodbye* ($12.95 plus $3 shipping from them at 435 Hudson St., New York, NY 10014)**. This is a reprint of a 1992 hardback published by Pharos Books. The book is good, but it is passionless. One gets the impression Ms. Lewin was never a part of the rat race. She tells about *other* people's reasons for leaving or wanting to leave corporate America, but it is difficult to believe Ms. Lewin comprehends just how much of a grind being a cog in a mindless company bent only on downsizing can be. That said, the book does lay out a rational and practical plan for escape, and it provides enough charts to make you look forward to doing your taxes.

For those who just can't stand to get rid of anything and, as a result, are inundated with stuff, there's **Clutterer's Anonymous.** They have a twelve-step program similar to that of Alcoholics Anonymous. For more information send a self-addressed, stamped envelope to them at **P.O. Box 25884, Santa Ana, CA 92799-5884.**

K. D. Shanahan sent a copy of *Money Magic: Discover Your Hidden Wealth* **($6.40 postpaid from Alpha Company, Memorial Ave., P.O. Box 295, Allendale, SC 29810).** The very first page of this 111-page book has advice for single people one rarely sees in print: You don't need life insurance. Needless to say, I was intrigued by this unconventional (but valid) approach. And the rest of the book does not disappoint. There's even a chapter on unnecessary insurance policies. The book covers more than insurance, of course. There's advice on buying a home, a new or used car, and more. All in all, I would say this book is an excellent value. And it would be an even better value if you could get your library to order it for you as well as for their other patrons.

Olaf Egeberg's *Non-Money: That "Other Money" You Didn't Know You Had* is a practical guide to exchanging goods and services as well as a blueprint for better communities. You may recall that I mentioned I needed a lamp and was able to get two lamps in exchange for a garbage can that, because of a change in my city's garbage collection procedure, had become worthless to me. Mr. Egeberg's book discusses just this sort of thing, but he goes beyond this simple type of exchange. He goes into exchange networks, exchanges in lieu of rent, etc. Much of the 191-page book discusses setting up neighborhood exchanges, using an existing Maryland neighborhood exchange as an example. **The book is a healthy $18.50 from The McGee Street Foundation, P.O. Box 56756, Washington, DC 20040**, but it is not copyrighted, and the author advises, "Anyone wishing to reproduce this book may do so."

Jordan L. Cooper, whose book *Shadow Merchants* was reviewed in Issue 26, is back. His new book, *Second-Hand Success: How to Turn Discards into Dollars* **($18.95 including shipping from Loompanics Unlimited, P.O. Box 1197, Port Townsend, WA 98368—Washington residents add 7.9 percent sales tax)** is a fun read. He tells how, for example, one man makes a fairly good living by removing items from apartments of college students who are going home for the summer and selling these items at swap meets. The students are happy to have the stuff hauled away, so the man's investment is minimal. Mr. Cooper then discusses other ways to make money on discarded items, from paperback books to Dumpster items to vintage aircraft parts. The book is a tad pricey, but, if you have any interest in starting a recycling business, it may be for you. As always, Loompanics will include their $5 catalog free with an order.

Sherry L. Eskesen sent a copy of her often-humorous 1991 book, ***Save and Survive in a Difficult Economy: 429 Ways to Save Money When Times Are Tough ($8.54 from SLE Publishing, P.O. Box 231603, Encinitas, CA 92023-1603)***. Some of Ms. Eskesen's suggestions are quite good (use the clothesline instead of the dryer, use self-serve gas), and some are quite humorous (accept all invitations to dinner, move back in with Mom and Dad, move in with your kids). The humorous suggestions are mingled with the serious, so beware. If you read this book on a plane or a bus, you will laugh often enough that your fellow passengers are going to wonder just what is so funny about surviving in a difficult economy.

Scott Humphrey's brand-new book, ***How to Save a Million Dollars ($19.95 postpaid from Screen Communications, P.O. Box 17162, Hattiesburg, MS 39404-7162)***, was a difficult read for me because of Mr. Humphrey's writing style, but it was well worth the effort. Some of his most sage advice is that you must be your own money manager. The 144-page book shows how to set realistic goals, which, with the magic of compound interest, can result in a substantial nest egg given enough time. I would highly recommend that you ask your library to order this book so that it will be available to readers in your community.

Garrett Publishing, Inc. sent a copy of Arnold Goldstein's ***How to Settle with the IRS for Pennies on the Dollar ($24.45 postpaid from Garrett Publishing, Inc., 384 S. Military Trail, Deerfield Beach, FL 33442, or call 800-333-2069)***. Mr. Goldstein advises how to protect assets from the IRS (evidently there are attorneys who specialize in asset protection), and then he goes on to explain the "Offer in Compromise" program, which allows you to negotiate with the IRS. I found this book interesting in a depressing sort of way. On the one hand, I suppose it is good that people who owe the IRS more than they can pay can reach a compromise. On the other hand, is it fair to those of us who pay what we owe to subsidize other taxpayers?

For those who can't pay the IRS or anyone else, Alice Griffin has written ***Personal Bankruptcy: What You Should Know ($13.95 postpaid from The Cakewalk Press, P.O. Box 1536-NL, New York, NY***

10276). This book was written for those who have serious financial difficulties. Ms. Griffin discusses how bankruptcy works, why a bankruptcy lawyer is essential and how to find a good one, and, finally (and fortunately) alternatives to bankruptcy.

The folks at Dearborn Trade sent some books my way recently. The first, *It's Never Too Late to Get Rich*, by James Jorgensen, contains many useful suggestions for (primarily) baby boomers who are concerned about retirement. I don't necessarily agree with all of his suggestions (especially when it comes to bonds), but you may. The $17.95 (plus shipping) book should be available in your library or bookstore. The second book, *Scrooge Investing*, by Mark Skousen, lists 122 "cost-cutting tips." Many of these are interesting if somewhat risky (buy bonds of bankrupt companies for pennies on the dollar, for example). Some are fairly obvious (use a discount broker). Some are downright questionable (there's a whole chapter on silver and gold). The book is $19.95 plus shipping.

Briefly, here are some other books Dearborn has recently published:

- *How to Build a Fortune Investing in Your Spare Time*, by Stephen Littauer (**$16.95 plus shipping**), provides some good, albeit basic, information on investing. The 246-page book concentrates a bit too heavily on stocks and mutual funds for my taste. Mr. Littauer also gives short shrift to investing in bonds (except bond funds).

- Kathryn Shaw's *Investment Clubs* (**$14.95 plus shipping**) discusses setting up and operating an investment club. While I am certain some of these clubs are successful, *Money* carried an article some time ago about the investment club from hell. And a club with which I am familiar (I am not and have never been a member) has had its share of problems. I believe the investments have done well, but arguments about where to put the club's money have tested many friendships and ended a few of them. Personally, I believe it's best to invest on your own and keep quiet about where your money is.

- Ted Nicholas's 147-page *The Corporate Forms Kit* (**$19.95 plus shipping**) contains forms corporations need to keep legal.

- Mr. Nicholas has also written ***The Business Agreements Kit ($19.95 plus shipping)***, which contains just about every type of form a business may need and then some. Each of these "kits" comes with an IBM PC-formatted computer disk that presumably will allow the forms to be customized.

- Nan L. Goodart's ***The Truth About Living Trusts ($16.95 plus shipping)*** in 157 pages answers common questions about living trusts. The book is a good primer, but laws do vary from state to state, so you will need to do some additional research if you decide a living trust might be for you.

- David S. Magee has written a very helpful book, ***Everything Your Heirs Need to Know ($19.95 plus shipping)***. This book really lives up to its name, and I wish such a thing had been around in my grandparents' time. In addition to listing insurance policies, bank and savings accounts, investments, real estate, etc., the book has a section for sharing a personal history. Believe me, many of your heirs will appreciate this information as much as they will appreciate the other information in this book. My family recently had a "close call," and I gave my copy of this book to my parents. I hope they use it!

- ***Make Your Connections Count***, by Melissa Giovagnoli **($15.95 plus shipping)**, discusses in 226 pages establishing and using your network to enhance, promote, and, when necessary, replace your career.

- An early entry in Dearborn's "Upstart Guide" series of guides for starting your own business is ***The Upstart Guide to Owning and Managing a Bed and Breakfast***, by Lisa Angowski Rogak. I'll confess that going into the bed-and-breakfast business is not something I plan to run out and do, but this book gives good and surprisingly detailed information not only on its subject, but on determining whether this type of business is right for you. Other books in this series include guides on owning and managing a bar or tavern, a desktop publishing business, and a résumé service. **The "Upstart Guide" books are $15.95 each.**

The Dearborn books should be available in your library or bookstore. If you want to order direct, **Dearborn's address is 155 N. Wacker Dr., Chicago, IL 60606-1719; their toll-free number is 800-245-2665. Shipping costs are $5 for the first book**, and they suggest that, if you order more than one book, you call to get the exact charges.

When garage sale signs decorate front lawns from sea to shining sea, you might turn to Michael and Pam Williams's book titled *Garage Sale Magic* **($13.45 including shipping from Freedom Publishing Company, 400 W. Dundee Rd., Buffalo Grove, IL 60089, or toll-free 800-717-0770)** to help you maximize your garage sale profits. This book has a lot of good ideas, including a suggestion to join with your neighbors to create a neighborhood, condo, or apartment sale, the theory being more people will be drawn to a multifamily sale. While I'm in favor of garage sales, I'm also in favor of garage sale prevention. In other words, don't buy garage sale fodder—you won't make money by buying retail and selling garage sale.

One of the best and most original newsletters I've seen in quite a while is *Simple Living News* **($20 per year—10 issues—from P.O. Box L1884, Jonesboro, GA 30237-1884; for a sample issue, send a long self-addressed, stamped envelope)**. In the premiere issue, Edith Flowers Kilgo analyzes her former job and shows how it *cost* her nearly $16,000 (over and above what she was earning) to work the fifty-five to sixty hours a week her employer expected. This newsletter is a refreshing and intelligent breath of fresh air that our workaholic world needs.

Jack Heinowitz, Ph.D., has written a timely book, *Pregnant Fathers: Entering Parenthood Together* **($14.95 from Parents as Partners Press, 4019 Goldfinch St., Suite 170-BL, San Diego, CA 92103)**. In an era in which even our president takes note of "missing fathers," Dr. Heinowitz advocates approaching not only parenthood but pregnancy and birthing as a team, and the team approach includes older children as well.

The National Center for Financial Education (P.O. Box 34070, San Diego, CA 92163) advises that, if you get an unwanted credit card in the mail, you should cut it up and return it rather than throwing it away. If you don't, they advise, the credit card will show as an open account on your credit report. This may result in your not getting credit when you want it. (I agree this is not fair; a company should not be able to damage you by sending you something you don't want and didn't ask for, but we must live in the world as it is.) If unwarranted problems pop up on your credit report, NCFE offers a *Do-It-Yourself Repair Guide* for **$12 postpaid**.

Good Advice Press offers a cassette called *Smart Credit Strategies for College Students* (**$15.95 postpaid from them at Box 78, Elizaville, NY 12523**). The 30-minute cassette is narrated by Gerri Detweiler, an expert on credit matters. Also available from Good Advice Press is *The Banker's Secret Audio Kit*, which dispels some of the common mortgage myths of our time. This 30-minute tape is **$22.95 postpaid**. (You'll also receive a certificate that will entitle you to an individual analysis of how you can pay your mortgage off early.)

If you're looking for new furniture, M. Katherine Gladchun has just come out with the third edition of her *The Fine Furniture and Furnishings Discount Shopping Guide* (**$14.95 postpaid plus Michigan tax if applicable from Resources, Inc., P.O. Box 973, Bloomfield Hills, MI 48303-0973**). This 235-page book is a virtual who's who in the discount furniture business. She lists not only their addresses and phone numbers, but also what products they provide and which manufacturers they work with. Although this is an excellent resource for those in the market for new furniture, you should be aware that furniture depreciates very rapidly. Therefore, the best way to save money on furniture is to buy it used.

Vicki Lansky is a contributing editor to *Family Circle* magazine, and I've had the pleasure of reading some of her other books. Now she's written *Baking Soda: Over 500 Fabulous, Fun and Frugal Uses You've Probably Never Thought Of*. The 108-page $6.95 book should be available in your library or bookstore, or you may order it for **$9.45 postpaid from Practical Parenting, 18326 Minnetonka Blvd., Deephaven, MN 55391, or call 800-255-3379**. Be advised some of the suggestions are a bit over the edge (making arrows or footprint directions on carpets—to be vacuumed up later), but many are excellent cleaning and cooking uses that I had never before been aware of.

I came across Neil Balter's *The Closet Entrepreneur* (**free from your library, $14.95 in bookstores, or $18.45 postpaid from Career**

Press, P.O. Box 34, Hawthorne, NJ 07507, or toll-free 800-CAREER-1). Subtitled *337 Ways to Start Your Successful Business with Little or No Money*, the 280-page paperback discusses just about every facet of starting a business from coming up with a concept to maintaining a professional image and generating free publicity. And the author knows what he is talking about. He started the California Closet Company when he was seventeen. He sold his business for $12 million before he turned thirty.

If you're thinking of starting a business based on something you've developed, Sonny Bloch's *Selling Your Idea or Invention: The Birthplace to Marketplace Guide* may be just what you're looking for. Published by the **Carol Publishing Group (600 Madison Ave., New York, NY 10022), the $29.95 hardback should be available in your library or bookstore**. In 237 pages, Mr. Bloch discusses a range of topics from intellectual property to trademarks.

The Employee Strikes Back, by John D. Rapoport and Brian L. P. Zevnik, is a valuable book to have in these times of corporate downsizing, salary cuts, and institutionalized greed. The 309-page paperback discusses your right to pursue litigation in certain circumstances, including sexual harassment, age discrimination, drug testing, polygraph abuse, unfair performance appraisals, and wrongful termination. Unlike the few books on this subject I have seen, the book also assesses the risks of pursuing legal action against your employer. The $10 book was published by Collier Books and should be available in your library or bookstore.

Leila Alpel has written four attractive books on sewing clothes for your family: *Easy Halloween Costumes for Children*, *Easy Sewing for Adults*, *Easy Sewing for Children*, **and** *Easy Sewing for Infants*. The books are each about 125 pages, and **they retail for $12.95 plus $1 per book for shipping**. Ms. Alpel is making a special offer to *LCN* readers. **You can order one or all books for US$5 each postpaid from her at P.O. Box 203, Chambly, Quebec, Canada J3L 4B3.**

Remember the hoopla when the National Rifle Association sent out a fund-raising letter in which some federal agents were called "jackbooted thugs"? What a tempest that letter set off! Former President George Bush resigned his NRA membership, and NRA Executive Vice President Wayne LaPierre was forced to join other talking heads on various current events television shows. Mr. LaPierre finally apologized for his group's rhetoric. Did anyone else notice the discussions focused not on what the NRA's letter said but how the NRA said it? The letter listed several specific instances of alleged government abuse, but all we heard discussed was whether federal agents should be called jackbooted thugs. Good grief! Aren't Americans used to hyperbole in political speeches and campaign literature? After all, the Speaker of the House of Representatives has been quoted in the media as referring to the President as a "Counterculture McGovernick" and the First Lady as something one normally would call a female canine. If all this sounds to you like the media have become a group focused on image rather than substance, you might want to read *By Invitation Only: How the Media Limit Political Debate*, by David Croteau and William Hoynes. This 218-page paperback also demonstrates how the media often provide us with "false choices." It should be available in your library or bookstore for $9.95, or you can order it from **Common Courage Press (Box 702, Monroe, ME 04951, or 800-497-3207) for $12.45 postpaid**.

If you're looking for a job, either in your current location or in a new one, JIST Works, Inc., offers several titles:

- J. Michael Farr's *America's 50 Fastest Growing Jobs* (**$14.95 plus shipping**), a 162-page (plus appendixes) 8½″ × 11″ paperback, lists not only the fastest-growing jobs, but the prospects for other jobs as well. The book is interesting, and it may be helpful for some people. Still, when I see titles like this, I can't help remembering those who pursued an engineering career in the 1960s only to find too many others had done the same thing. And teachers in the 1970s. And so on.

- David F. Noble's *Using WordPerfect in Your Job Search* (**$19.95 plus shipping**) is a 454-page paperback on the subject of preparing a résumé, writing cover letters, keeping a calendar, keeping track of networking and contact lists, and more with WordPerfect. As I browsed through this book, the only words I could come up with were *overkill* and *overpriced*.

- Fred. E. Jandt's and Mary B. Nemnich's *Using the Internet in Your Job Search* (**$16.95 plus shipping**) is, in my opinion, the best of the three. It covers its subject from understanding the Internet to preparing an electronic résumé, to declining an offer politely to keeping your job once you have one. And it does all this in 224 pages.

JIST's shipping charges are 7 percent of the price of the order, with a $4 minimum. Their address is 720 N. Park Ave., Indianapolis, IN 46202-3431; their toll-free order number is 800-648-5478.
For those of us who are too independent or too tired of résumés, interviews, etc., Canadian author Wendy Priesnitz has written ***Bringing It Home: A Home Business Start-Up Guide for You and Your Family***, which starts with the logical question, Can I work at home? Assuming the answer is yes, the 190-page paperback then discusses setting up a home office, marketing your products, understanding zoning laws, and more. Ms. Priesnitz also publishes *Natural Life*, a bimonthly newspaper focused on environmental concerns. **The book is $12.95; the newspaper is $15 per year. The address is P.O. Box 60, Lewiston, NY 14092-0060.**
For those who want to know what's new in newsletters of all stripes, there's *Newsletter Times* **(P.O. Box 92051, Santa Barbara, CA 93190)**. Nowadays, with the proliferation of personal computers, if you have an interest, odds are there's a newsletter out there for you. Bill Brown, the publisher of *Newsletter Times*, is offering **a discounted rate of $8.88 for *LCN* subscribers (the regular rate is $15.88). An introductory issue is $2**.
To help you make your decisions when Election Day rolls around, there's **Project Vote Smart (129 N.W. Fourth St., #204, Corvallis, OR 97330)**, which offers a free *U.S. Government: Owner's Manual*, a 64-page book telling how to get in touch with your elected representatives, how your representatives are rated by various "think tank" groups, how their campaigns were financed, and how they voted on key issues.
Russ Walter's twenty-first edition of ***The Secret Guide to Computers*** is out. **It's $15 postpaid from him at 22 Ashland St., Floor 2, Somerville, MA 02144-3202.** The book comes with twenty-four-hour technical support (from Russ himself). The 638-page 8½″ × 11″ paperback is a good source of information on computers. The section on Macintosh computers demystifies the confusing Macintosh hierarchy better than anything I've seen elsewhere, and he gives the real price of each model, which comes in very handy if you're buying a used model. If you

don't need this minute's information on computers, Russ is offering his huge but dated eighteenth edition for $5 postpaid. Massachusetts residents must add sales tax to all orders.

If you or someone you know is preparing to put on a wedding, Sharon Naylor's ***1001 Ways to Save Money and Still Have a Dazzling Wedding* (Contemporary Books, 1994)** may be just what the caterer hoped you didn't order. The 308-page paperback discusses ways to save money on everything from the engagement notice to planning the honeymoon. **It should be available in your library or bookstore for $11.95** (Contemporary is not set up to take direct orders). One option I would like to have seen discussed in the book is not to have a formal wedding at all and use the money that would have gone to this one-day extravaganza for a down payment on a house, a car, or something that would be of lasting use to the bride and groom.

I don't usually read books that contain such buzzwords of our time as *paradigm*, *reinvent*, or *proactive*, but R. Theodore Benna's ***Escaping the Current Retirement Crisis* ($24)** turned out to be an exception because *proactive* didn't appear until I was almost through the book. The book contains some good advice, but in many ways it seems to me that Mr. Benna, who helped devise the 401(k) plans that have made a comfortable retirement possible for more people, puts the cart before the horse. Retirement, in his eyes, seems to be the reason for working, so Mr. Benna advises us to stay with one employer and work as long as we can. If you like what you are doing, this advice is great. But if you find yourself with a toxic employer (been there), is it wise to stay with a job that is sure to be bad for your health (done that) for the sake of a retirement you may not live to see? This book is sure to be in your library soon (especially if you request it). Get it there.

On a brighter note is Chuck Chakrapani's ***Financial Freedom on $5 a Day* ($13.95 postpaid from Self-Counsel Press Inc., 1704 State St., Bellingham, WA 98225)**, which even has eight pages of information on my favorite financial instruments, bonds (and that's about eight pages more than most investment books have). Dr. Chakrapani discusses the options available for small investors, and he even warns that in the beginning it will appear investors are not making much headway. But, as he demonstrates, if you stay on course, you can have financial freedom.

Alvin Dannenberg's ***21½ Easy Steps to Financial Security*** is geared for those who are interested primarily in mutual funds. If that is you, the small 216-page paperback is **available for $13.16, which includes a 10 percent discount and $1.50 shipping, from International Publishing, 625 N. Michigan Ave., Suite 1920, Chicago, IL 60611**.

California has made it illegal for women to be charged more than men for the same item or services. I was not aware there was such a discrepancy, but *Women Pay More (and How to Put a Stop to It)* by Frances Cerra Whittelsey and Marcia Carroll provides 180 pages of proof that women are often gouged for things men get cheap or free. The book should be available in your library or bookstore. Its price tag says, "Women $9.95; Men $11.95 (Just Kidding)."

I'm always amused at how many people claim to have "started" the frugality movement. Such is the case with Lee and Barbara Simmons's *Penny Pinching* **(Bantam, 1995)**, a $4.99 paperback generally available in bookstores and libraries everywhere (a friend found the copy I read in a used-book store). I'm amazed how many people believe they are somehow helping themselves by putting others' efforts down, as the Simmonses do with frugality newsletters, and they assure us they have no intention of starting a newsletter of their own. First, for the record, my book *Living Cheap: THE Survival Guide for the Nineties* was published fully eighteen months before the first (September 1991) edition of *Penny Pinching*. Second, I don't claim to have started the frugality movement; I've found frugality books from the 1960s at estate sales, and frugality was big in the 1970s. In fact, frugality was big in Emerson's and Thoreau's time. And before. Second, newsletters provide a two-way communication. Have you ever seen a "letters to the editor" column in a book? Books are good, but a book is a lecture. A newsletter is a discussion. That said, once the reader gets past the introduction, the Simmonses' book is a pretty good one. While some of the ideas will not be new to readers of LCN, others will be, and the Simmonses provide a wealth of resources. I wish the Simmonses continued success with their writing, and I hope to see a more objective and less self-congratulatory introduction in their next edition.

Brian Boyer, who recently graduated magna cum laude from Southern Illinois University, sent a copy of his *The Slacker Handbook: A Financial Survival Guide for College Students* **(a very reasonable $5.95, which includes shipping, from him at P.O. Box 2137, Decatur, IL 62524-2137)**. The 8½″ × 11″ book is 34 pages, stapled, concise, and really good. I'd be willing to bet Mr. Boyer is saving his $7 per day for retirement already! I wish he'd been around to write this book when I was in college.

Linda Slater, former editor of *The Thrifty Times*, offers a $5 booklet, ***How to Save Money on Travel, Clothing, and Entertainment.*** **Checks should be made payable to her and sent to 6135 Utica St., Arvada, CO 80003**.

LCN COUPON • YOU MAY PHOTOCOPY THIS COUPON

AVAILABLE FROM

LIVING CHEAP PRESS
7232 BELLEVIEW AVE.
KANSAS CITY, MO 64114-1218

Beating the System: The Next American Revolution, by Larry Roth. Even if you love your job, you'd better be prepared to do without it. This book tells you how. $14.95 ppd. with this coupon.

Living Cheap News. Published ten times yearly (monthly except January and July), this nationally recognized newsletter addresses issues affecting your financial well-being and provides tips on keeping cheap. $12.00 per year.

Living Cheap News: The First Two Years. CLOSE-OUT SPECIAL! All issues from 1992 and 1993 in one volume. $5.95 ppd. with this coupon.*

Living Cheap: THE Survival Guide for the Nineties. CLOSE-OUT SPECIAL! The 1990 book that started it all. $4.95 ppd. with this coupon.*

Miserly Moms: Living on One Income in a Two Income Economy (1994). The subtitle says it all (reviewed on p. 231). $5.95 ppd.

*While supplies last.   Missouri residents add 6.475%.

LCN COUPON • YOU MAY PHOTOCOPY THIS COUPON